Parish
School

Parish School

American Catholic Parochial Education
from Colonial Times to the Present

Timothy Walch

A Crossroad Herder Book
The Crossroad Publishing Company
New York

1996

The Crossroad Publishing Company
370 Lexington Avenue, New York, NY 10017

Copyright © 1996 by Timothy Walch

Printed in the United States of America

Library of Congress Cataloging-in-Publication Data

Walch, Timothy, 1947–
    Parish school : American Catholic parochial education
from colonial times to the present / Timothy Walch.
        p.   cm.
    Includes index.
    ISBN 0-8245-1532-3 (hc)
    1. Catholic Church—Education—United States—History.
    2. Catholic Church—Education—Social aspects—United States—
History.   I. Title.
    LC501.W28   1996
    377'.82–dc20   95-20308
                                                        CIP

FOR VICTORIA IRONS WALCH

*"No cord nor cable
can so forcibly draw,
or hold so fast,
as love can do
with a twined thread"*
—ROBERT BURTON, 1621

Contents

Acknowledgments

T HIS BOOK was researched and written over the past twenty years, and during those years I have received the advice, encouragement, and assistance from many historians and scholars. Among those individuals who have contributed to the chapters that follow are Robert L. Church and Michael W. Sedlak, both of Michigan State University; Jay P. Dolan and Philip Gleason, both of the University of Notre Dame; Robert Trisco and the late John Tracy Ellis, both of the Catholic University of America; George M. Frederickson of Stanford University, and Rudolph C. Miller of *Religious Education*.

I am particularly grateful for the support of three friends. Archie Motley, the dean of the Chicago archival community, provided critical assistance in the location of vital source materials for this book and a previous volume. Christopher Kauffman, professor of church history at the Catholic University of America and editor of the *U.S. Catholic Historian*, provided sources to consult and issues to be addressed.

Finally, Edward R. Kantowicz, formerly professor of history at Carelton University in Canada and historian of Chicago Catholicism, read the manuscript in its entirety and provided vital historiographical advice and editorial assistance. The book is immeasurably better for his effort. Every writer should have a friend like Ed Kantowicz.

This book would not have been possible had it not been for the love and support of my family. My mother-in-law, Mary Winslow Irons, generously opened her home each summer to the Walch family and allowed me the time and the setting to think and write about parish schools. Many of these chapters were first drafted on the Victorian secretary in her parlor. My wife, Victoria Irons Walch, to whom this book is dedicated, provided the time, encouragement, and sympathy that sustained me on the long journey of discovery from idea to concept through research and on to draft after draft, arriving finally at a finished if imperfect manuscript. *Parish School* is truly her book as much as it is mine.

In the end, however, the ideas that follow are my own and the book must stand or fall on the quality of those ideas. So also the flaws and mistakes are my own. For those errors I can only say "mea culpa" and ask for the mercy of the reader.

Introduction

MORE THAN two hundred years ago, Philadelphia Catholics established what is thought to be the first Catholic parish school in the United States. It was not the first church-sponsored school in the country. In fact, it was not even the first *Catholic* school in the country.

But this largely unnoticed event began one of the most ambitious social movements in American history. Over the next two centuries, Catholic parochial schools would educate tens of millions of American citizens without direct financial assistance from federal, state, or local governments.

By the middle of the 1960s, when the Catholic parochial school movement had reached its high point, there were more than 4.5 million children in parish elementary schools — fully 12 percent of all of the children enrolled in the United States at that time. It is an achievement that has never been duplicated anywhere else in the world.

At the heart of the Catholic parochial school movement is the unwavering belief that the education of children is a primary responsibility of the family and the church, not the government. Until the middle of the nineteenth century, this also was the prevailing view of most American citizens.

But rapid industrialization and urbanization, in concert with the arrival of millions of immigrants from Ireland and Germany, made many Americans fearful of social and political unrest, and common public schools that would educate all social classes were seen as an important tool in the campaign to preserve social order. Public schools would mix together children of various social classes, nationalities, and creeds to inculcate the proper values for success in American society.

1

The end result would be patriotic, law-abiding, deferential, and diligent American citizens. Community leaders argued that the state had both a right and a responsibility to provide such education as a means of preserving order in the republic.

Catholic leaders opposed these public schools not only because these institutions usurped the traditional role of the church in the educational process, but also because the curriculum of the early common schools included heavy doses of Protestant instruction and anti-Catholic propaganda. The movement to establish Catholic schools was, above all else, an effort to prevent Catholic children from abandoning their religious faith.

In this manner the competition for the hearts and minds of Catholic children and their parents began in the middle of the nineteenth century and continues to the present day. Catholic parents in the 1990s face educational choices similar to those faced by their great-grandparents a hundred years ago: Can I afford to send my children to the parish school? Is the Catholic school curriculum just as good as the public school curriculum? Will my children be better Catholics if they go to parish schools? Will my children lose their faith if they go to public schools? Each generation has answered these questions a little differently, and how they answered these questions deeply affected the development of Catholic schooling.

Surprisingly, given how important Catholic education has been to the history of the American church, the subject has not appealed very much to historians. That there have been only four historical surveys of Catholic parochial education written since 1900 qualifies the topic as one of the most neglected in American historiography. Early in this century, James A. Burns published the first work on Catholic schools, and the fact that his two volumes are still in use is a testament to the lack of scholarship in the field. Bernard Kohlbrenner abridged Burns's work in 1937 and transformed the two volumes into "a textbook for normal schools and teachers colleges." He also added several chapters bringing the story up to 1937. A third general history appeared in 1970. Its author, Harold A. Buetow, provided extensive annotation but relied almost exclusively on previously published sources. Buetow revised and republished some of his historical research in the mid-1980s in a general study of Catholic schooling. Glen Gabert published the fourth study more than twenty years ago. None of these histories offered the depth of research or the sophisticated analysis that the topic demands.

This book is an effort to trace the contours of American Catholic parochial education from its origins in the missionary and colonial eras and analyze the importance of these schools to successive generations of American Catholics. Beginning with a few informal efforts to educate Native American children in the sixteenth century, the Catholic school movement grew into this nation's second largest school system by the turn of the twentieth century. It is a dramatic story of a social institution that adapted itself to almost constant change without abandoning its goals of preserving the religious faith of Catholic children and preparing them for productive roles in American society.

Several themes emerge in the chapters that follow. The first is survival. Beginning in the middle of the sixteenth century, Catholics struggled to sustain their religion and its few churches in a hostile land. Spanish and French missionaries suffered great hardship in a largely futile effort to educate the nation's native population. English missionaries struggled to sustain their small flock of colonial Catholics in the face of a hostile Protestant majority. It was not clear until the 1820s that Catholicism in general, and Catholic schools in particular, would survive in this country.

A second theme is immigration. What secured the future of Catholic education in this country was the arrival of tens of millions of immigrant Catholics during the years from 1820 to 1920. Impoverished but ambitious, concerned about the preservation of their religion and their culture in the New World, many of these immigrants embraced parish schools as the answer to their concerns. It was the determination of these immigrant Catholic parents that took parish schooling from a few dozen schools in 1820 to nearly ten thousand schools 140 years later.

A third theme is the variety of responses to the parish school movement. Contrary to the popular belief that American Catholics uniformly supported these schools, less than half of the Catholic school-age population attended these schools. To be sure, many immigrant Catholics were eager and enthusiastic supporters of parochial education, but most Catholic parents did not join the cause. Indeed, not all Catholic bishops and pastors were uniformly supportive of parish schools. In truth, there was a wide range of responses to the Catholic school movement.

Yet a fourth theme is adaptability. The success of parochial education was insured by the willingness of Catholic educators over many generations to change and revise the parochial school curriculum in response to changes in the public school curriculum and the desires and aspirations of Catholic parents. Catholic educators realized that a rigid, doctrinaire curriculum would force Catholic parents to choose between their religious faith and their children's future. By incorporating many of the elements of public schooling into the parish school curriculum, Catholic educators promised to secure both the faith and the future of its children.

A fifth theme is community. Perhaps the greatest asset of parochial schooling — even to the present day — is that these schools reflected the goals, aspirations, and even the prejudices and fears of the neighborhood Catholics who supported these institutions. Public school teachers often lived outside the neighborhoods where they taught, and the curriculum was established by a school superintendent or a school committee downtown.

But parish schools were community-based in every sense of the word. Each immigrant group established their own "national" parishes with their own ethnic Catholic schools. Parents had a sense of involvement in these schools. To be sure, these immigrants deferred to their pastors and to the nuns in the classrooms, but pastors and teachers alike were well aware that parental support was vital if parish schools were to thrive.

A final theme in the book is identity. For most of its existence, the Catholic school was seen as a safe haven for a religious minority that did not feel welcome in the public schools. But after the Second Vatican Council in the 1960s, and for the next generation, the differences between Catholics and non-Catholics on educational issues seemed to fade away. The justification for maintaining a separate, very costly school system seemed less compelling. Many schools were closed and those that remained were redefined.

At its most basic level, this book is a synthesis of a wide range of source materials and a broad spectrum of ideas from many scholars. Yet the book has no pretensions of being definitive. It is more properly an invitation to the community of scholars and educators to focus more attention on this long neglected but very important social institution.

The history of American Catholic parochial education is a dramatic story of a social institution that ingeniously adapted itself to almost constant change in American society without abandoning its two basic goals — the preservation of the religious faith of Catholic children and the preparation of these children for productive roles in American society. It is a story that is worth telling.

Chapter 1 _____

The Origins of Catholic Education

T HE ORIGINS of Catholic education in America can be found in the 250-year effort to convert a continent to Christianity. From the middle of the sixteenth century to the end of the eighteenth century, Spanish, French, and English missionaries preached the gospel to Native Americans and colonists in what is now the United States. The hardship and deprivation suffered by these priests were extraordinary, but they persisted because they believed they were doing God's work in a new territory uncorrupted by sin.

The Spanish focused their missionary efforts on the South. Florida settlements came first in 1565, followed by the New Mexico missions at the end of the sixteenth century, Texas and Arizona in the seventeenth century, and California in the eighteenth century. Major American cities such as San Antonio, Santa Fe, San Diego, Los Angeles, and San Francisco all trace their origins and their names to Spanish missions.

Spanish priests were not alone in their quest to do God's holy work. The famous French "black robes" fanned out from Quebec in Canada to educate the Native Americans in what is now the northeastern and midwestern United States. Like their Spanish counterparts, French priests were partly responsible for the foundation of dozens of settlements that later became American towns and cities. Detroit, St. Louis, New Orleans, Mobile, and other cities have French origins.

The least ambitious missionary effort was led by English priests. Because Catholicism was a prohibited religion in all the English colonies except Maryland and Pennsylvania, colonial

7

Catholics — especially priests — kept a low profile. Unlike the Spanish and French, English priests largely ignored the Native Americans and concentrated on sustaining the religious faith of their compatriots in the New World.

Not surprisingly, these three European cultures had different approaches to religious education of Native Americans in the New World. "Spanish civilization crushed the Indian," wrote Francis Parkman. "English civilization scorned and neglected him; French civilization embraced and cherished him." Even though Parkman simplified a complex response to the Native Americans, there is truth in this dictum.[1]

※

In their attempt to dominate, civilize, and educate the Native Americans, the Spanish devised what became known as the "mission system." Under this system, the Spanish government provided financial support and physical protection for a series of small settlements to be established and administered by the Catholic Church. The general purpose of the mission system was to transform nomadic native tribes into a stable, docile work force that could be used for the benefit of the Spanish empire. The specific purpose of each mission was to provide religious education to the Native Americans, but missionary priests also taught cooking, sewing, weaving, farming, housing, cattle ranching, and other activities.

At its most basic level, the mission system was the spearhead of a cultural revolution. Spanish missionaries used every educational method known to them to transform the Native Americans from "savages" into "saints." Not surprisingly, the missionaries focused most of their time and effort on children. They were the first to be baptized, and they often received special instruction during the day. After the children, missionaries targeted adult leaders for conversion, theorizing that the rest of the tribe would follow.[2]

The educational methods used were crude but universal throughout the mission system. The chapel served as a classroom; the techniques used were memorization and religious pageantry. Missionaries were men of great faith, and to a man they believed that simple efforts would lead to lifelong conversion.

Yet these mission "schools" were more than efforts to convert Native Americans. Mission educational efforts also included occupational training and other aspects of Spanish civilization. In this manner, the missionaries and the government that supported them hoped to control Native Americans — to make them the bottom rung on the ladder of Spanish civilization. This purpose was succinctly captured by historian Herbert Bolton when he noted that "the missions were designed to be not only Christian seminaries, but in addition were outposts for the control and training schools for the civilizing of the frontier."[3] Yet the promise was never fulfilled.

Early missionary efforts in Florida, New Mexico, and Texas all started with promise, but ended in failure. Poor logistics, inconsistent leadership, native revolts, and threats from England and Spain all contributed to the demise of the Florida missions. The enslavement of Native Americans and their subsequent rebellion undermined the New Mexico missions, and Texas was a lost cause almost from the start. The church had little impact on these regions before the eighteenth century.[4]

If efforts in Florida, New Mexico, and Texas can be categorized as failures, the Arizona missions were qualified successes. This achievement was due in large part to one man — the Italian Jesuit Eusebio Kino — who arrived in Arizona in 1687 to work among the Pima Indians. Kino succeeded where others had failed because he accepted the tribe on its own terms. He did not try to force Catholicism on the Pima as many other missionaries did. Instead, Kino quietly introduced a number of improvements in the quality of Pima life. Simple innovations such as cattle ranching and the introduction of new grains of wheat and fruit improved the Pima diet without undermining their culture. But success was tied to Kino alone. His experiment among the Pima never flourished after his death in 1711.[5]

Just as the success of the Arizona missions was dependent

on one man, so also was the success of the California missions dependent on a single individual. Yet Junipero Serra, a Franciscan, was very different from Eusebio Kino. Kino had been an anthropologist, an explorer, and a cartographer. Serra was none of these; in fact, Serra's great strength was as an organizer and administrator. During his fifteen years in California from 1769 to 1784, Serra founded nine missions along the coast from San Diego to San Francisco.[6]

The success of the mission system in California was due to a number of other factors. Serra was able to gather around him a number of experienced, committed priests to staff each of his missions. Also, the California climate was conducive to raising cattle, growing fruit, and cultivating grapes for wine. Finally, the Native Americans of California were less hostile to the Spanish than the tribes of the Southwest; in fact, they were very responsive to the overtures of Father Serra and his colleagues, and the system continued into the nineteenth century.

For Spain and for the church, the California missions were an economic wonder. The use of native labor and the favorable climate allowed the missionaries to cultivate a vast quantity of land. The fruit, wine, and beef from California were among the best in the world, but the price was high. The hard labor killed off the native population, and the decline of the mission system in California followed the demise of the native population.

❖

As Spanish missionaries pushed north from Mexico, their French counterparts moved down from Canada. In superficial ways, French missionary activities were quite similar to the Spanish missionary system. Both efforts were administered jointly by church and government officials, and both efforts were dependent on the establishment of missions in strategic locations among native populations.

Beyond these similarities, however, the French missionary experience was very different from that of the Spanish. The French were not as committed to the New World as the Spanish, and fewer missionaries meant fewer mission stations and fewer conversions. The French sought only to trade with the Native Americans and convert the small number who would listen to the word of God.[7]

The French also faced a number of other obstacles unfamiliar to most Spanish missionaries. There were relatively few Native Americans in the Northeast and Midwest, and they were more sparsely settled and hostile to strangers. Long distances and frequent intertribal wars precipitated communications problems for the French and often forced them to choose sides. Adding to the confusion was the close proximity of the English colonists, who exacerbated the tribal wars to undermine the alliances between the Native Americans and the French. All of these problems were compounded by the cold climate and the short growing season, which limited the amount of travel and work that could be accomplished each year.

Like the Spanish missionaries, French priests concentrated their educational efforts on children as a prelude to converting adults. And like Spanish educational activities, the French efforts were largely a failure. When formal efforts would not work, the French tried other techniques. "When it came to persuading the Indians to accept Christianity," notes historian Jay Dolan, "no better technique could be used than to instill in them a fear of eternal damnation."[8] It was a crude but partially effective program of education and conversion.

Even though the French missionaries attempted to be systematic in converting the native population, success was heavily dependent on the commitment of individuals. The self-sacrifice of priests such as Jean de Brebeuf, Gabriel Lalemant, René Menard, and Isaac Jogues was legendary. These men literally devoted their lives to a valiant but vain effort to convert the Huron, the Algonquin, and even the Iroquois to Catholicism.[9]

From 1632 to 1649 Brebeuf and his colleagues established small but significant Christian communities among the Huron and Algonquin tribes, but these conversions came at a great price. The longstanding hostility between the Huron and the Iroquois put the missionaries in almost constant danger. Brebeuf, Lalemant, and Jogues, among others, all lost their lives at the hands of the Iroquois during the 1640s. Even though French civil authorities signed treaties with the Iroquois in the 1650s, the death of these Jesuit priests had a chilling effect on French missionary efforts.

The French missionary effort began to decline by the end of the seventeenth century. The generation that had produced heroic priests such as Brebeuf, Jogues, and later Jacques Marquette came to an end. Succeeding generations of French priests did not migrate to the New World in equivalent numbers, and those who did travel to Quebec worked among the natives who had already been converted to Catholicism. Gradually the French effort declined to the point that in 1749 only nineteen Jesuits remained in mission work in all of North America. This paltry number was cut even further by the French and Indian War (1754–63) between France and England and the suppression of the Jesuit order by the pope in 1763. By 1770, the French missionary presence in the United States had come to an end.[10]

The situation was not much better in the English colonies. Few Catholics chose to emigrate to the English colonies in the years before the American Revolution. Two priests and about a hundred lay people did settle in Maryland in March 1634, but this community grew slowly compared to the general population. Pennsylvania also accepted Catholics after the colony was founded in 1689, but the number of emigrants amounted to only a few thousand people. By 1765, there were only about twenty-five thousand Catholics in the English colonies out of an estimated population of nearly two million.[11]

Catholics who suffered through the perilous ocean voyage found a society even more anti-Catholic than the one they had left behind in England. Colonial editors published horror stories of alleged Catholic plots to usurp English liberties. Colonial clergymen preached sermons about the decadence of the pope in Rome and the conquests of his dreaded army of Jesuit priests. Colonial children learned of the evils of Catholicism in their primers and almanacs. The very idea of tolerating Catholics was regarded by many colonists as an act of weakness, a betrayal of English liberty and a denial of the righteousness of the Protestant faith.[12]

English colonial anti-Catholicism was codified into law in the years between 1690 and 1776. In Massachusetts, for example, Catholics were prohibited from holding religious services, preaching Catholic doctrine, or organizing their own congregations. In Maryland, Catholics were denied the right to vote, to practice law, or to hold public office. Priests in Maryland were subject to fines for celebrating the Mass or presiding at other religious services. Even though they had only a handful of Catholics, other colonies passed a series of laws similar to those of Massachusetts and Maryland. Only in Pennsylvania and Rhode Island — two colonies founded by religious dissenters — did Catholics have any measure of religious freedom.[13]

English Catholics struggled to maintain their religious faith in this hostile world. As one might expect, they turned to one another for mutual protection and solace. But they did not openly discuss their religious beliefs with others and attended Mass in private chapels in isolated locations. It was a hard life, a life full of restrictions and discouragement. "I will leave you to judge whether Maryland be a tolerable residence for a Roman Catholic," wrote one colonist in 1760. "Were I younger, I would certainly quit it."[14]

In the face of this overwhelming hatred and legal restriction, colonial Catholics made little effort to establish their own schools. The majority of Catholic children received their education at home. Occasional visits by traveling schoolmasters were opportunities to polish this home schooling. Rare visits by missionary priests were the time to obtain religious instruction.

Not all English colonial Catholic children were given such an informal education, however. Wealthy Catholics were very concerned that their children, especially their sons, receive rigorous formal instruction in both secular and religious subjects.

There is evidence, for example, that one Ralph Crouch, a former Jesuit novice, instructed Catholic children in St. Mary's County as early as 1640 and continued to do so for the next twenty years. His school at Newton Manor, a center of Jesuit activity in Maryland, was supported by gifts of land and cattle from the estates of wealthy Catholic families in the county. This school continued intermittently until the turn of the eighteenth century.[15]

A second Catholic school was opened in Cecil County, Maryland, in 1745 to provide preparatory training for young Catholics soon to enter the College of St. Omer's in Flanders. Among the first students at "Bohemia Manor," as the school was called, was John Carroll, who would become the first Catholic bishop in the United States, and his cousin, Charles Carroll, one of the signers of the Declaration of Independence. The school prospered during the middle of the eighteenth century by providing rigorous instruction to the sons of the Brents, the Neales, the Heaths, the Carrolls, and other prominent Maryland Catholic families.[16]

Newton Manor and Bohemia Manor were the only successful Catholic educational experiments in Maryland in the years before the Revolution. There were other attempts, of course. Mary Ann Marsh boldly opened "a popish seminary" in Baltimore in 1757, but it was quickly closed by the colonial government. Another attempt to open a Catholic school in Baltimore in 1774 ended when the school was attacked by an angry mob.

Pennsylvania's Catholics had a very different experience. Most important, they did not face angry mobs protesting the establishment of "popish seminaries." In fact, Catholics in Pennsylvania were free to build churches and schools as they saw fit. But this tolerance did not seem to matter much because there is no documentary evidence that the Pennsylvania Catholics ever established a school before the 1780s. Local tradition does claim that the German Catholics of Goshenhoppen organized regular Catholic instruction for children in 1741. Early histories also claim that Jesuit priests and an occasional layman conducted informal classes in other Pennsylvania communities. But Catholic education in the colony remained informal throughout the eighteenth century because these small, rural Catholic communities could not afford to support schools as well as churches. It was more a matter of economics than religious commitment.[17]

※

The dismal fate of colonial Catholicism in general and Catholic education in particular changed rapidly during the American Revolution. The anti-Catholicism of the colonial era diminished as a large segment of English colonial society — both Catholic and non-Catholic — united to fight Mother England. Protestant editors and clergymen turned their pulpits and pens away from the "evils of Catholicism" to attack all who gave comfort to the detested "red coats."

More important, state legislatures in the 1770s dropped legal restrictions keeping Catholics from full citizenship and added statutes on the freedom of conscience and religion. Pennsylvania passed such laws in September 1776, and Maryland followed in November with a constitution that eliminated all restrictions on the practice of Catholicism. Catholics responded by fighting for independence side by side with their Protestant compatriots.[18]

With the end of the war in 1783, some Catholics must have wondered if the freedoms they had been granted were permanent or if the nation would revert to the anti-Catholicism of the past. This uncertainty made Catholics apprehensive about their place in American society. For the most part, Catholics wanted to fit in, to be inconspicuous, to accept the dominant Protestant culture in all things but religious beliefs. But this goal proved difficult to achieve.

The first obstacle to assimilation was the foreign orientation of the church. In many European nations the church had been given privileged status by the government, but the church in America had to accommodate itself to being only one of many religions, none more privileged than another. The selection of John Carroll as first bishop of the United States was fortuitous in this regard. Carroll helped Rome to understand this new nation and likewise helped Americans understand Catholicism.

A second obstacle to Catholic assimilation was the rapid growth of the Catholic population through immigration. As early as 1790, tens of thousands of foreigners from Ireland, France, and Germany came to the United States, thereby reinforcing the dominant American view that Catholics were foreigners. Carroll and his episcopal successors faced the complicated task of Americanizing these foreign-born Catholics without compromising their religious faith. To a large extent the bishops relied on parish schools to achieve this goal.

Carroll's initial campaign for parish schools was motivated by a simple concern. Without Catholic schools or some similar social institution, untold numbers of Catholics would be lost to the church through intermarriage and what Carroll called "unavoidable intercourses with non-Catholics." In his first pastoral letter to the American church in 1792, Carroll emphasized the importance of Christian education as a means of instilling principles that would preserve religious faith. He called on parents to educate their children while they retained "their native docility and their hearts are uncorrupted by vice."[19]

Carroll acknowledged that the expense of Catholic schools would be great and many parents would have to sacrifice to support these institutions. What may have surprised Carroll was that Catholic parents would want a say in how these schools were administered. Through elected trustees, Catholic parents pooled their funds, built parish schools, hired Catholic teachers, and decided on the curriculum. Trustees saw no reason to consult the parish priest about educational matters.

When Bishop Carroll and his priests attempted to exert their right to control parish schools as specified in canon law, the laity rebelled. During the years from 1815 until the late 1830s, trustees in Norfolk, Charleston, Philadelphia, New York City, and elsewhere fought with priests and bishops over the appointment of pastors and the financing of churches and schools. "Trusteeism," as it was called, proved to be the most significant conflict in the American church in the years before the Civil War.[20]

⁂

Catholics in Philadelphia established the first of these parochial schools in 1783. From the beginning, St. Mary's School was a collaboration between the pastor and his parishioners. Certainly the pastor, Father Robert Molyneaux, was the first among equals on the school committee, but he did not have the power to make educational decisions unilaterally.[21]

The most difficult task facing St. Mary's trustees was hiring and keeping effective teachers. There were no orders of teaching sisters in the country at the time, and few lay people considered teaching to be anything but temporary employment on the way to a law practice, a farm, or a shop. Since few candidates for teaching jobs had much experience, it was difficult to select the most able from among the applicants. It is not surprising, therefore, that St. Mary's School had eight different schoolmasters from 1787 to 1800. Some of them left voluntarily; others were fired.[22]

Raising funds to sustain St. Mary's School was another trustee responsibility. The funds to purchase and refurbish the school building came from subscriptions, and there is no indication that the trustees had any difficulty raising the necessary funds. Operating funds came from several sources — tuition, donations, and annuities. Additional funds were raised by Father Molyneaux through a "charity sermon" given once a year for the benefit of the school. Finally, a small endowment was established through the donations of parishioners. Money did not seem a problem during the first years of Catholic schooling in Philadelphia.[23]

St. Mary's was not the only Catholic parish to build a school in Philadelphia during those years. In 1788, the Germans broke away from St. Mary's and established Holy Trinity church and school. For the first fifteen years classes were held in the church basement, but in 1803 the trustees were finally able to raise enough money to build a school. The school prospered largely because of the growth of the German Catholic community in Philadelphia and its commitment to Catholic education. A third school in Philadelphia was established in St. Augustine parish in 1811, but the parish was unable to sustain the school and closed in 1815. The Catholic community in Philadelphia supported only two schools until the arrival of large numbers of Irish and German immigrants in the 1830s.[24]

Less is known of Catholic schools in other cities in the early years of the nineteenth century. New York had a growing Catholic population during these years, and the Catholic schools in the city were never able to meet the need. The thirteen hundred Catholics in New York in 1800 were able to establish a school in conjunction with St. Peter's parish, but the school provided for only a small share of the Catholic children in the city. Even so, by 1806, St. Peter's was the largest denominational school in New York, with an enrollment of 220 pupils. The cost of maintaining the school was substantial, and the parish was fortunate to receive a share of the state school fund to assist in paying expenses. Indeed, the Catholic Church in New York began to depend on this share of the state school fund and consider it a right rather than a privilege.[25]

As the Catholic population of New York grew through immigration, St. Peter's School could not keep pace. By 1810, for example, the Catholic population had grown to more than fifteen thousand and the number of Catholic children to over thirty-one hundred. St. Peter's was providing schooling for only five hundred of those children.[26]

Some relief did come in the years from 1815 to 1820. In 1815 St. Patrick's parish established a school, and the Sisters of Charity opened two schools in the next few years. But even the addition of three new schools was not enough to meet the demand. St. Peter's was forced to take a desperate measure to make more room for students; the school was converted to the monitorial system, in which the oldest students taught the youngest students, out of necessity. By 1820, the Catholic population of New York was up to twenty thousand with about four thousand Catholic children. Only seven hundred of these children were enrolled in Catholic schools.[27]

The biggest blow to the struggling Catholic schools in New York was the end of public funding. In 1825, the Public School Society, a nominally Protestant civic organization, convinced the state assembly to end its support for denominational schools in New York City in favor of supporting the nondenominational Protestant schools sponsored by the Public School Society. Without state subsidies, the growth of Catholic schooling came to a virtual halt in the late 1820s. By 1830, there were thirty-five thousand Catholics in New York and only five schools for the seven thousand children of school age. The church in New York was falling farther and farther behind in educating its children.[28]

The story of Catholic education in Boston during these years is largely a tale of frustration and failure. In 1806, a group of Catholics sought the permission of the Massachusetts legislature to hold a lottery to raise money for a school; the petition was never answered, and they looked for other ways to raise the needed funds. A subscription drive in 1807 did bring in nearly $600, and Father F. A. Matignon of Holy Cross parish was optimistic enough to purchase land for a school. But the dream was never realized. "Our only affliction here," Matignon wrote to John Carroll, "is our inability hitherto and perhaps for years hence to finance a Catholic school which is absolutely indispensable for us."[29] Matignon did not live to see his school.

It was not until 1820 that Jean Cheverus, the first bishop of the Boston diocese, was able to establish a parochial school in that city. Under the direction of the Ursuline Sisters of Montreal, the institution opened in September of that year with students attending half-day session at first. The school seemed to operate without problems until 1823–24 when three of the original four sisters died of consumption. The school struggled along during the rest of the decade with an enrollment of between fifty and sixty pupils. The institution did little to meet the needs of an ever-expanding Irish Catholic population in that city.

The ability of Catholics to staff parish schools was aided substantially by Elizabeth Bayley Seton, an unassuming convert to Catholicism who became the first native-born American saint. It was Seton's vision of an order of teaching sisters that became the framework for the growth of Catholic schooling during these formative years and the decades that followed. Staffing no fewer than fifteen schools in eleven cities in the years between 1809 and 1830, Seton's Sisters of Charity brought stability and order to an otherwise chaotic pattern of Catholic educational development. Indeed, Seton's sister-teachers often made the difference between success and failure in many Catholic parishes. It was an extraordinary achievement — even for an American saint.[30]

Seton's journey of faith took her from New York City to Italy, back to New York, to Baltimore, and finally to the small Maryland community of Emmitsburg. Along the way, Seton suffered the death of her husband, converted to Catholicism, was shunned by her family, and established a Catholic school in Baltimore. Her journey ended when she established the American branch of the Daughters of Charity. The motherhouse at Emmitsburg became the nerve center of a national educational enterprise.

Seton received a number of invitations to establish schools in other Catholic communities. In response, she turned her attention to providing care for the orphans and poor children in the major cities of the new republic. She sent three sisters to Philadelphia in 1814 to open St. Joseph's orphan asylum and sent four sisters to New York three years later to establish a similar institution. Seton sisters would go on to establish asylums in Baltimore and Frederick, Maryland; Washington, D.C.; Harrisburg, Pennsylvania; Albany, New York; Cincinnati, Ohio; Wilmington, Delaware; and New Orleans, Louisiana, during the 1820s. More importantly, most of these asylums doubled as the first formal schools for Catholic children in those communities. Elizabeth Seton earned her reputation as the founder of the Catholic parochial school movement in the United States.[31]

※

The origins of American Catholic parochial education can be found in the European quest for God, gold, and glory. During the sixteenth, seventeenth, and eighteenth centuries, colonial Catholics struggled with a vast unexplored territory. To say that missionary work in the New World required exceptional faith and heroism is an understatement. Indeed, the limited success of the church in all of the colonies — Spanish, French, and English — was due largely to the personal sacrifices and skills of a few great priests. Their willingness to give all, including their very lives, left a Catholic imprint on virtually every region of the United States.

Several themes emerged repeatedly in the history of Catholic education in the colonial era. First, Catholics had to overcome significant obstacles before they could build their own schools. The very survival of Catholicism as a religion in America was in doubt until after the Revolutionary War. After the war, the church faced the challenge of tens of thousands immigrants to be acclimated to the new nation. Carroll and his fellow Catholics struggled to keep up with the demand for parish schools. Their record was mixed at best.

The second theme in these early decades was the central importance of women religious to the eventual success of parish school development. The hard work and persistence of Elizabeth Seton and other women like her led to a steady supply of devoted sister-teachers who were the backbone of the parish school system for nearly 125 years.

Yet the most important theme — one that pervades the history of Catholic education from its earliest days — is sacrifice. For more than two centuries, Catholics from many nations and a wide range of professions were willing to risk their personal safety for the greater glory of God. To be sure, some of these Catholics were motivated by the hope of personal gain. Yet one cannot dispute that most colonial Catholics — missionaries and colonists alike — were willing to sacrifice their well-being for the sake of education. They all knew that the future of the church in the New World was tied to educating the next generation in the ways of the faith. It was a goal worthy of great personal sacrifice.

Chapter 2

Strangers in the Land

A MERICAN SOCIETY was turned upside down in the decades between 1820 and 1870. Over five million Irish and German immigrants arrived in the United States during those years, bringing cultural diversity to the largely English culture of the new nation. At first the number of immigrants was small; a mere 150,000 arrived in the 1820s. But the trickle quickly became a stream and then a flood with each succeeding decade: 600,000 arrived in the 1830s, 1.7 million in the 1840s, and 2.3 million in the 1850s. It was the beginning of a century-long social phenomenon that shifted the population of many nations, particularly the populations of Europe, to the United States.

The general population was ambivalent about these new arrivals. European immigrants came to the United States when the nation desperately needed more workers if its economy was to continue to grow. But these immigrants also arrived at a time when the native-born population was still too unsure of its nationality and uneasy about ethnic cultures and foreign religions. As the number of immigrants increased, so also did social tension and class division.[1]

There were hundreds of reasons why the peasants of Europe were both pushed and pulled to the New World. The population of Europe had doubled between 1750 and 1815, putting a strain on the food supply. The introduction of large-scale farming and the rise of the factory system displaced millions of peasants and forced them to find new ways to support themselves. Social, political, and religious upheaval unsettled the lives of additional millions. Handbills and cheap newspapers inviting and encouraging American emigration circulated in every country in Europe. These are among the most obvious reasons for the arrival of millions of immigrants on America's shore in the years from 1820 to 1860.[2]

These new arrivals constituted the potential work force for the growing number of factories, farms, and public construction projects, but they were hardly the ideal work force. These immigrants were largely illiterate, impoverished, and, worst of all, Catholic. Religion seemed to stand out as the focal point of contention. "I think that the Catholic religion has erroneously been regarded as the natural enemy of democracy," observed Alexis de Tocqueville.[3]

Native-born Americans focused on the Catholic Church as the symbol of all that was wrong with the foreign-born. Attacks against Catholic churches, priests, nuns, and the laity took place in many major cities during the years before the Civil War. Boston, New York, Philadelphia, Baltimore, Cincinnati, Detroit, St. Louis — each was the setting for violent street fighting. Two specific confrontations stand out as important case studies of anti-Catholicism: the burning of the Ursuline convent at Charlestown, near Boston, in 1834 and the Philadelphia Bible Riots of 1844. The repercussions of these and other anti-Catholic incidents lasted for generations.[4]

The Ursuline Sisters had operated a convent school for girls from upper-class Protestant and Unitarian families from the time of their arrival in Boston in 1818. But beginning in the 1830s, Congregationalist ministers used their pulpits to attack the convent school as a symbol of the coming Catholic dominance of Boston's ruling class. Tension in the lower-class neighborhoods near the convent increased as the pulpit attacks became more numerous and vociferous during the early months of 1834. The nervous breakdown and "escape" of one of the Ursuline sisters in July 1834 added grist to the rumors of barbarity and immorality in the convent. Urged on by Congregationalist ministers, the working classes rallied and burned the convent and an adjoining farmhouse on August 11. A later trial of the arsonists was a farce, and the accused were not only exonerated but also applauded as heroes.[5]

The emergence of organized anti-Catholicism in Philadelphia in the form of nativist "American-Republican" clubs led to the worst anti-Catholic rioting in American history. Campaigning in the municipal elections of May 1844, the American-Republicans held a rally on the edge of one of the city's Irish neighborhoods, and fighting broke out between the nativists and Catholics on the edge of the crowd. Bricks and bullets flew and a young Protestant boy was killed.

The Protestant response was both massive and immediate. The north side of the city became a battleground: Catholic homes were set on fire; a Catholic church and a rectory were attacked and burned. Even though order was restored on May 9, the tension never subsided, and a second Catholic church was attacked and destroyed on July 5. The riots of May and July 1844 left the Catholic community of Philadelphia embittered.[6]

The violence in Boston, Philadelphia, and other cities was the result of an anti-Catholicism deeply rooted in the American mind. Catholicism had been anathema since the establishment of the British colonies. The Catholic Church was mocked in both the popular and religious press, in novels, histories, children's books, and even in almanacs. Three points were repeated in these publications: that Catholicism was not a Christian religion but a form of idolatry, that Catholicism was irreconcilable with democracy, and that the American acceptance of the Catholic moral standard would lead to the nation's demise.

Using the pulpit and the press, Protestant ministers and social reformers warned the nation to be on the watch for Catholic conspiracies to deprive America of its liberties. But exposing Catholicism as a national threat did nothing about millions of Catholic immigrants already in the country. Native-born Americans searched for ways and means of transforming the Catholic foreigner into productive, God-fearing citizens.[7]

※

Among the social institutions that promised to "homogenize" foreigners was the common school, or public elementary school. "It was not their exclusive purpose," notes historian Carl Kaestle, "but it dominated the thinking of schoolmen. Because poverty, social deviance and religious differences were seen in highly charged moral terms, the schoolmen did not conceive of homogenization as a process which would produce a stable mixture of original ingredients, but rather as a sort of alchemy, in which some undesirable members of society would be transformed into useful members."[8] Even though they had no proof that this transformation process would work, common school advocates spoke as if it were only a matter of time before immigrant children were acting and thinking like native-born children.

Common school advocates proposed to undertake two tasks in their effort to Americanize immigrant children. First, common schools would be used to promote universal literacy. An enlightened citizenry would be the best line of defense against foreign conspiracy and the enemies of democracy. Literacy would open the minds of immigrant children, allow them to think for themselves, and make them less dependent on parish priests and foreign-born parents for guidance. Second, by mixing children from all backgrounds and social classes, common schools would forge a common national identity, an identity based on deference, diligence, honesty, thrift, and other conservative social values. Immigrant children would be encouraged to abandon their ties to their parents, homeland, and religion and embrace the American republic and Protestant religion. Reformers argued that the twin goals of literacy and national identity would insure the new nation of homogeneity in its national culture.[9]

The curriculum of the common schools was nondenominational but distinctly Protestant. At the core of the curriculum was the King James Bible, which was used as a textbook for inspiration, example, and moral instruction. It never occurred to common school advocates that the use of the King James Bible would cause controversy or that Catholics would object to its use. In the minds of common school advocates, this version of the Bible was an essential tool in the effort to forge a common national identity.

In addition to the Bible, common school advocates depended on the moralistic schoolbooks of William Holmes McGuffey. The popularity of these schoolbooks was understandable because McGuffey never forgot that the Bible was the keystone of the common school curriculum. As historian Timothy L. Smith notes, McGuffey's *Readers* were "handbooks of common morality, testaments to the Protestant virtues which a half a century of experience had elevated into the culture-religion of the new nation."[10] The stories and vignettes in these little books mirrored the values of the native-born middle class in America but made little effort to appeal to the sensibilities of Irish and German immigrants.

The overtures of common school advocates generated very different reactions from the wealthy, from the middle class, and from immigrant Catholics. The wealthy agreed with the message of common schooling in the hope that it would produce a docile, deferential work force, but gave no thought to sending their own children to these "common" schools. The middle class also agreed with the message of common schooling in the hope that it would break down class barriers and contribute to their own material well-being but did not want their children associating with poor Catholic children. Immigrant Catholics agreed with the social values implicit in common schooling, but objected vociferously to the Protestant overtones of the common school curriculum. In fact, immigrant Catholics presented a serious challenge to the basic assumption that common schools should be a major force in the lives of their children.

In proposing to establish a common school system, social reformers grossly underestimated the objections and determination of the Catholic Church. Common school advocates had worked out compromises with other Christian denominations, and they expected to do the same with the Catholic Church. These common school advocates failed to understand that there were fundamental differences between their own educational assumptions and those of the Catholic Church. Their misunderstandings led to frustration and anger in the decades before the Civil War.

The differences between the two sides, notes historian Carl Kaestle, can be divided into textual, catechetical, and cultural. The textual issue concerned which version of the Bible — King James or Douay — would be used to teach Catholic children. Even though this was a minor difference, common school advocates were irritated that the Catholic Church was unwilling to join other religions in the use of a "common" version of the Bible. The church, for its part, was upset with the notion that Catholic children would be educated with a Protestant Bible.

A second issue separating the two groups was catechetical. Protestant ministers and public school advocates claimed that reading the Bible without note or comment was nonsectarian and nondogmatic. Catholic leaders vehemently disagreed and charged that Bible reading without guidance was a Protestant concept and therefore unacceptable for the education of Catholic children. On both the textual and the catechetical issues, no agreement could be reached because few Catholic leaders were convinced that there was any common ground on which to compromise. To Catholics, education without denominational doctrine was more dangerous than no education at all.[11]

But the major Catholic concern about common schools was cultural, a concern that struck at the very premise of the common school. Public school advocates never defined the Americanization process; children of all religious faiths and cultures were to be mixed together with liberal doses of deference, patriotism, Christianity, and the good moral example of a righteous teacher, and the end result would be "Americanized" children. Common school advocates were quite clear in their argument that Americanization and education were the responsibility of the state.

Catholic leaders challenged both of these arguments. They accused common school advocates of incorporating large doses of Protestant doctrine into the "nonsectarian" common school curriculum. Catholics further accused common school advocates of a subtle campaign to win the allegiance of Catholic children and at the same time to denigrate the Catholic Church and the Irish and German cultures. The end result, noted Catholic leaders, was a generational conflict between these "Americanized" children and their immigrant Catholic parents. How could Catholic parents send their children to common schools knowing that the children would return alienated from their families and their religion? It was clear to church leaders and many Catholic parents that the common school was not acceptable for the education of Catholic children.[12]

The church also disputed the claim that the state had any role in the education of children. For hundreds of years, indeed during the formative years of the American republic, education had been a private matter, handled by the churches in consultation with parents. The state had no role in the education of children, the church argued; the establishment of common schools was a usurpation of the right of parents to choose schools that reflected their own moral code and culture.

In defining their position on the question of common schools, Catholic leaders consistently turned to the newly emerging Catholic press for amplification and dissemination. Catholic editors obliged by giving statements on Catholic education prominent display on the front pages of their publications. As the number of these publications grew from a single paper in 1822 to more than twenty by 1842, so also did their impact. The *U.S. Catholic Miscellany* in Charleston, the *Truth Teller* in New York, the *Jesuit* in Boston, and the *Catholic Herald* in Philadelphia defended immigrants and their children against the attacks of nativists, Protestants, and reformers and at the same time proclaimed the Catholic position on education.

In fact, Catholic newspapers and pamphlets were the main means of contact for immigrants with the world outside the ghetto. The press was also the main means of religious education for adults. For this reason, Catholic arguments attacking public schools were not written to convince non-Catholics of the injustice of these institutions — non-Catholics never saw Catholic newspapers. These lengthy and laborious polemics were to build unanimity of opinion *within* the Catholic community, to convince lax Catholic parents to withdraw their children from public schools, and to encourage loyal Catholics to fight for a share of the state school funds. Catholic bishops used these newspapers to speak to their flocks on the issues of the day, and no one issue was more important than the education of the young.[13]

The bishops also spoke to the Catholic population through pastoral letters that were issued at the close of periodic provincial councils. Beginning in 1829 and continuing until 1849, the Catholic hierarchy met every two years to discuss the issues affecting the Catholic Church in America. The resulting pastoral letters were meant to guide both the temporal and the spiritual lives of American Catholics. As was the custom in such letters, the advice was very general, reflecting the bishops' concern for various social problems, but offering no specific solutions. It remained for the Catholic press to interpret what the bishops wanted done.[14]

The pastoral letters on education warned Catholic parents about the dangers of public schooling. "In placing [your children] at school," noted the bishops in 1829, "seek for those teachers who will cultivate the seeds which you have sown; for of what avail will it be, that you have done so much, if the germs which begin to put forth shall now be stifled or eradicated; and should tares be sown where you have reaped the soil?"[15] Throughout the 1830s, the messages from the councils were very similar; in 1833, and again in 1837, the bishops reminded the laity of their duties as parents and implied that their only possible choice was Catholic education.[16]

The bishops were less than pleased with the response of the laity and they were particularly alarmed at the large number of Catholic children who attended public schools or no schools at all. But the bishops were not so much concerned with illiteracy as they were with religion. "The great evil," they concluded in 1840, "is the danger to which [the children] are exposed, of having their faith undermined, the imperfect instruction which they receive, if they get any, upon the most important subject of religion, the nearly total abandonment of their religious practices and their exposure in their tender youth to the fatal influence of shame which generally arises from the mockery of the superciliousness of those who undervalue their creed."[17]

In 1843, the bishops were even more direct. "We have seen with serious alarm," they stated, "efforts made to poison the fountains of public education, by giving it a sectarian hue and accustoming the children to the use of the Bible made under sectarian bias."[18] In the final assessment, the bishops said, the eternal salvation of all children rested with their parents. "Let them avail themselves of their natural rights," concluded the pastoral letter of 1843, "and see that no interference with the faith of their children be used in the public schools and no attempt made to induce conformity in anything contrary to the Catholic Church."[19]

The bishops were quite explicit on what parents could do to protect the spiritual lives of their children. "It is no easy matter to preserve the faith of your children in the midst of so many difficulties," noted the pastoral of 1840. "We are always better pleased to have a separate system of education for the children of our communion because we have found by painful experience, that in any common effort it was always expected that our distinctive principles of religious belief in practice should be yielded to the demands of those who thought it proper to charge us with error."[20]

The message was clear in 1840, and the rhetoric became more vigorous in succeeding councils, particularly in the plenary councils of 1852, 1866, and 1884. Catholic parents had a moral responsibility to provide for the spiritual lives of their children, and the best means of providing that spiritual life was through parish schools. Catholic parents were never *required* to send their children to parish schools until 1884, but not to do so was to incur the displeasure of the organized church.[21]

The message of pastoral letters was filtered through the pens of Catholic editors to the laity. The letters served as the justification for the seemingly endless editorials in favor of Catholic education that appeared in the Catholic press. Were the pastoral letters and the subsequent editorials effective tools in rallying the support of the Catholic population? The answer has to be a qualified yes, for without the strong support of the hierarchy, there would have been few parish schools. But the influence of the bishops was limited; even with all their cajoling, only about half of all Catholic children ever attended Catholic schools.

❖

Even though the bishops had only limited influence as a group, they did have substantial influence as individual leaders of specific dioceses. Some bishops — Benedict Fenwick of Boston, for example — chose to minimize their involvement in educational matters. Others were able to do very little because ethnic conflict and poverty had created far larger problems than the establishment of parish schools. Still other bishops were tireless advocates of parochial education, and in their dioceses their word was church doctrine. Two of these men — Francis Kenrick of Philadelphia and John Hughes of New York — were so forceful as to become national leaders of the Catholic school movement.[22]

Of the two, Kenrick was considered the moderate. No less an advocate of parochial schools than Hughes or his brother bishops, Kenrick saw no value in dramatic confrontations. He saw no need to rally his flock against Protestant or "infidel" common school reformers. From the time of his arrival in

Philadelphia in 1830 until his death as archbishop of Baltimore in 1863, Kenrick quietly and consistently stressed the need for parish schools.[23]

He had been born in Dublin in 1796, the son of a clerk. After entering the seminary to study for the priesthood, young Francis was quickly recognized as a scholar and sent to Rome to complete his education at the Vatican College of Propaganda. After his ordination in 1821, he accepted an invitation to teach at St. Thomas Seminary in Bardstown, Kentucky, where he distinguished himself as a writer and pulpit orator. His administrative skills as secretary to the First Provincial Council in 1829 impressed the assembled bishops, and Kenrick was nominated to succeed the aging Henry Conwell as bishop of Philadelphia.

During his tenure in Philadelphia, Kenrick faced numerous tests of his leadership. In 1831, he was challenged by the trustees of St. Mary's Church over control of parish affairs, and he quickly put the congregation under interdict. His firm resolve not to negotiate and pressure from the parish members to once again hear Mass in their church forced the trustees to agree to Kenrick's demands. All future donations and property at St. Mary's were in the name of the bishop, and Kenrick had no more trouble with the trustees of St. Mary's parish or any other parish in the diocese.[24]

With the exception of the trustee problem, Kenrick counseled moderation and compromise on all issues. His regular consultations with the priests of his diocese minimized misunderstandings within the diocese, and the weekly publication of the *Catholic Herald* provided guidance and instruction to the laity. His moderate policies led to an agreement with public school officials that permitted Catholic children to use the Douay version of the Bible in the common schools. In fact, it was Kenrick's counsel of moderation that minimized the retaliatory violence of the Catholic population of Philadelphia after the horrible anti-Catholic riots of the spring and summer of 1844. It was Kenrick's quiet but persistent resolve, rather than confrontation or polemics, that led to the establishment of a parochial school system in Philadelphia in the early 1850s.

Kenrick's moderation was in sharp contrast to the confrontational style of John Hughes of New York. Hughes was a suspicious, abrasive leader who fought for his own rights and those of his flock. Born in June of 1797 in County Tyrone in the north of Ireland, Hughes and his family emigrated to the United States in 1816 just as young John reached manhood. Determined to become a priest, he worked as a gardener to pay for his seminary education. He was ordained in 1826 and assigned to St. Augustine's parish in Philadelphia, where he distinguished himself as a curate. Over the next seven years, Hughes served in several posts, including secretary to Bishop Kenrick, theologian at the First Plenary Council, founder and editor of the *Catholic Herald,* and pastor of the trustee-plagued St. Mary's parish. But Hughes gained his reputation as a church militant through a series of polemical newspaper exchanges with the Reverend John Breckinridge, a Presbyterian minister and bitter foe of the Catholic Church. Carried on between 1833 and 1836, these "debates" gave Hughes national exposure as a defender of the faith.[25]

Hughes's activities and reputation made it almost inevitable that he would be chosen to lead one of the country's most beleaguered dioceses. In January of 1838, the pope selected Hughes to assist and eventually succeed John DuBois, the aging bishop of New York. "Hughes immediately seized control of the diocese," wrote historian Richard J. Purcell, "for so forceful a character could hardly qualify as a subservient assistant. He found an apologetic people who were groping toward active citizenship and improved social and economic position, and he left a militant people insistent on the rights to which their growing numerical strength entitled them."[26] Hughes was the key figure in the transformation of the church into an important force in New York urban affairs.

Hughes's combative style and unwillingness to compromise made it inevitable that he would clash with city leaders over public education. In fact, the bishop's campaign against the

Public School Society between 1840 and 1842 received national attention in the press, and it is often considered by historians to be a turning point in the church's effort to establish parish schools.

Unlike Kenrick, however, Hughes did not give up when his campaign for a share of the state school fund was unsuccessful. He formed a coalition that garnered enough votes to prevent a Democratic victory in the municipal election of 1841. With votes as leverage, Hughes was able to persuade the state legislature to remove control of New York City's share of the state school fund from the Public School Society. If the Catholics of New York could not have a share of the state school fund, he would also deny that privilege to private Protestant schools.[27]

Hughes's self-image was that of a protector; it was a mode of social behavior that would predominate among the American hierarchy for the next century. "I had to stand up among them as their bishop and chief," Hughes wrote in his memoirs, "to warn them against the dangers that surrounded them; to contend for their rights as a religious community; to repel the spirit of faction among them; to encourage the timid and sometimes to restrain the impetuous; in short to knead them into dough, to be leavened by the spirit of the Catholic faith and of Catholic union."[28] Hughes articulated and typified the ghetto mentality that dominated most of the American Catholic Church throughout the nineteenth century. In short, Catholicism in America was a religion under siege, and Hughes and his fellow bishops were the commanders. It remained for the men and women in the pews to fall into formation and be good soldiers.

Rapid social change accompanied by misunderstanding, hostility, and resistance were important ingredients in the process of educational development in the years from 1830 to 1870. The grand plan was to use a common school system to transform a diverse population of children into a homogeneous, deferential, and very American citizenry. But there was a major flaw in the plan. In the mind of common school advocates, to be American was to be Protestant, and this was a premise that was wholly unacceptable to an emerging Catholic population. Catholics resisted these efforts by retreating into ethnic ghettos and building their own schools. The prevailing state of inter-denominational relations in the mid-nineteenth century was persistent conflict.

Yet the two sides did have an influence on each other. The tensions between public and Catholic school advocates forced the two sides to modify the content of their curricula. After a decade of violence in the 1840s, both sides sought other ways of winning the hearts and minds of the Catholic population. Public school advocates took measures to make their schools less sectarian. Catholic school advocates countered with measures to make their schools more secular. Both sides were competing for the attention and loyalty of Catholic parents and their children. It is a competition that would continue well into the twentieth century.

Chapter 3 _____

A Range of Educational Experiences

E VEN THOUGH the American bishops spoke with one voice on parish schools, the responses to their call were different from one diocese to the next. In Boston and other Massachusetts cities, little effort was made to build parish schools; Catholic parents were satisfied to send their children to common schools. But in New York and Philadelphia, many Catholics would have little to do with public schools, and some were involved in dramatic, sometimes violent confrontations over the use of the Bible and the equitable distribution of state school funds. In Chicago, Cincinnati, and other midwestern cities, Catholics were active in the establishment of both public and parochial schools, and there was little of the acrimony that marked the history of Catholic schools in the East.[1]

The local bishop's influence was often the decisive factor in determining whether parish schools were built. If parish schools were of little interest to the bishop, little was done. If the bishop promoted parish schools, Catholic education flourished.

Another factor was the support of the immigrant laity for parish schools. The Italians showed little interest in building parish schools. The Irish had mixed feelings about parish schools, and many sent their children to public schools. The Germans, however, were unswerving in their support for parish schools. Other nationalities fit within this spectrum of divergent views on Catholic schools.

A third factor affecting parochial education was the availability of public schools at the time Catholics arrived in different regions of the country. In the East, common schools were widely available, and Catholic schools were branded by many as a divisive element in the public order. But in the Midwest, where common schools were few in number and overcrowded, Catholic schools were often praised as important supplements to public education. The various combinations of these and other unique factors precipitated a variety of Catholic educational experiences in the years before the Civil War.[2]

The paucity of parish schools in Boston was due to several of these factors, most notable the intense poverty of the immigrant Catholic population and the low priority given to the establishment of parish schools by the priests and bishops of the diocese. Parish pastors were well aware that Catholic parents could ill afford to send their children to any school, let alone pay for the establishment of parish schools. Catholic children were needed as wage earners to contribute to the welfare of their families. Keeping the family together was their first priority, and that meant that everybody worked. Parish pastors understood the plight of their flock and asked for nothing more than the establishment and support of a church. Bishops Benedict Fenwick and John Williams accepted this state of affairs with some reluctance, but understood that they were powerless to change matters.[3]

Yet in spite of the poor response to the call for parish schools, there was Catholic educational activity in Boston during these years. Throughout the 1830s and 1840s, the diocese operated three Catholic schools, but these institutions could provide instruction for only a few hundred of the twelve to seventeen thousand Catholic children in the diocese during those years.[4] The one Catholic educational venture that did achieve a measure of success was the Catholic Sunday school. By 1845, Boston Catholic Sunday schools were enrolling more than four thousand children a year, and these schools continued to grow throughout the decade and into the 1850s. But Sunday school was a short-term measure, and parish schools in Boston were virtually nonexistent in the years before the Civil War.

In this climate of inactivity there emerged in Lowell, Massachusetts, an educational experiment that was to have important implications for the history of Catholic education throughout the United States. In an effort to "consider the expediency of establishing a separate school for the benefit of the Irish population," the Lowell town meeting of 1831 appropriated fifty dollars for the support of the local Catholic school. At the time, most Massachusetts schools were affiliated with religious denominations, and the grant to the Catholic school seemed the most logical way of providing for the education of Lowell's small but growing Irish population. The relationship worked well, and by 1835 three Catholic schools in Lowell were being supported with public funds.[5]

The terms of the agreement between the town school committee and the parish pastors were straightforward. The committee reserved the right to examine and appoint all teachers working in parish schools; to prescribe and regulate the "textbooks, exercises and studies" used in the schools; and to examine, inspect, and supervise the school on the same basis as other town schools. The parish pastors insisted that qualified Catholics be appointed as teachers in their schools and that the textbooks contain no statements offensive to Catholics or the Catholic Church. The committee and the pastors mutually agreed that parish school buildings were to be provided and maintained by the parishes and that teachers were to be paid by the school committee.

The plan worked well throughout the 1830s and 1840s, and enrollments increased from a few hundred in 1835 to more than thirty-eight hundred a decade later. As late as 1850, Barnabas Sears, secretary of the Massachusetts Board of Education, wrote that he had no schools equal in quality to the Catholic schools of Lowell. But the "Lowell Plan," as it was later called, quickly ended in 1852 when one Catholic parish, unable to find qualified lay Catholic teachers, invited the Sisters of Notre Dame to staff the school. Catholics claimed that the school staffed by the sisters was just as worthy of support as the other Catholic schools, but the Lowell school committee objected to the nuns, and this experiment in cooperation ended in acrimony and bitterness.[6]

Even though educational cooperation ended in Lowell in 1852, the idea was too powerful and appealing to die. One small community in Massachusetts had solved the problem of public funding of parochial education, and the plan worked well for almost twenty years. Other communities in other states also would try the Lowell plan with varying degrees of success in the later decades of the century.[7]

⁂

The low profile of Catholic schools in Massachusetts generally, and the cooperation in Lowell specifically, were in dramatic contrast to Catholic educational experiences in New York. Catholic schooling in New York in the years before the Civil War was a marginal operation that struggled to survive in the face of the overwhelming poverty of the faithful and competition from the Public School Society. The parish schools in New York during these decades were held in damp and crowded church basements and conducted by poorly prepared teachers.[8]

The clergy persisted in their efforts to establish schools they could ill afford to support because they strongly objected to the Protestant-oriented public schools on doctrinal and cultural grounds. The public schools sponsored by the Public School Society used only the King James version of the Bible and taught that Catholicism was a backward religion at best, and in some cases depraved.

The Catholic clergy believed that these public schools were an effort to wean Catholic children from the religion of their parents and encourage them to become Protestants. Thus the clergy persisted in establishing parish schools no matter what the cost because the very existence of the church in America depended on these institutions to protect future generations. By 1840, the clergy had succeeded in establishing eight free schools and a few pay schools enrolling about five thousand children, one-fourth to one-third of the Catholic children of school age in New York at that time.[9]

The clergy quickly realized that Catholic education for every Catholic child in New York would not be possible until the church obtained additional support, most particularly a share of the state school fund. With the support of Governor William H. Seward, who had supported the establishment of schools taught by teachers who shared the immigrants' language and religion, the Catholic clergy petitioned the New York City Common Council for a share of the state school funds allocated to the city.

The Public School Society challenged the petition as a threat to the very notion of a common school system. The council agreed and rejected the Catholic petition, although the legislative body continued to hear arguments both for and against the petition, including an acrimonious debate between fiery bishop John Hughes and the virulent nativists Hiram Ketchum and Theodore Sedgewick. In January of 1841, searching for an end to the controversy, the council decided to purge anti-Catholic passages from the Public School Society textbooks. But Hughes and the Catholic clergy wanted a share of the state school funds and would settle for nothing less.[10]

Encouraged by Hughes and their pastors, New York Catholics petitioned the state legislature for relief. In response, Secretary of State John Spencer, acting in his capacity as state superintendent of schools, introduced a plan to decentralize the control of New York City's public schools and break the Public School Society's monopoly on public aid.

But Spencer's plan settled nothing; in fact it added fuel to the controversy. Catholics generally favored the plan, although they thought it far short of their goal. The Public School Society was appalled and petitioned the legislature to reject the plan. An effort to pass the plan reflected the deep division over the issue; the Senate rejected the Spencer plan by one vote.

Catholics were not about to give up, and during the summer they pressed Democrats in the legislature to endorse the Catholic position or face opposition in the fall elections. Catholics made their point in November as the only city Democrats to lose were those who opposed the Spencer plan. A bill based on Spencer's first report was passed by the legislature in April of 1842. The new law ended the control of state school funds by the Public School Society and put the public schools under the control of publicly elected ward commissioners. Amendments to the bill also provided for a central board of education and prohibited sectarian teaching in the schools.[11]

But the new law was no victory for the Catholics. To be sure, control of New York City's public schools had changed from private to public control, but the majority of New Yorkers were Protestant, and in all but a few of the city's wards the public schools remained largely Protestant in tone and curriculum. In fact, the newly elected superintendent of the city's schools continued the tradition of Bible readings in each of the city's schools — including those in the Catholic wards. The public schools of 1843 were much the same as those of 1841.

Yet the Catholic campaign was not a failure. Hughes had not succeeded in gaining a share of the state school fund, but there is no reason to believe he ever expected to achieve this goal. He had, however, succeeded in uniting the diverse elements of his diocese into a common cause. "My people were composed of representatives from almost all nations," Hughes recalled in his memoirs. "It was necessary that they should be brought together to coalesce as one flock. They were surrounded by many inducements to diverge from the unity of the Church both in profession and practice." By uniting his flock, Hughes had created a siege mentality among Catholics, forcing generations to come to choose between loyalty to their religion and winning acceptance and respectability in American society.[12]

The school fund campaign also generated new support for parochial schools. Parish schools moved out of church basements, and enrollments jumped from five thousand students in 1840 to more than twenty-two thousand in 1870. Yet this tremendous growth in parish school enrollments barely kept pace with the growth of the Catholic population as a whole.

In 1870, after thirty years of sustained growth, the Catholic schools were educating only a small percentage of Catholic children in New York. No matter how hard he tried, Hughes could not raise the funds necessary to provide a Catholic education for every Catholic child.[13]

For most Catholic parents, therefore, the choice was between sending their children to public school or no school at all. Some parents, either by design or by neglect, chose the latter course; illiteracy among Catholics remained high throughout the century. But a great many Catholics, ignoring the warnings of their parish pastors, sent their children to public schools.

The number of Catholics in New York public schools increased throughout the 1840s and 1850s as these institutions became increasingly secular and hired Catholics to work as teachers. In fact, the change was rather dramatic, and by 1849 one newspaper estimated that one-half to three-quarters of the children enrolled in public schools were Catholic.

Hughes's success in bringing the public schools under public control and purging the Protestant bias from the curriculum made these institutions more appealing to Catholics than in the past. Thus John Hughes, tireless champion of Catholic schools, should be given credit for increasing the Catholic enrollments in the public schools as well as in the parochial schools.

❖

The tension between Catholics and Protestants over public education drifted south from New York to Philadelphia in the 1840s. One might have thought that the so-called City of Brotherly Love, with its moderate Catholic bishop, Francis Kenrick, would have been able to resolve peacefully any differences over public education. But this was not the case; in fact, the failure of Philadelphians to find a solution to the public school crisis led to the worst anti-Catholic violence in American history.[14]

Unlike New York, the issue in Philadelphia was not the control of the state school fund. Kenrick saw no value in waging a campaign he could not win, but he did feel that he was justified in asking the school board to allow Catholic children in public schools to use their own edition of the Bible instead of a Protestant version. To Kenrick this was a matter of simple justice and respect, a matter of conscience for Catholics. But Philadelphia nativists saw this request as a conspiracy to cut the heart out of public education, and they opposed any compromise with the Catholics. The school board excused Catholic students from reading the Protestant Bible but would not allow them to use the Catholic edition. Dissatisfaction with this decision led to weeks of tension and days of rioting in the spring and summer of 1844.[15]

The campaign to allow Catholics to use their own edition of the Bible was largely Kenrick's idea. Writing in 1839 under the pseudonym "Sentinel," Kenrick called on Catholics to oppose the use of the Protestant Bible to teach their children. "Is it just to place the Protestant Bible in the hands of Catholic children," he asked, "to make them commit its text to memory and to respond to the questions which sectarian teachers may put as to its contents?"[16] The answer, of course, was no, and in later editorials Sentinel proposed a variety of ways of protesting this injustice, including the removal of Catholic children from public schools. But Sentinel's calls for action received few letters of support. Catholics apparently intended to leave their children in public schools whether Sentinel liked it or not.

Failing to marshall popular support for a boycott, Kenrick changed his tactics. If Catholics would not remove their children from public schools, perhaps they would support a campaign to allow Catholic children to use their own edition of the Bible. In December 1842, acting on behalf of the Catholic parents of the diocese, Kenrick petitioned the school board for this right. "We do not ask you to adopt the Catholic version for general use," he wrote the board, "but we feel warranted in claiming our conscientious scruples to recognize or use the other be respected. In Baltimore, the Directors of the Public schools have thought it their duty to provide Catholic children with the Catholic version. Is it too much for us to expect the same measure of justice?"[17] In addition, Kenrick asked that Catholic children be excused from all devotional prayers and hymns since these were also Protestant exercises. It seemed like a simple and reasonable request to Kenrick.

But nativists saw dark designs in Kenrick's appeal to the board; many were convinced that the petition was a diversion, the first step in a campaign to undermine the Christian curriculum of the public schools. In the nativist mind, Catholics were interfering with the will of the majority. "Protestants founded these schools and they have always been in the majority," noted the editor of the *Presbyterian*. "Were Roman Catholics forced to send their children to these schools, their complaints would be well-grounded; but there is no compulsion; they act in the full knowledge of the facts, and therefore should not complain."[18] Nativists and Protestant ministers saw no reason to compromise with these Catholic outsiders, and they warned the board not to give in to Catholic demands.

A month later, in January of 1843, Kenrick received a reply to his petition in the form of two school board resolutions. First, the board resolved that no children would be required to read from the Bible in public schools if their parents objected, and, second, they agreed that children whose parents preferred a particular version of the Bible without note or comment could use the preferred edition. The board also agreed to enforce standing rules against sectarian religious services in the public schools.

The decision of the board satisfied no one. Although the Catholic community did not complain, Catholics were resentful that the board would not permit the use of the Douay edition because it contained commentaries. Nativists were livid that the board had excused Catholics from Bible readings and other devotional exercises; these were core elements in the public school curriculum, and no one should be excused. Throughout 1843, nativist publications harped on the indignity of this compromise with the Catholic Church and the rhetoric became increasingly inflammatory as the year progressed. During the municipal elections held in the spring of 1844, nativist charges of Catholic conspiracies against American liberties precipitated acrimony and distrust between the Catholic and non-Catholic

communities in the city. Philadelphia became a powder keg
ready to blow.

⚎

The incidents that touched off the worst anti-Catholic rioting in
American history were calculated efforts to instigate violence.[19]
With tension between the two groups running high, the nativists organized a rally in the heavily Catholic neighborhood
of Kensington. The nativists gathered on the night of May 3
only to be driven off by a gang of Irish Catholics. A second
nativist rally in Kensington on the afternoon of May 6 was dispersed by a thunderstorm. As the crowd was running for cover,
shots from an undefined location killed a young Protestant boy.
Nativists pointed to the windows of a nearby Irish Catholic
house as the source of the gunfire and attacked the house. Before order was restored, a band of Irish laborers countered the
nativists and forced them to retreat for a second time.

The next morning, nativists gathered to hear speakers ha-
rangue against the Catholic Church and to read of the "bloody
hand of the Pope stretched forth to our destruction" in the
anti-Catholic press. Spurred on by this inflammatory rhetoric,
mobs returned to Kensington, shouting insults and damaging
Irish homes in the neighborhood. Before the attack was over,
the nativists had destroyed over thirty Irish homes.

The third day of the rioting was even more violent, as
nativists returned once again to Kensington bent on the systematic destruction of the entire neighborhood. Entire blocks
of homes went up in flames, but this was not enough for the
crowd as they moved on to destroy Catholic churches and a
seminary. Throughout the Catholic community, priests, nuns,
and lay people fled for their lives — refugees in a war of hate.

The wanton destruction of sacred structures marked an end
of the violence in Kensington. With the aid of the press and
public opinion, the mayor and the city militia moved in to
exercise public order. A semblance of peace returned to Philadelphia by the middle of May.

But the peace was no more than a truce. The nativists were

determined to rid their city and their schools of the Catholic menace, and they bided their time until they could attack again. A clash between Irish laborers and American nativists, in combination with a rumor that guns were being stored in St. Philip's Church in Southwark, touched off more violence on July 5. Determined to avoid a repeat of the May riots, the mayor sent large numbers of the city militia to defend the church.

For two days the militia skirmished with the nativists outside the church, but on the third day the nativists gained an advantage by breaking into the church. Efforts by the militia to retake the building escalated the fighting, and combatants exchanged gun and cannon fire for several hours. In an effort to relieve the mounting violence, the mayor withdrew his troops on the morning of July 8. This proved to be an effective tactic, and the nativists dispersed without doing any further damage to the church. The casualty list was shocking: thirteen dead and fifty wounded in three days of fighting.

The riots changed nothing in Philadelphia. Anti-Catholicism was just as virulent in the autumn of 1844 as it had been four months earlier. In fact, there was not a hint of remorse for all the violence and destruction. Efforts to repay Catholics for the loss of their property were thwarted by nativist protests, and official city inquiries into the cause of the riots ascribed the troubles to "efforts of a portion of the community to exclude the Bible from our Public schools." Perhaps the mood of the city was best summed up by one Quaker merchant who was appalled by the violence, but who also believed "that the Papists deserved all of this and much more. It were well if every Popish church in the world were leveled with the ground."[20]

The riots and the unwillingness or inability of the public school committee to compromise on the use of the Bible in the common schools forced Kenrick to undertake a campaign to build parish schools. Unlike his colleague in New York, Kenrick did not look forward to the task because he knew what a burden this would be for the impoverished laity. He wrote in 1850 that he was "fully sensible of the importance of Catholic schools, but I do not know how we are to establish them. Teachers of religious character are not easily had and schoolhouses are wanting."[21]

But Kenrick also knew that he had little choice. During his remaining years in Philadelphia and during his tenure as archbishop of Baltimore, he encouraged the establishment of parish schools. Kenrick's successor in Philadelphia, Bishop John Neumann, continued the school campaign by establishing a central Catholic school board in the diocese in 1852. The board was charged with raising funds to support Catholic schools, reviewing Catholic school materials, and planning for the construction of new schools. It was the first Catholic school board in the United States.[22]

※

The tension and violence that gripped the school campaigns in New York and Philadelphia were not part of parish school development in the Midwest. In fact, while Catholics in New York and Philadelphia were building barricades, Catholics in Cincinnati, Chicago, Milwaukee, St. Louis, and other cities went about the business of building parish schools.[23]

There were, nevertheless, significant educational disagreements in these cities. As in the East, Catholics in the Midwest campaigned for public funds and criticized the sectarian nature of the public school curriculum. But in the Midwest, the response from non-Catholics was different. There were no riots and no violence. Non-Catholics put up a spirited defense of the concept of the common school without any of the paranoia that gripped the response in eastern cities. "There is often need of improvement," noted the *Chicago Tribune* in 1853, "and we hope our Catholic fellow citizens will help us accomplish it."[24] Midwestern common school advocates envisioned the cooperation of all the Christian denominations in the establishment of a common school system. Catholics were invited to join in this common cause.

Several factors account for the tolerance of Catholics and their educational views in the Midwest. Certainly the size and economic role played by the Catholic communities in these cities affected the attitudes of non-Catholics. In all of the cities of the Midwest, immigrants generally and Catholics specifically were important for their sheer force of numbers; immigrants frequently constituted more than half of the populations of midwestern cities.

More important, these immigrants provided cheap, dependable labor that fueled the economic development of these cities in the years before the Civil War. Thus it was in the public interest for non-Catholics to tolerate the Catholic community and its schools. Such tolerance in the age of nativism all but amazed Father Michael Heiss of Milwaukee. "Here we have four daily English papers in which you can hardly ever find anything that could be called an attack on the Catholic faith," he wrote to a friend in 1853. "It is true that in some cases it is nothing but politics, for everything depends on elections; those that 'run' for office must reckon with the great number of Catholics."[25] There were a few efforts to organize nativist opposition to the church in the Midwest, but these groups were insignificant by comparison with their counterparts in the cities of the East.

A second factor that affected denominational relations in the Midwest was the important role played by Catholic social institutions in the urban development process. The impact of these hospitals, asylums, and schools varied from one city to the next. In the East, Catholic social institutions served immigrants almost exclusively. Protestant benevolent associations, school societies, and municipal law had established hospitals, schools, and asylums long before the arrival of the church. When the Catholic Church began to grow in these cities in the 1830s and 1840s, there was no role for Catholic social institutions outside the immigrant neighborhoods.

The Catholic experience in the urban Midwest was different. When the church came to that region in the 1830s and 1840s, the cities had only a few public institutions, and these were badly overcrowded. It is not surprising, therefore, that the establishment of Catholic schools, hospitals, and asylums had an impact on both the Catholic and the non-Catholic populations. These institutions frequently operated in quasi-public capacities and received public aid from municipal and state governments. Civic leaders and citizens on the urban frontier naturally applauded the efforts of the church because such assistance was in the best interest of their communities. These initial establishments were used by non-Catholics for only a short time; other denominations eventually established their own institutions after 1850. Yet the influential role played by these Catholic hospitals, schools, and asylums had a substantive effect on the attitudes of non-Catholics toward the church.[26]

The debate over the financing and content of public and private education in Chicago was typical of the debate in other midwestern cities. During the early 1850s, Chicago Catholics were concerned about the Protestant bias of common schools and said so in the pages of the *Western Tablet*, the diocesan paper. Chicago Catholics also worked against the passage of a state law to provide tax support for public schools. As in other cities, many Catholic children attended public schools. "We have a large number of Catholic children in our schools," noted School Superintendent William H. Wells in 1858, "but I have not heard so much as a suspicion expressed in any quarter that any of the teachers were attempting to exert a sectarian influence."[27] Education was not much of an issue in Chicago or other midwestern cities.

It needs to be emphasized, however, that this lack of protest is not an indication that midwestern Catholics generally accepted the Protestant bias of public schools. Indeed, they did not. But midwestern Catholics had learned from their co-religionists in the eastern dioceses that protest would not change public schools. Midwestern Catholics quickly concluded that putting their time and energy into building parish schools would be more profitable than trying to change the public schools. Except for the occasional protest over new education legislation or the "godlessness" of public education, midwestern Catholics devoted themselves to raising monies to build parish schools and finding qualified teachers to staff these institutions.

No group was more committed to this plan than the German Catholics who dominated the dioceses of Cincinnati, St. Louis, and Milwaukee and were sizable minorities in Chicago and Detroit. They built their schools quickly with no complaint about cost. Funds were raised through pew rentals, voluntary donations, and funds received from mission societies in Europe. To provide continuing support, many German parishes organized school societies that had the responsibility of raising additional funds. German missionary priests working in America traveled to Europe to convince superiors of religious orders to send a few sisters to the Midwest to teach in the parish schools. By the 1860s, it was hard to find a German Catholic parish without a thriving school. It was an altogether remarkable achievement.[28]

The rapid growth of German Catholic schools in Cincinnati was typical of what was happening in other midwestern dioceses. In 1834, German Catholics established their first parish school in Cincinnati and enrolled an unspecified number of pupils; additional teachers were added in the late 1830s as the enrollment increased. By 1843, with the addition of a second school two years earlier, enrollment was up to six hundred pupils. Less than five years later, after an influx of new German immigrants, the number of German Catholic schools had jumped to six and enrollment was over eighteen hundred. This pattern of growth in the number of pupils and schools continued throughout the years of German emigration to Cincinnati. It is not surprising, therefore, that Cincinnati Archbishop J. B. Purcell would note with pride that "one of the chief pleasures of our episcopacy ... consists in the generous response given to our call by all our flock, but especially the German portion thereof, for the last twenty years, in providing for the education of our children."[29]

German support for parish education was motivated primarily by the fear that the public schools would "Anglicize" their children and turn them away from "heim und kirche" — home and church. German Catholics firmly believed that language keeps the faith and one way to ensure the teaching of the German language and culture was to establish their own schools. "Where the Germans had their own German schools and spoke only German," noted one German missionary, "they are as faithful to their Religion as they or their parents were a hundred years ago when they left the ship." The predominantly Irish Catholic hierarchy applauded the German campaign to establish parish schools, but the bishops were not sanguine about the plan to use these schools to preserve their German language and culture. Indeed, concern over this matter would become a major issue within the American Catholic Church in the 1880s and 1890s.[30]

One important manifestation of the conflict between public and Catholic school advocates in the 1840s was experimentation. If either side was to predominate, it had to respond to the perceived needs of Catholic parents and their children. In some communities — Boston, for example — public schools prevailed even in Catholic neighborhoods. But in other cities such as New York and Philadelphia the parish school was a dominant institution in every Catholic neighborhood. Most communities fit in between these two extremes as if points on a spectrum of educational development in the years before the Civil War.

Chapter 4 _____

The Campaign for Control

═══

I N 1852, more than decade after the New York school controversy and more than eight years after the Philadelphia
school riots, the Catholic bishops of the United States met
in a plenary council to address the state of Catholicism in the
nation. The intervening period had not changed much; time
had not healed old wounds. Catholic leaders were still determined to obtain their share of public funds to support their
own schools. And public school advocates were just as determined to resist any effort to divide tax monies or to change the
public school curriculum to accommodate Catholic concerns.
This campaign for control changed over the next forty years,
but the contest between Catholic and public school advocates
was largely a stalemate.[1]

There was one notable difference between the 1840s and
later decades. The bitter violence and confrontation of the 1840s
had given way to relative calm a decade later. Surprisingly
it was John Hughes, one of the movers in the campaign for
a share of the state school fund, who changed the debate.
"How are we to provide for the Catholic education of our children?" he wrote in the *Freeman's Journal* in 1850. "I answer:
Not by agitating the question on constitutionality, legality, or
expediency of state schools. Let us leave these points to be
settled by the politicians.... Let us leave the public schools to
themselves."[2]

The plenary council of Catholic bishops endorsed the resolve
shown by Hughes. It was a historic occasion for the American
church. Growth in the number of communicants and growth

in the number of dioceses and provinces meant that by 1852 American Catholicism was truly national — from the archdiocese of Baltimore in the East to the archdiocese of Oregon City in the West. The pronouncements of this first national council had a more substantial impact than the previous pastoral letters of the provincial councils.[3]

One message that certainly came through clearly was the firm resolve of all the bishops to support and establish parochial schools. "Listen not to those who would persuade you that religion can be separated from secular instruction," the bishops warned. "Listen to our voice, which tells you to walk in ancient paths; to bring up your children as you yourselves were brought up by your pious parents; to make religion the foundation of the happiness you wish to secure for those whom you love so tenderly. . . . Encourage the establishment and support of Catholic schools; make every sacrifice which may be necessary for this object."[4] The words of the bishops encouraged Catholic school advocates to redouble their efforts to establish a Catholic school in every parish.

But such efforts did not mean peaceful coexistence with the public school establishment. Thousands of Catholic children were educated each year in the public schools and their rights also were to be protected. Friction between Catholics and non-Catholics emerged over this point of contact many times over the next four decades.

The conflicts were familiar ones. Catholic children were required under pain of expulsion to read from the King James edition of the Bible. Local parish priests protested to no avail; the school committees would not compromise on the matter. "We are determined to protestantize the Catholic children," one public school advocate allegedly said. "They shall read the Protestant Bible or be dismissed from the schools; and should we find them loafing around the wharves, we will clap them in jail." Some Catholic children did refuse to read from the Bible and were promptly expelled. In response to such crises, local Catholic parishes opened schools.[5]

Such incidents reminded Catholics of the unwillingness of public school committees to make changes to accommodate the Catholic conscience. Other warnings appeared on a weekly basis in the Catholic press written by a growing cadre of editors, essayists, and novelists. Among the most influential of these writers were James A. McMaster, editor of the *Freeman's Journal* in New York, and Mary Ann Madden Sadlier, a popular novelist and short story writer. Both McMaster and Sadlier saw only danger for Catholics in the public schools.

McMaster was a convert who used his paper as a bully pulpit to promote parochial schools and attack public education.[6] Although he never wavered in his Catholic faith, McMaster never quite abandoned the Calvinist viewpoint of his youth. He was a great one for confrontation, publicly criticizing friend and foe alike in the pages of the *Journal*. McMaster spurned and castigated priests and bishops as well as lay persons whom he regarded as lukewarm in their support for parish schools. One biographer referred to him as "a stormy petrel in Catholic circles," and it is not likely that his rhetoric won McMaster any friends.

But McMaster saved his most vituperative rhetoric for his attacks on the "godless" and "pagan" public schools that he blamed for every manner of crime and moral decay. Throughout his years as editor from 1848 to 1886, McMaster never let up; he was a moral crusader in endless battle. His energy, rhetorical skill, and religious orthodoxy made him an important, national voice in the Catholic school campaign.[7]

But McMaster's fiery rhetoric and combative style was not the only way of convincing the laity to support parish schools and abandon the public schools. Mary Anne Madden Sadlier used fiction to emphasize the importance of Catholic schooling and the dangers of public education.[8] Serialized in Catholic newspapers and later compiled into novels, Sadlier's fiction depicted the everyday lives of American Catholics in a melodramatic fashion. Each chapter touched upon the temptations, ambitions, problems, and issues that filled their lives. Many of the stories showed dramatically, if fictively, what would happen if Catholic parents ignored the call for Catholic schools. As literature, Sadlier's fiction was third-rate, but as propaganda it was a masterpiece.[9]

Sadlier's novels with American settings — *Willie Burke, The Blakes and the Flanagans, Con O'Regan,* and four other books — were the core of her popularity. *Willie Burke,* for example, sold seven thousand copies within a few weeks after publication. The response was gratifying, but Sadlier had a far more serious intention for her books than entertainment. Her goal was "to reach those who will not read pious or denominational books and to foil the spirit of the age with his own weapons. Such and no other have been the actuating motive of all the tales I have written."[10] It is not surprising, therefore, that Sadlier was an important if not obvious leader in the campaign to establish parish schools.

On the last two pages of *The Blakes and the Flanagans* Sadlier summarized the didactic themes that pervaded all of her novels. "Ah, it would be well if Catholic parents would think more of these things than they do," she wrote with passion. "If they would only consider that they are accountable to God and his Church for the precious gift of faith, and are bound under the pain of deadly sin, to transmit it to their children pure and undefiled, they would not dare to send those children to godless schools, where they are sure to lose their precious inheritance, or having it so shorn of its splendor, so poor and feeble, that it is no longer worth having."[11] To that, Catholic school leaders could only add "amen" and thank the Lord for the likes of Mary Anne Sadlier.

But not everyone in the Catholic community agreed with McMaster, Sadlier, and the Catholic school leadership. There were, for example, hundreds of thousands of the faithful who sent their children to public schools in spite of all the real and perceived dangers. There also was one Catholic essayist, Orestes Brownson, who challenged conventional Catholic views on the benefits of parochial education and the dangers of public education.

In countless lectures and a few key essays, Brownson argued forcefully that most parish schools were of low academic caliber, not yet up to the intellectual standards of the church. He also argued that children from good Catholic homes would not be hurt by attending public schools. In fact, Brownson argued, pious Catholic children would be a positive force in changing public education. Above all, Brownson beseeched the laity to develop their intellectual skills and to play active roles in American society. Brownson sought to bridge the gap between the emerging Catholic ghetto and the larger American society. It was a goal he never achieved.[12]

The decade before the Civil War was a time of persistent tension in Catholic education. The leaders of the American church struggled to refine and articulate a philosophy of education that would win over the hearts and minds of their co-religionists. Public school advocates worked just as hard to attract Catholic parents to their cause.

Not surprisingly, Catholic parents received unsolicited advice from both sides. Using popular media such as newspapers, novels, and magazines, Catholic writers such as McMaster, Sadlier, and Brownson propagandized and ultimately persuaded thousands of Catholic parents of the righteousness of parochial education. It was a significant achievement that would not have been accomplished without a united front.

The post–Civil War growth of Catholic parochial schools caused serious concerns among Catholics as well as non-Catholics, but for very different reasons. Most Catholic leaders were generally pleased with the rapid growth of the parish schools, but some Catholics — conservatives for the most part — were not satisfied. In fact, conservatives were appalled with the large number of Catholic parents who continued to send their children to public schools in spite of papal instruction to the contrary. They looked for a way to force reluctant pastors to build more schools and require recalcitrant Catholic parents to send their children to these schools.[13]

Non-Catholics viewed the growth of parochial schools from a very different perspective. The continued vitality of parish schools surprised and concerned many non-Catholics. Many public school advocates had hoped that Catholics would abandon their parish schools once public schools became truly non-sectarian. But it became increasingly clear that parish schools were not going to die out; in fact they would continue to be a significant part of the American educational system.

Non-Catholics were particularly concerned about the ethnic or foreign cast of many of these schools, and public school advocates and legislators sought ways of influencing the content of parochial education. Non-Catholics also sought ways to end the Catholic campaigns to gain state funds for their schools. Throughout the 1870s and 1880s, Catholics and non-Catholics conducted separate campaigns to increase their influence over the growth and content of parochial schools. Confrontation between these two groups was inevitable.[14]

The campaign to force Catholic parents to send their children to parochial schools was spearheaded by James McMaster, who argued that "the time has come for enforcing everywhere the general law of the Catholic Church, that Catholics must not send their children to any schools but Catholic schools!" McMaster was vigorous in his advocacy, and when his call was ignored by Catholic prelates and pastors as well as by Catholic parents, he schemed to involve the Vatican in his cause.[15]

In February 1874, McMaster presented a formal memorandum to Vatican officials asking if Catholic parents could send their children to schools "not under the supervision of the Catholic clergy." In an effort to influence the answer, he sent along several articles on the horrors of public education in the United States.

The Vatican responded quickly, asking the archbishops of the United States about the "evils" of public education. Specifically, the Vatican wanted to know why some Catholic parents sent their children to public schools. Was there an effective way to reverse this trend? Why did some Catholics advocate the denial of sacraments to parents who sent their children to public schools? Could such a policy be instituted without harm to the church and would it be effective?[16]

The American archbishops meeting in Cincinnati responded to these questions and countered other conservative allegations. The archbishops noted that "public schools are not non-Catholic in the sense that they have in their very nature something which is directly and purposely opposed to the Catholic religion, but are proudly secular in which, to be sure, are handed down the elements of secular knowledge with the omission of all religious education."[17]

The archbishops doubted the wisdom of denying absolution to parents who sent their children to public schools. They responded to each of the Vatican's questions. Why did Catholics send their children to public schools? The archbishops noted that many rural communities had no Catholic schools and in many large cities parochial schools were clearly inferior to public schools. This trend would change in time, they argued, as the quantity and quality of parish schools caught up with the Catholic population. This was the only effective solution to the problem. "Denial of the sacraments," the bishops added, "would only serve to exasperate feelings and stir up hatred against the Catholic religion among our non-Catholic fellow citizens."[18]

The response from Rome, in the form of an "instruction," did not please the American hierarchy. Issued in November 1875, the eight-point document strongly supported the position taken by McMaster and his conservative colleagues.[19] The Vatican called on the prelates to do everything in their power to prevent Catholic children from attending public schools. "Every effort must be made to increase the number and quality of parochial schools and the obligation to support Catholic schools should be especially brought to the attention of the more wealthy and influential Catholics and members of the legislature."[20]

The Vatican did acknowledge that certain circumstances

might permit Catholic parents to send their children to public schools, but only in cases where no Catholic school existed
or where the Catholic school was clearly inferior to the public
school. On the question of absolution, the document was eva-
sive. Absolution could be denied to "obstinate" parents who
sent their children to public schools even though they could
afford to send them to a "good and well-equipped Catholic
school" in the same neighborhood. The document did not define any of the many vague terms in its statement, preferring
that the bishops set standards for their own dioceses.

Yet few American bishops had the economic resources to
provide a desk in a parish school for every Catholic child in
their diocese. It just was not possible, regardless of the Vatican's instruction, for every Catholic child to attend a Catholic
school. The status quo prevailed and the document was largely
ignored, regarded by many of the bishops as an embarrass-
ment. Yet the *Instruction of 1875* was not without impact, for
it later served as the framework for the discussion of parochial education that took place at the Third Plenary Council of
Baltimore nine years later.[21]

❖

The intervening years between the publication of the Instruction and the Baltimore council did little to resolve the conflict
within Catholic education. To be sure, Catholic schools continued to grow at unprecedented rates. In fact, the number of
parish schools jumped from fourteen hundred in 1875 to over
twenty-five hundred in less than a decade. But in spite of this
growth, hundreds of thousands of Catholic children continued
to attend public schools. What could be done to change this
latter trend? Could the church ever provide enough schools
for an ever-expanding Catholic population? These were among
the questions facing the bishops as they arrived in Baltimore
in 1884.

Much of the discussion of parochial schools was tactical.
How can we convince the laity of the vital importance of parish
schools? Should the council take a clear-cut stand and require

pastors to build parish schools? Should they require recalcitrant parents, under the pain of sin, to send their children to parish schools? It was clear to all the bishops present that the tone of their message would be as important as the content.

The result was an effort to take the middle ground. The pastoral letter on the "education of youth" was gentle. "No parish is complete," concluded the letter, "till it has schools adequate to meet the needs of its children and the pastor and the people of such a parish should feel that they have not accomplished their entire duty until the want is supplied." There were no harsh words in the pastoral concerning pastors and parents who did not agree with the bishops or follow their advice.[22]

The decrees of the council were another matter, however, and reflected a firm commitment to the belief that every Catholic child belonged in a Catholic school. The first decree stated bluntly that a parish school must be built near every Catholic church. The second decree provided for the removal of parish pastors who were "gravely negligent" in erecting parish schools. The third decree promised spiritual "punishment" for any parish that failed to support their pastor's effort to build a school. A final decree stressed that "all Catholic parents are bound to send their children to parochial schools unless at home or in other Catholic schools, they provide sufficiently and fully for their Christian education." The implementation of the four decrees was reserved for the bishops themselves.[23]

The decrees were a setback for the liberal prelates who wanted to encourage Catholic parents to send their children to parish schools but stop short of imposing sanctions on those parents who chose not to follow. But the conservatives had argued persuasively that decades of "encouragement" had not stopped the tide of Catholic children from attending public schools. It was time, the conservatives argued, to require these fair-weather Catholics and recalcitrant pastors to build and support parish schools.

Yet there was a vast chasm between this new policy and its implementation, and the education decrees had only limited impact on the pattern and rate of parochial school development during the balance of the century. Like the *Instruction of 1875*, the education decrees of the Third Plenary Council failed to face the clear fact that the American church lacked the economic resources to provide a Catholic education for every child.

The decrees did, however, have a significant impact on the organizational structure of parochial schools. For more than a century the Catholic schools had been administered at the parish level by pastors and trustees. Most dioceses were patch-works of semi-autonomous parish schools as different from one another as the cultures that made up American Catholi-cism itself. But the educational discussions of the Third Plenary Council gave momentum to an effort to coordinate parish schools through diocesan school boards. The establishment of boards in most dioceses in the years from 1885 to 1920 was the first major step in the long campaign to standardize and establish control over parochial schools.[24]

✄

The Catholic bishops were not alone in their efforts to influ-ence and control the development of parochial schools. Fearful of the growing power of the Catholic Church, non-Catholics launched two separate legislative efforts, one to prohibit the use of public money for parochial schools and a second cam-paign to monitor and control the content of parochial school curricula.[25]

In an effort to stop the endless Catholic efforts to obtain public funds for their schools, many state legislatures con-sidered amending their constitutions to prohibit the use of public funds for religious institutions. Such amendments were approved by voters in Illinois, Pennsylvania, and Colorado, but defeated in New York, Michigan, Ohio, and New Jersey. The campaign escalated in September 1875 when President Ulysses S. Grant condemned the use of public funds for re-ligious schools. "Encourage free schools," Grant proclaimed, "and resolve that not one dollar of money appropriated to their support, no matter how raised, shall be appropriated to the support of any sectarian school." Grant's speech made a national issue out of the various Catholic campaigns in the states.[26]

Grant followed his speech with a December message to Congress calling for a constitutional amendment to prohibit any state from giving funds to religious schools. Soon after Grant's speech, Congressman James G. Blaine of Maine introduced a bill in Congress to accomplish Grant's proposal. Not surprisingly, Catholics throughout the nation were very vocal in their opposition. In fact, the *Catholic World* suggested rather caustically that Congress should prohibit the use of public funds for "sectarian" and "atheistic" public schools as well. Catholic protests may have had an effect on Congress. Even though the amendment passed the House of Representatives in August of 1876, it failed in the Senate.

The national campaign to prohibit public money for parochial schools ended as quickly as it began, and many Catholics dismissed the matter as little more than politics. But this was wishful thinking. The Blaine Amendment, as it was called, had a significant effect on the states. Between 1877 and 1917, some twenty-nine states incorporated the amendment into their constitutions. Indeed, some state legislatures looked for ways to exert public control over portions of the parish school curricula.[27]

In the late 1880s, as the tide of foreign-born Catholics increased, legislators began to worry about the persistence of foreign nationalism and culture in the United States. Were there no mechanisms for transforming these foreigners into Americans? Indeed, there were the local schools, both public and private. But American-born legislators must have been disappointed by the foreign overtones of many parish schools — those modeled on institutions established by an earlier generation of German Catholics.

To many legislators, parish schools were part of the problem rather than part of the solution. Some thought there ought to be a law that required parochial schools to conform to public school standards. This idea materialized in law in Illinois and

Wisconsin in 1889, and the resulting controversy reverberated around the nation. The implication of these laws — state control over private schools — was unprecedented, but the vigor of the Catholic backlash came as a surprise to many Americans. To most Americans, it was just another law; but to Catholics, it was a threat to the very purpose and independence of their schools.

The battleground for this controversy was the Midwest, principally the states of Illinois and Wisconsin. In 1889, the Illinois General Assembly passed a law requiring children between the ages of seven and fourteen to attend public schools or private schools approved by local school boards.[28] To be approved by local boards, private schools had to certify that their curriculum was taught in the English language and included reading, writing, arithmetic, as well as the history of the United States and geography.[29]

The act clearly gave the state the right to regulate private education. When the impact of the law became known, Catholics and Lutherans joined forces to fight for repeal. Indeed, the law became the focal point of state elections in 1890 and 1892, with the Democrats capitalizing on Catholic and Lutheran anger. The Democratic victories in both elections were painful political lessons for the Republicans.[30]

The controversy arose in Wisconsin almost simultaneously with the one in Illinois. After months of wrangling, the Wisconsin legislature passed a law that was almost a carbon copy of the Illinois law and with the same result. German Lutherans and Catholics joined forces to protest the new law.[31]

The state election of 1892 in the Dairy State also mirrored the results in Illinois. The Democrats swept to power on the tide of the Lutheran-Catholic coalition.[32] "The school law did it," noted one defeated politician, "a silly sentimental and damned useless abstraction."[33] The Republicans in Wisconsin, like their colleagues in Illinois, had learned a valuable political lesson.

Republican miscues to the contrary, the victory won by the Catholic-Lutheran-Democratic coalition in Illinois and Wisconsin was significant. Most important, Catholics learned that victory could come if they were willing to join with other denominations in a common cause. Had the Catholics stood alone against these laws, they probably would have lost. But in joining the Lutherans, the church found political strength.

Such coalitions were only temporary, of course. It is doubtful that the Catholics and the Lutherans could agree on anything other than their joint opposition to these laws. But when such common causes emerged, victorious coalitions were possible. Catholic leaders henceforth looked for ways to appeal to other religious groups to join in their campaigns. The defeats of these laws marked the end of a long period of political struggle for the Catholic Church. By 1890, they understood how the system worked and had enjoyed the victory.

❖

The defeat of the private school laws constituted a turning point in the campaign for control over parochial education. For the next thirty-five years, Catholics shifted their attention to controlling the growth and development of Catholic education from within the denomination. The disagreements with the start over who would control the parochial schools were set aside for a generation. This did not mean that the disagreements had ended. In fact, both sides shared one common belief — that education was a vital part of American society. "If on any one point the friends and enemies of the Catholic Church are a unit," wrote Father Josef Salzmann in Milwaukee, "it is on the question of the importance of the schools. Both hold the view that the future belongs to him that controls the schools."[34]

Both Catholic and public school advocates learned important lessons in their efforts to control parochial education during the last half of the nineteenth century. It was not enough to promulgate decrees or pass legislation. Neither side could have much of an impact on parochial education unless they could persuade Catholic parents of the righteousness of their cause. Catholic leaders could not force Catholic parents to send their children to parish schools. State legislatures could not mandate public control over parochial institutions. Both sides learned that control of parochial education was elusive. Successful campaigns must be based on patience, persistence, and persuasion.

Chapter 5 _____

New Models for Parish Schools

===

T HE FIVE DECADES from the end of the Civil War to the end of World War I were years of upheaval and so-cial change within the Catholic Church. As the nation moved toward an urban base and an industrialized economy, it attracted millions of new immigrants from Europe. Since the majority of these new arrivals were both poor and Catholic, the American church was a primary source of their support, both spiritual and corporal.

In addition to this challenge, the church also was confronted by a new generation of American-born Catholics who were at-tracted to the fruits of American life and hoped to prepare their children for increasingly productive lives in American society. The loyalty of foreign-born Catholics to their native cultures and the strong desire of American-born Catholics to participate fully in American society pulled American Cathol-icism in opposite directions and affected the pattern of devel-opment of parochial education.[1]

It comes as no surprise, therefore, that parochial schools developed in different ways depending upon the balance of the two groups within each Catholic community. In fact, the presence of both foreign-born and American-born Catholics in each diocese forced the church to sponsor separate educational models for each faction and administer these models at the parish level.

During these decades three models predominated: the pub-licly supported parochial school, an experimental plan imple-mented in about a dozen small communities; the Americanized

Catholic school, the most popular model utilized by American-born Catholics; and the ethnic Catholic school, which was the model developed by German Catholics and utilized by the Germans and other nationalities. Each of these models made important contributions to the evolving history of parochial education.

※

Of these three models, the publicly supported Catholic school generated the most controversy and educated the fewest students. From 1831 to 1916, Catholics in at least twenty-one communities in fourteen states attempted to bridge the gap between parochial and public education. The specific terms of agreement between parishes and school boards varied slightly. In almost every community where the experiment took place, the school board leased a school from a local parish for a small sum and paid the salaries of teachers in those schools. The teachers were selected jointly by the school board and the parish pastor. The board regulated the curriculum, selected the schoolbooks, and conducted periodic examinations, but the parish pastor had the right to insure that all of the elements of the curriculum were acceptable to the Catholic Church. Most important, however, was the fact that the school day at these publicly supported Catholic schools was the same as at any other public school. No religious instruction was conducted until after classes were dismissed.

These schools were experimental and in most communities the experiment was short-lived. But in three communities — Lowell, Massachusetts, from 1831 to 1852; Savannah, Georgia, from 1870 to 1916; and Poughkeepsie, New York, from 1873 to 1898 — publicly supported parochial schools educated several generations of Catholic children. Even though the number of Catholic children educated in these schools was small, the publicly supported Catholic school was an important grassroots effort to resolve the outstanding differences that separated many Catholics from public education.[2]

The publicly supported parish school in Poughkeepsie is

worthy of closer attention not only because of its longevity, but also because it received national attention as the representative example of cooperative education efforts in other communities. The "Poughkeepsie Plan," as cooperative efforts came to be known, began when the Reverend Patrick F. McSweeney, pastor of St. Peter's parish in Poughkeepsie, informed the local school board in the spring of 1873 that his parishioners could no longer afford to maintain St. Peter's two schools. Starting in the fall, McSweeney noted, the eight hundred children who attended St. Peter's two schools would enter the public school system.

This news must have caused grave concern among Poughkeepsie school board members. At the time there were only sixteen hundred children enrolled in all of the Poughkeepsie public schools, and the board was not prepared for a 50 percent increase in enrollment. In fact, the board committee investigating the problem noted in its report that most of the Catholic children who would enroll in the fall lived "in the lower part of the city where the school buildings are already occupied to their full capacity." Clearly the board faced an emergency that required extraordinary measures.[3]

It seems that Father McSweeney not only precipitated the problem, he also had the solution. With the permission of Archbishop John McCloskey of New York, McSweeney proposed that the school board lease his two school buildings for a dollar per year. In addition, the board would be required to keep the buildings in good repair and insure them against loss or damage. McSweeney proposed that the board use the buildings to conduct public school classes for the children of St. Peter's parish "according to the [board's] rules and regulations now or hereafter adopted." Religious instruction would not be part of the public school curriculum but would be conducted in the building after normal school hours. Participation in religious exercises would be completely voluntary for all students.

The new public schools were to be staffed by teachers selected, employed, and paid by the board "in the same manner as other teachers in its employ." But McSweeney made it clear that the board should hire Catholic teachers for the schools so long as they met school board requirements. As if to underline the experimental nature of the agreement, McSweeney added that "either the board or the owners may terminate the lease at the end of any scholastic year by giving the other thirty days previous notice of its intention to terminate." The board agreed to McSweeney's terms and further agreed that the parish school would retain unrestricted use of the building outside of regular school hours. A lease agreement was signed on August 21, 1873.[4]

Not everyone was happy with this arrangement, however. Protestant ministers and the local lodge of the American Protestant Association objected to the plan and to the board's decision to abandon Bible reading in the high school. The ministers appealed to the board for a return to the "secular education" that emphasized religion and morality as taught in the Bible. These clergymen argued that abandoning the Bible would undermine the values necessary to transform young children into enterprising citizens.

In response to this claim, the president of the school board invoked Roger Williams's famous defense of the rights of conscience. "The feeblest Roman Catholic child in that common school," he added, "has rights which I, its committeeman, am bound to protect."[5] Local criticism of the plan faded in the face of the community-wide goal of assimilating the foreign-born into American society. The agreement between the school board and St. Peter's parish continued year after year without further criticism from the general public.

Even though this plan was accepted by American-born Catholics in Poughkeepsie, it was not accepted by all their co-religionists. Poughkeepsie's German Catholics looked askance at any plan that would require their children to participate in the public schools. Conscious of their native culture, language, and religion, the German Catholics of Nativity parish put their faith and their funds into their own parochial school as a way of preserving their treasured traditions.

The very thought of a cooperative education program that would have deemphasized German language and culture must have upset the German Catholic community. As late as 1896, twenty-three years after the implementation of the plan, the parish pastor at Nativity warned his parishioners that "parents who send their children to public school thereby commit a major sin and cannot be absolved until they have taken their children out of that school."[6] German Catholics were determined to maintain their own school regardless of the cost; they would have nothing to do with the Irish Catholics and their "Poughkeepsie Plan."

The eventual termination of the plan in 1899 was precipitated by factors far beyond the Poughkeepsie city limits. Throughout the 1890s, particularly after the Third Plenary Council of Baltimore in 1884, the plan came under attack by conservative Catholic newspapers. Even though these attacks — and scattered criticism from Protestant journals — did not undermine the agreement, they did create an air of tension and controversy throughout the period.

But the agreement held fast until 1895, when New York State School Superintendent Charles Skinner ordered the Poughkeepsie school board to break the agreement or lose state aid. Skinner based his actions on two grounds: the wearing of religious garb by the nuns who taught in St. Peter's School, and the long-term rental of parish buildings for the purpose of public education. Thus ended in January of 1899 the most innovative and visible effort to bridge the gap between parochial and public education.[7]

✥

The second model utilized by Catholics in the last quarter of the nineteenth century and the first decades of the new century was the American Catholic school, the prototype for the contemporary parochial school. The American Catholic school was the result of a desire on the part of American-born prelates, pastors, and parishioners to establish parish schools that were fully competitive with local public schools.[8]

In fact, these Catholics desired to establish parish schools that were superior to public schools in secular as well as religious instruction.

As always, Catholic school advocates were concerned that Catholic parents would be tempted to send their children to the public schools. "Our objective," noted one editorial in the *Western Catholic* of Chicago, "is to place Catholic schools not only on an equality with public schools, but to elevate them to such a standard of efficiency as well as to make them objects of envy of our non-Catholic neighbors."[9] It was a lofty goal, but many American Catholics were committed to achieving this end.

Yet this seemingly simple task of establishing American-ized Catholic schools was fraught with difficulties. As Catholic schools became increasingly similar to public schools, their independence and very reason for existence was threatened. "Advocates of English language parochial schools," noted historian Howard Weisz, "were faced with the difficulty of arguing both that the schools were American and that they were different from all other American schools. If parochial schools were not demonstrably American they could not survive pressure from their enemies and if they were not different, then they had no reason to exist."[10]

In fact, growing similarities between parochial and public schools caused concern among some Catholics. One editor, Patrick Hickey of the *Catholic Review,* argued that the parochial school, in its effort to Americanize, had strayed from the true path; to Hickey's way of thinking, the worst thing that could be said of parochial schools was that they were similar to public schools.[11] Another editor, Maurice F. Egan, was critical of the growing number of different courses offered by American Catholic schools. "It savors too much of the pretentious system of brain stuffing and stifling adopted in the public schools," he added.[12] In spite of these and other criticisms, advocates of the American Catholic schools were undeterred in their campaign.

In an effort to counter the arguments that parish schools were inherently un-American, Catholic educators mixed large doses of patriotism and civil piety into the parish school curriculum. "We have no flag but the stars and stripes, "noted one New York City pastor, "which we fly on every occasion over the school and rectory, speak no other language than United States, and when we sing, you can always hear 'Hail Columbia,' 'America,' and 'The Star Spangled Banner,' etc."[13] In fact, American Catholic educators went so far as to claim that the establishment of a parish school was in and of itself an act of patriotism and good citizenship.

But flags and anthems were not the best evidence of the American undertone of the typical parish school curriculum; the best evidence was the content of Catholic school books. Even though these texts do not provide evidence of the total classroom experience, such books necessarily made an impression on Catholic children if only because long passages were committed to memory. A careful examination reveals very few differences between public and parochial texts in form and content.[14]

Ruth Miller Elson has shown convincingly that public school textbooks were the "guardians of tradition." The hundreds of schoolbooks published in the last quarter of the nineteenth century emphasized the same values: patriotism, piety, deference, thrift, honesty, and diligence. These values were expressed repeatedly through the use of three story lines: the lessons learned from nature, the lessons learned from the lives of American statesmen, and the lessons learned from proper social behavior.

Educators repeatedly turned to such stories to encourage docility, diligence, and patriotism in their students. Teachers sincerely believed that a large part of their duty was to help their students and readers adapt to the rigors of an industrialized society. The values implicit in public school books were believed to contribute to "success" and were therefore highly valued by most Americans.[15]

The social values and stories in late nineteenth-century

Catholic school books were very similar to those in public school texts. The most popular Catholic texts were those published by D. and J. Sadlier of New York. The Sadlier Company dominated Catholic publishing in the late nineteenth century, and it is not surprising that their "Excelsior Series" was the most popular text of its kind.[16] What is surprising is how very similar the style, content, and themes of the Excelsior texts were to those used in the public schools.

Like public school texts, Catholic school books emphasized the lessons to be learned from nature. A buzzing bee, for example, taught the value of work to a lazy boy. The growth of an oak tree from an acorn underscored the importance of patience in reaching a goal. A number of texts included the famous parable of the grasshopper who fiddled away his summer only to starve in the winter. Often the lessons focused on the loyalty of dogs and the freedom of birds.[17]

These texts also stressed proper social behavior as reflected in the lives of American heroes such as George Washington and Benjamin Franklin. Even more to the point, Catholic school books urged cooperative behavior. "There are many ways of being useful," began one lesson. "You are useful — you who from a love of order and a wish to see everybody happy, watch carefully that nothing should be injured, that everything should shine with cleanliness." The lesson went on to stress that "usefulness" also meant that students should "keep silence" and be "humble and good natured."[18]

In 1874, the publishing firm of Benziger Brothers entered the competition by introducing the "Catholic National Series of Readers." Because the author of the series was Richard Gilmour, the conservative bishop of Cleveland, the books were particularly attractive to conservative parishes. Yet there were few differences between the Benziger series and its competitors. The familiar themes about nature and social values were repeated.[19]

The overwhelming majority of Catholic school books were in complete thematic agreement with public school texts. Yet it would be erroneous to think of the two types as exactly the same. On one particular point, parochial school texts differed: the Catholic perspective on the American past was clearly partisan. Catholic school books, to be sure, agreed that America was superior to other nations. Yet these texts also emphasized the continuing involvement and contributions of Catholics in American history. Lesson after lesson recalled the exploits of American Catholic heroes from the obvious, such as Commodore John Barry and Bishop John Carroll, to the preposterous, such as Bishop Gorda, a missionary to Greenland.

Parochial school advocates hoped that such instruction would encourage Catholic children to become involved in American affairs. "We desire that the history of the United States should be taught in all our Catholic schools," noted one school advocate. "We must keep firm and solid the liberties of our country by keeping fresh and noble memories of the past and thus sending from our Catholic homes, into the arena of public life, not partisans, but patriots."[20]

The purposes of both Catholic school and public school historical lessons were identical in spirit, but Catholic school advocates wanted American Catholic children to be proud of both components of their heritage. Young Catholics were to render their spiritual loyalty to the Catholic Church and their temporal loyalty to the United States.

Textbooks were only one indication of the values taught in the American Catholic classroom, but they provide a good impression of those values. Even though American Catholic schools remained distinct from the public schools in one important area — intensive religious instruction — they became increasingly similar in other areas. "The parish schools came into existence not only to further the Catholic faith," noted historian Howard Weisz, "but also to serve as a surrogate for the public schools. Pressure to emulate those public schools came from parents jealous of the educational advantages of others."[21] The values implicit in Catholic texts reflected the increasing Americanization of the English-language parochial schools during the last quarter of the nineteenth century.

⠭

The third model used by Catholics was the ethnic parish school, an institution designed to cultivate and preserve foreign languages and cultures as well as to preserve religious faith and provide literacy. First established in the 1830s and 1840s by German Catholics and Lutherans, the ethnic parish school was an important and popular model until the 1930s.[22]

The commitment of German Catholics was almost unanimous, and not surprisingly special emphasis was placed on the preservation of the German language.[23] "Our German language," noted one German American editor, "is to us the treasure that is inseparable with our being. We are better citizens, better men, and better Christians if we give expression to our noblest feelings in our own tongue unhindered. We desire to be faithful American citizens; we desire to remain devoted children of the Catholic Church, but we also desire to find an unhindered expression of the soul in our own language."[24] As long as native language and culture had meaning for the immigrants, the ethnic parish school played an important role.

It is hard to overestimate the importance that most immigrant Catholic groups placed on these schools. "The schools they set up," notes historian Philip Gleason, "performed the functions, in addition to intellectual and religious training, of transmitting the ancestral language, orienting the young to the national symbols of the group through successive generations."[25]

Yet support for ethnic parish schools was not unanimous, varying from one immigrant group to the next. The Germans had been the first to establish ethnic parish schools in the nineteenth century and were its most ardent supporters. But by the turn of the century, most German parish schools had felt the impact of Americanization and were using English as the main language of instruction. The Poles, who continued to arrive in this country in large numbers during the first two decades of the twentieth century, were enthusiastic supporters of ethnic parish schools. Other Slavic groups also established ethnic parish schools in proportion to their numbers.

The Italians took a different course, however, and turned away from the ethnic parish school. In spite of their large numbers and their willingness to build extraordinary churches, the Italians showed little interest in parish schools. This unique response to education — one so different from the Slavic response — perplexed the stolid, Irish American bishops of the American church.

Certainly the Italians posed the biggest challenge for these church leaders.[26] "Experience has amply proved that the Italians will not send their children to parochial schools if they have to pay for them," noted one Italian priest.[27] Even when the bishops built and paid for Catholic schools in Italian parishes, the classrooms were not full.

Many Italian parents simply preferred a public education for their children. "Despite strenuous efforts to bring Italian children into parochial schools," adds historian Rudolph Vecoli, "only a small minority of them ever received a Catholic education.... Thus, as late as 1924, there was only one school for every six Italian churches."[28] It was a fact of American Catholic life that Italians would not support parochial education.

Concern about the impact of education on their children was not peculiar to the Italians. Other immigrants — Eastern European Catholics — shared in this belief. Yet the concerns of Bohemian, Slovak, Ukrainian, and Polish Catholics were not the same as the concerns of the Italians. Eastern Europeans saw a very specific and important purpose for education — to sustain cultural, linguistic, and religious values in the next generation. These Slavic Catholics embraced education for these purposes but questioned the value of education for social advancement or social mobility. It is not surprising, therefore, that Slavic Catholics were willing to build their own parish schools and reluctant to send their children to public institutions.[29]

Like the Italians, Slavic Catholics were skeptical of the value of education beyond the elementary level. During the years from 1890 to 1930, most Eastern European Catholics removed their children from school after the sixth grade and sent them to work. "Slavic parents," notes historian John Bodnar, "not only influenced their children by the example of hard work and the demands of family survival, but also imparted definite views concerning education. A typical Slovak father stressed to his son that it was more important to learn a manual skill than attend school."[30] It is not surprising, therefore, that fewer than 10 percent of Slavic children went on beyond elementary school. Like their parents before them, second-generation Slavic American Catholics went to work at an early age.

There were, of course, differences between specific Slavic Catholic nationalities in their pattern of parochial school support. For the minority of Bohemians who were practicing Catholics, parochial schooling was the logical extension of a European culture dominated by Catholicism. The Bohemian parish school in America was a mechanism to maintain a bond between parents and their children. "The school became something very intimate in the life of the Bohemian Catholic family," notes historian Joseph Cada. The schools "served as agents in closing the cultural gap between the old and the young generations."[31]

It is no wonder, then, that Bohemian Catholic school enrollments never declined in the years from 1895 to 1945. In 1895 the Bohemians maintained 42 schools with a total enrollment of 8,673; by 1915, the number of schools had increased to 68 and the enrollment was up to 13,790, and by 1925, there were 76 schools with 16,517 students. By 1945, long after the end of Bohemian emigration to the United States, Bohemians continued to support 94 parish schools with 16,809 students. Such statistics were a testament to the devotion of the Bohemians to their native culture and religion.

The Slovaks also were devoted to parochial schools as the major means of sustaining national identity and religious heritage. In Europe, the Slovaks had willingly established church schools in the 1870s and 1880s. But with the domination of

Hungary over Slovakia at the turn of the century, the Slovak people were forced to send their children to public schools that emphasized Magyar culture and language.

Hungarian efforts to subjugate Slovak culture and language left a bitter impression among those Slovaks who emigrated to the United States. These emigrants vowed to fight all efforts to undermine their heritage. This viewpoint came through clearly in the American Slovak press and was expressed best by one writer who denounced public schools because "whether in Hungary or America, [these schools] denationalize our children."[32]

The Slovaks, therefore, went on to build their own schools to insure that the next generation would remain loyal to its native culture and religion. The unanimity of opinion on the school question is evidence of their determination. "Catholic leaders valued parochial schools above all else," adds historian Mark Stolarik, "they worried much more about their children's moral and national upbringing than about social mobility and they had no use for public schools."[33]

By 1930, the Slovaks had built schools in over half of their 241 parishes in the United States, and the majority of children in those parishes attended parochial schools. The Slovaks did everything possible to live up to the motto: "our own church, our own school, and worship in our own language."[34]

The enthusiasm of the Slovaks for parish schools was exceeded only by the Poles, who were acknowledged leaders along with the Germans in the establishment of ethnic parochial schools from the time of their arrival in this country in the mid-nineteenth century. At first the number of schools was small, but as the number of Polish emigrants increased after 1890, so also did the number of schools. Their reasons for building the schools were the same as those of the Slovaks — parish schools would preserve ethnic identity and religious devotion — but their strength in numbers made the Poles far more visible than the Slovaks. By 1910, the Poles had established more than 350 parish schools in more than a dozen states.[35]

The dramatic growth of Polish Catholic education was fueled

not only by the commitment of Polish parents, but also by the simultaneous establishment of several congregations of Polish American sisters who devoted themselves to teaching. In 1882, four nuns from Cracow established the Felician congregation in Detroit as the first order of Polish American teaching nuns. The Sisters of the Holy Family of Nazareth arrived in the United States in 1885. The Polish Sisters of St. Francis were established in 1893. The Sisters of the Resurrection arrived in 1900, and the Polish Sisters of St. Joseph were founded in 1901. Other orders quickly followed as the demand for Polish teaching sisters increased. By 1914, there were twenty-two hundred Polish American nuns teaching in parish schools in two dozen states.[36]

The conditions faced by these sisters were primitive by contemporary standards. Parish schools were frequently located in cramped and unheated church basements. To make matters worse, students were literally crammed into classrooms. It was not unusual for a single sister to face seventy-five students at a time, and some of these dedicated nuns had as many as a hundred children in their charge. "So many of our young people were suffocating in cramped, poorly ventilated classrooms," remembered one parishioner in Chicago. "It was a pity to see them packed like herrings in a barrel during the hours of instruction poring over their books."[37] Such conditions were typical of schools in Polish parishes across the country at the turn of the century.

The tools for teaching — books, maps, blackboards — were in short supply. "The lack of educational aids led to inventiveness," notes historian Anthony Kuzniewski. "At one school, children wrote with chalk on stone lids instead of slate tablets."[38] The Felician sisters did take the initiative in compiling texts for use in Polish American parish schools, but the number of books was never sufficient to meet the demand.

Ethnic Catholic schools faced their greatest challenge in the years from 1910 to 1930, the result of a concerted effort to

"Americanize" these schools. It was a campaign waged on several different fronts, starting with the government. State law in the early 1920s mandated that all instruction in private schools should be conducted in English and frequently required that private school teachers meet state standards in teacher training.

The Catholic hierarchy also joined in the campaign for Americanization through their instructions to pastors, and diocesan school boards asserted the right to approve the languages and courses of study used in parochial school classrooms. In fact, the hierarchy took a vocal and visible role in this process. Bishops such as James Gibbons, George Mundelein, and John Ireland led the campaign. "Ours is the American Church," noted Ireland, "and not Irish, German, Italian, or Polish — and we will keep it American."[39]

As important as these external forces were, the most important force for Americanization came from within the ethnic Catholic communities themselves. As the older generation of priests and lay persons gave way to an American-born generation, the Old World ways were abandoned. Native language and culture were less important to American-born Catholics than to their parents. The new generation did not object to an Americanized curriculum; in fact, they welcomed it. By the 1930s, native language and culture had become extracurricular subjects in most parochial schools and dropped altogether at some of these institutions.[40]

All ethnic schools came in for the same treatment, and perhaps it was inevitable. The ethnic parochial school was tolerated as temporarily expedient by most Americans — both Catholic and non-Catholic. It was assumed by all that national parishes and foreign language usage would die out as the new immigrants acclimated themselves to American society. But many of these immigrants held on to their native languages and customs with a fierce determination that must have disheartened the American public.

World War I, with its propaganda campaign against all things foreign, ended the tolerance of the American public for ethnic parochial schools. The American public in general, and the Catholic hierarchy in particular, would no longer accept the argument of ethnic leaders that immigrants could maintain their native languages and cultures and still be loyal to their new nation. The American public rejected this argument as contradictory and pressured the foreign-born to openly pledge their total allegiance to the United States. Ethnic parochial schools were a casualty of this war-time loyalty campaign.[41]

The ethnic Catholic school was a key element in the rapid growth of parochial education for the fifty years following the Civil War. More important, these schools served as the bridge from the old world to the new for many immigrant children. Yet these schools were destined to be temporary and transitional. With the pressure of American nationalism both during and after World War I and the end of mass immigration in 1924, the ethnic Catholic school gradually lost its value to the Catholic Church.

❖

Catholic parents faced a variety of educational choices in the years between the Civil War and World War I, and their responses were determined largely by their perceptions of the values and dangers of common schooling. A significant percentage of Catholic parents — perhaps a majority — had relatively few qualms about public education. In fact, these parents saw the public school as the best means of insuring the future prosperity of their children in American society.

A second group of parents could not quite accept the idea of a curriculum totally devoid of religious instruction, but they were not willing to abandon the goals of public education. Their choice was to build formal working relationships with local school boards that provided for publicly supported secular institutions taught by Catholic teachers in parish owned classrooms; religion was an after-school activity.

A third group of parents spurned formal relationships with public school boards, but nevertheless adapted many of the fundamental elements of the public school curriculum for use in parish classrooms. The result was the prototype for the

Catholic parochial school that would come to dominate the educational landscape in the twentieth century.

A fourth group of parents, most of whom were immigrants from Europe, not only spurned the public schools, but also established parish schools that heavily emphasized native culture, language, and religion. Taken together these four distinct responses underscore the important fact that there was no single prototype for Catholic education in last half of the nineteenth century and the first quarter of the twentieth century. The style and substance of Catholic parochial education varied from region to region, diocese to diocese, and even from parish to parish across the United States.[42]

Chapter 6 _____

The School Controversy

===

THE APPROACH of a new century saw the emergence of a struggle among American church leaders over the content and purpose of parochial schools and their relationship to American society. Liberal Catholic bishops argued that the purpose of the parish school was to preserve the religious faith of children and at the same time prepare them for productive roles in American society. Liberals, moreover, were inclined to acknowledge the positive contributions made by public schools to the general welfare of the nation.

Conservative bishops wholeheartedly accepted the premise that parish schools should protect the religious faith of Catholic children, but these prelates disagreed with the liberals on the value of public education generally and the specific role of parochial education in American society. Conservatives argued that the church should be wary of making parish schools too American in tone and content, lest these institutions lose their distinctive Catholic qualities. In fact, the conservatives saw little in public schooling worth adopting. To their way of thinking, these institutions were hotbeds of materialism, hedonism, and immorality.

The men caught up in this conflict were an interesting assortment of energetic individuals.[1] The majority were American-born of working-class immigrant heritage. All were intelligent, and each man was tapped at an early age for leadership posts in their respective dioceses. But these bishops were not cut

from a common mold: one was the descendent of a distinguished Maryland family; two had been born in Ireland and
one in Austria; one was an orphan and one a convert.

The diversity in their backgrounds was mirrored in the gra-
dations of their views on parochial education. For purposes of
clarity these men can be grouped together as liberals or conservatives, but in truth they fit into a spectrum of opinion with
each bishop differing slightly from his colleagues. They were,
indeed, individuals with their own distinctive views.

Certainly the most liberal of the prelates was John Ireland.[2]
Ireland's philosophy of education was but one aspect of his
larger view of the relationship between the church and American society. In fact, Ireland devoted his life to eliminating
the sources of conflict between Catholics and non-Catholics
and sought ways to unite the Catholic Church with American values. "The principles of the former," he preached, "are
in thorough harmony with the interest of the latter."[3]

To Ireland's thinking, most of the conflict between his
church and his nation had nothing to do with church dogma
or values, but was fostered by the cultural baggage of the foreign immigrants who dominated the American church in the
nineteenth century. As these immigrants became increasingly
American, so also would Catholicism become an American religion. It is not surprising, therefore, that Ireland used every
means available to encourage Americanization among his
flock. One means to that end was parochial education.

Ireland was deeply committed to the fundamental principles
of parochial education, that is, the critical tie between religious
and secular instruction in publicly funded, publicly controlled
schools. As one historian put it, "This was the bedrock upon
which Ireland based all of his educational proposals."[4]

There is no question that Ireland's views on the unification of public and parochial schools were the most liberal
among Catholic Church leaders. In fact, many churchmen were
shocked and scandalized by Ireland's views, and efforts to
implement some of his ideas precipitated the major Catholic
educational controversy of the nineteenth century. But Ireland

was not alone in his basic belief in the rapprochement between public and parochial education. Other church leaders, most particularly James Gibbons, the archbishop of Baltimore, were sympathetic to this view.

As the archbishop of Baltimore, Gibbons was the nominal head of the church in the United States. In this capacity, he represented American Catholicism to the Vatican. Much to the dismay of conservative bishops, Gibbons refused to join in the condemnations of public education and encouraged efforts to find a common ground between the two systems. In fact, Gibbons defended Ireland's efforts to develop specific plans for cooperative schools in two Minnesota communities and obtained official approval for Ireland's plans. On education, as on other social issues, Gibbons sought ways of harmonizing the tenets of the Catholic faith with the principles of American democracy.

At the other end of the spectrum were the conservatives and their complaints. Liberals, they argued, were undermining more than fifty years of Catholic educational progress by introducing the notion of compromise, cooperation, and conciliation with the public schools. The conservatives accused the liberals of bargaining away the very essence of Catholic education just to make the parish schools more American. The conservatives vowed to fight.

The leader of the conservative faction was Michael Augustine Corrigan, the archbishop of New York. Corrigan was, of course, an ardent supporter of parochial education throughout his life.[5] Yet he was not a philosopher given to writing and publishing his views on educational issues. He did express himself through a voluminous correspondence with fellow bishops, and most of what he had to say concerned tactics. Corrigan concentrated on two issues: how Catholics could obtain public funds for the support of their schools and how they should respond to the liberal challenge of Archbishop Ireland and his cohorts.

Corrigan saw no need to defend the Catholic schools to the world. The Holy Father and the Third Plenary Council had spoken clearly and in no uncertain terms on the issue: every Catholic parish should build and support a school. Corrigan intended to do just that in New York and oppose any bishop who opposed this policy. To Corrigan's thinking, the time for debate was over.

Corrigan was joined in his cause by a number of conservative bishops, among them Bernard McQuaid, the first bishop of Rochester and outspoken supporter of Catholic education.[6] "Many battles have been fought, many victories won," noted McQuaid at the midpoint of his career, "but the schools are my greatest glory."[7]

McQuaid would consider no compromise with the public schools in his diocese and openly clashed with prelates and priests who did not share his views. One colleague described McQuaid as "a crusty old ecclesiastic who in perfect good faith felt that he alone was fighting the battles of the Church."[8] McQuaid was the most visible conservative in the campaign against Ireland and other liberal prelates.

The energetic individuals who dominated the parochial school movement in the last quarter of the nineteenth century shared common commitment to the importance of religious-based education. All of these men, regardless of the place on the philosophical spectrum, agreed that Catholic schooling was a necessity if the church was to survive and flourish in Protestant America.

Beyond that simple common commitment, these men could agree on little else. Were parish schools an unfortunate necessity or a moral alternative to public schools? Should the church seek out cooperative educational ventures with the public schools or should parents be required to build and support parish schools? As long as these issues were discussed in private, there was an uneasy peace between the liberals and the conservatives. But in 1890, at the annual meeting of the National Education Association, Archbishop John Ireland spoke out on the relations between "state schools and parish schools"

and the truce was broken. The speech precipitated a controversy characterized by misunderstanding and bitter feelings.[9]

When Ireland spoke to members of the National Education
Association on a hot summer day in 1890, he hoped to build a
bridge between two competing but not contradictory philoso-
phies of education. He was well aware that the education of
the young had divided Catholics from non-Catholics for almost
fifty years. In fact, acrimony and bitterness had prevailed between the two groups since the days of John Hughes and the
New York school controversy.

Ireland was convinced that the differences between public
and parochial education were not insurmountable. In fact, Ireland proposed a compromise plan that he hoped would lead
to a merger of the two school systems. "In the circumstances
of the present time, I uphold the parish school," he noted. "I
sincerely wish that the need for it did not exist. I would have
all schools for the children of the people be state schools."[10]
Ireland hoped that his remarks would contribute to a greater
understanding and communication between Catholic and public educators. Little did he realize that his speech would cause
havoc and controversy within the American church.[11]

Unlike previous confrontations, which pitted Catholics
against non-Catholics, the school controversy of 1890–93 was
a struggle *within* the American church. Liberal Catholics, especially John Ireland, argued that the church should be open to
compromise and cooperation with public schools, particularly
on the matter of the secular curriculum.

The liberals' scheme was essentially the Poughkeepsie Plan
writ large and would use public funds to support Catholic
teachers to instruct Catholic children on secular subjects in
classrooms located in parish buildings. The hours from nine
to three would be devoted to secular subjects; religion would
be taught after the end of the school day. The liberals never
claimed that these hybrid schools were substitutes for parish
schools, but they did hope that the plan would insure the religious as well as the secular instruction of children in parishes
that would not or could not support parish schools.[12]

Conservative Catholics, particularly Bernard McQuaid, were outraged. Compromise indeed; the conservatives would have nothing to do with the "godless heathenism" of the public schools. The conservatives accused Ireland and the liberals of abandoning the dictates of the Third Plenary Council of Baltimore that had required every parish to establish a parochial school.

If only the American bishops would stand together as a unit, argued the conservatives, and *require* Catholic parents to send their children to Catholic schools, there would soon be no Catholic children attending public schools and no need to talk about compromise with public education. The conservatives considered compromise to be synonymous with capitulation. Cooperation with public educators and admitting that the state had certain rights in the education of children badly weakened the case for state-supported denominational schools. Thus conservatives vowed to oppose any liberal effort to compromise with public education.[13]

Ireland saw his NEA speech as an opportunity to propose the general use of the compromise school plan that had been in existence in Poughkeepsie and elsewhere for nearly twenty years. He believed that this plan offered the hope of a viable working relationship between the public and the parochial schools. Ireland hoped that his remarks would generate a positive response from the assembled public school teachers and administrators. What the archbishop of St. Paul was not expecting was the extensive criticism he received from within his own church.[14]

The fact that Ireland's remarks precipitated a controversy had little to do with the substance of his remarks. Ireland focused his remarks on the fundamental importance of religion in the educational process. "Do the schools of America fear contact with religion?" Ireland asked. "Catholics demand the Christian state school. In doing so, they prove themselves the truest friends of the school and the state."[15] One means of establishing "Christian state schools" was to encourage parish pastors to implement the Poughkeepsie Plan in their communities. The plan was not new, and Ireland did not think that he was suggesting anything controversial. He thought that he was merely adding his support to an accepted solution to the church-state-school question.

What made Ireland's remarks so controversial was the enthusiasm and support the archbishop expressed for the principles of public education. "Free schools!" he exclaimed. "Blest indeed is the nation whose vales and hillsides they adorn, and blest the generations upon whose souls are poured their treasures. No tax is more legitimate than that which is levied in order to dispel mental darkness and build up within the nation's bosom intelligent manhood and womanhood."[16] In addition to this effusive praise, Ireland also proclaimed that the state had a *right* to educate the young.

Many Catholics were shocked to hear such scandalous remarks from the mouth of a Catholic archbishop. Quotes from Ireland's speech were printed out of context in diocesan papers and roundly condemned by conservative Catholic educators from coast to coast. Conservatives saw Ireland's support for the Poughkeepsie Plan and his support for the concept of public education as a plot to undermine the existing parochial school system. In the mind of the conservatives, Ireland was preaching heresy, and they intended to appeal to the Holy Father to have this "consecrated blizzard" stopped.[17]

The furor created by his speech gave Ireland cause for concern, and he wrote to Gibbons in December to explain his remarks. Ireland began the letter by indicating that he had read the criticism of his speech, had reread the speech, and had found nothing deserving of censure. "The general purpose of the discourse," he noted to Gibbons, "was to state plainly to the country the grounds of Catholic opposition to the state schools and to lead up, if possible, to an alteration permitting the removal of this opposition. I was anxious too, to ally the angry feeling which reigns between non-Catholic Americans and

Catholics in so far as their feeling rests on a misunderstanding of our position."[18]

Ireland also defended his comments on public education. "What was I to do to gain their ears," he asked, "but to confess to all the good in the system and then, when their sympathy is won, to tell them of the defects." On reflection, Ireland saw nothing wrong with his remarks or his tactics.

Going beyond his speech, Ireland raised some fundamental concerns about the Catholic campaign against the "evils" of public schooling. He thought that the conservatives had gone too far in demeaning public schools. "They are not hotbeds of vice," Ireland added. "Neither do they teach unbelief or Protestantism. Teachers are often good Catholics, or at least are gentlemen or ladies decorous in conduct and generous toward our faith."[19]

Ireland emphasized the fundamental reasoning behind the liberal campaign to improve relations with the public schools. "There is a danger," he noted, "that never shall we have schools for all Catholic children, or Catholics will grow tired of contributing. At present nearly half of the Catholic children of America do not attend parish schools. The true solution, in my judgment, is to make the state school satisfactory to Catholic consciences, and to use it."[20] Ireland clearly had no intention of abandoning his campaign for a compromise school plan.

Gibbons agreed with Ireland in principle and thought it best to write to Rome on his friend's behalf. Gibbons had received regular reports during the fall that protests had reached the Vatican and that the text of Ireland's speech was being examined for errors. Gibbons defended Ireland's remarks in a December 30 letter to Pope Leo XIII, explaining the unique nature of public education in the United States. Gibbons noted that Ireland, more than any other prelate, understood the antagonism between the American public and the Catholic Church.

Gibbons defended Ireland's comments on public education. "It appears to me, Holy Father," he wrote after quoting at length from Ireland's speech, "that the various sentences in their context have no other meaning than this: The Catholics are not against state schools in principle."[21] In all of Ireland's remarks, Gibbons could find nothing unreasonable, and he hoped that the Holy Father would agree.

As Rome was considering the implications of Ireland's remarks, the acrimony between liberal and conservative Catholics again came into public view. This time, however, it was not Ireland or his views at the center of attention, but rather Thomas Bouquillon, a relatively obscure professor of moral theology at the Catholic University of America.

Bouquillon had entered the controversy as an innocent. At the request of Cardinal Gibbons and other Catholic leaders, Bouquillon had prepared a paper on the rights and responsibilities of the state in the education of children. The paper was initially submitted as an article to the *American Catholic Quarterly Review,* but it was rejected on the ground that the author had given too much authority to the state and not enough to the parent.

Unwilling to revise his views to meet the sensibilities of the *Review,* Bouquillon turned to Gibbons for advice. With Gibbons's financial support, Bouquillon published the article as a pamphlet under the title *Education: To Whom Does It Belong?* The booklet appeared in November of 1891, just a few weeks before the annual conference of the American archbishops.[22]

In the pamphlet Bouquillon argued that education was a responsibility of mankind, individually and collectively, through families, churches, and states. He stressed that education was the responsibility of all three, not one alone. The professor further argued that each of these entities had "special and proper" rights in the education process. He noted that the state's right to educate did not stem from the rights of parents, but was a separate right to "preserve the temporal welfare of the commonwealth." In fact, Bouquillon went so far as to argue that the rights of the state were co-equal with the rights of parents and their families. It was on this particular point that the conservatives vociferously disagreed.

Education: To Whom Does It Belong? was answered by the conservatives two weeks later in a pamphlet, *The Parent First,* written by René Holaind, a Jesuit theology professor at St. Francis Xavier College in New York. Holaind refuted Bouquillon's claim that the state had special rights in education. "The parent has the priority both in concept and in fact," he wrote. "The Church has the supreme direction because she has the noblest and most sacred union. By her side stands the state aiming at the public good without interfering with public or domestic rights, but ready to answer the call of the humblest member of society, ever watching over that order on which depend the peace and happiness of nations." Holaind's pamphlet was published with funds provided by the conservative archbishop of New York, Michael Corrigan.[23]

The Bouquillon and Holaind pamphlets came to summarize the fundamental liberal and conservative positions on the church-state-school question. In fact, the timing of the pamphlets gave these publications an importance far greater than was ever expected. Less than three months before publication of the Bouquillon pamphlet, Archbishop Ireland gave his permission to pastors in the small communities of Faribault and Stillwater, Minnesota, to sign agreements with local school boards to implement cooperative educational programs for Catholic children. Even though there was no tie between the Bouquillon pamphlet and the "Faribault Plan," as it came to be called, the conservatives saw these unrelated events as part of the same liberal conspiracy to destroy the parish school.[24]

The conservatives were particularly suspicious because the Bouquillon pamphlet appeared only a few weeks before the American archbishops were scheduled to meet and discuss the merits of the Faribault Plan. With that conference in mind, Holaind rushed his rebuttal into print. The conservatives were satisfied that both sides of the issue would be heard when the archbishops met in St. Louis. Unfortunately for both sides the archbishops' conference led to no resolution of the conflict, and the pamphlets went on to have lives of their own. Well into 1892, the issues raised by Bouquillon and Holaind were front-page news in the Catholic press and received extensive coverage in the secular press as well.[25]

The Bouquillon pamphlet had done little to resolve the school controversy as Gibbons had hoped. In fact, the little booklet had exacerbated the problems over schooling. At the beginning of 1892, the liberals tried a new strategy: a direct appeal to the pope for a vindication of Ireland and Bouquillon. To further this cause, Ireland traveled to Rome in January of 1892.

Gibbons also joined the campaign by sending the pope a lengthy summary of the proceedings of the conference of archbishops held the previous November. He indicated that there had been no criticism of Ireland or his Faribault Plan and a few of the prelates present offered their compliments. The letter bolstered Ireland's case and the early word from members of the Curia was that Ireland would be completely vindicated. "God bless the Pope," noted Gibbons with satisfaction. "It is not the Faribault school that is on trial, but the question to be decided is...whether the Church is to be honored as a bulwark of liberty and order or to be despised and suspected as an enemy of our institutions."[26] But Gibbons's optimism was premature. Ever mindful of the conservatives, the pope's statement on the Faribault Plan had all the wisdom of Solomon.

After more than a year of investigation and consideration, the pope issued a decision on Archbishop Ireland, his educational philosophy, and his school plan. The statement acknowledged the fundamental righteousness of the school legislation of the plenary councils of Baltimore, but noted that, after a consideration of all the facts and circumstances, the Faribault Plan could be "tolerated."

The statement was carefully nuanced so as not to offend either liberals or conservatives but at the same time to end the controversy. Unfortunately, the conflict had gone too far for either faction to drop the matter, and both the liberals and the conservatives claimed victory after the statement was made public.

Perhaps it was inevitable that such a subtle letter would be open to misinterpretation. The liberals interpreted the message as a vindication of Ireland and the concept of cooperative education. The conservatives countered by arguing that the pope had upheld the Third Plenary Council mandate that every parish should have a school. The Faribault Plan, argued the conservatives, was to be tolerated as a special case. Rather than calming the waters, the pope's message stirred up the acrimony between the two sides. As spring turned to summer, the American church was no closer to solving its school controversy than it had been two years earlier.[27]

Archbishop Corrigan and the conservatives took the initiative in the early summer of 1892 in claiming that Ireland and Gibbons had misinformed the pope about the condition of the church in the United States. Through his agent in Rome, Corrigan obtained a copy of Ireland's letter to the pope on the school controversy. In the letter Ireland had warned that the American church would suffer persecution if the pope sided with the conservatives. Corrigan countered that no such threat of persecution existed and that the pope should not allow such a spurious claim to influence his decisions on the school question. The pope responded to Corrigan and his colleagues with a plea for unity and a call for the bishops to work together for public funding for denominational institutions.[28]

Gibbons was in total agreement with the pope in praying for an end to the controversy. The cardinal was a realist, however. He knew that neither faction would accept such a neutral statement. "So long as certain periodicals will persist in minimizing and distorting the decision of Rome," Gibbons wrote, "advocates on the other side will not be wanting in maintaining their side and in keeping up the unhappy controversy."[29] Matters continued to deteriorate during the summer, and it was clear to Gibbons that the school controversy would again be the main topic of discussion at the upcoming conference of the archbishops.

But two factors would change the nature of the discussion that year. First, tension in Faribault and Stillwater over the use of nuns as teachers led to a termination of the cooperative agreements between the public and parochial schools in those two communities. Ireland's well-publicized plan, therefore, was no longer a "threat" to parish school development. A second and more important factor affecting the outcome of the conference was the presence of the pope's personal representative, Archbishop Francesco Satolli. Having Satolli attend the conference, reasoned the Vatican, would end the school controversy once and for all. Unfortunately, Satolli's presence had the opposite effect.[30]

Satolli was not a surprise to the archbishops when they opened their meeting on November 16. They knew in advance that he would attend the conference, and they all assumed that he would listen to the discussion. The American archbishops were surprised, therefore, when Satolli started the conference by reading a prepared statement listing fourteen points for consideration. After he completed the public reading, Satolli invited the stunned archbishops to agree to his points and sign the document.

The document was very close to the liberal position on the issue. Satolli espoused the establishment of new parish schools, but also permitted Catholic children to attend public schools with the permission of their bishops. He further proposed that the clergy could not withhold the sacraments from parents who sent their children to public schools. Another point noted the church's general support for public education, but also noted the church's particular objection to the lack of Christian denominational instruction. Satolli also proposed that the bishops make special provision for the religious education of Catholic children enrolled in public schools. Finally, the document proposed the acceptance of the compromise plan implemented in Faribault and Stillwater, Minnesota. Of all the archbishops present, only John Ireland came forward to sign the document.

The other archbishops greeted Satolli's propositions in stony silence. They were stunned. They had come to the conference expecting to discuss their differences over parochial education. Now they were being asked by the pope's personal representative to sign a document that none of them had read and one that many of those present found repugnant. It is not surprising, therefore, that the prelates refused to sign the document without substantial changes.

Satolli was taken aback. He had not expected such resistance to the pope's authority. He did, however, understand the value of compromise and agreed to modify his propositions. He arrived at the last session of the conference with a slightly modified version of his proposals.

But the changes were not enough for Corrigan and the conservatives, who asked for additional revisions. Unable to contain his anger, Satolli stormed from the room followed by Ireland, who was sent to console the Italian prelate and explain why the conservatives would not sign the document. Looking for a way out of this embarrassing situation without further compromising his position, Satolli added a note to his revised document that said "all these were read and considered at the archbishops meeting, the difficulties answered, and the requisite alterations made, November 17, 1892." Satolli also agreed not to publish his propositions until the conservatives had a chance to protest to the Holy Father.

The conservatives did, indeed, protest to Rome and did so with great vigor. "The American episcopacy does not oppose the public school," wrote Corrigan, "but only asserts that Catholics should be educated under the surveillance of the Church, that is, in parochial schools; if the state does not want to help us, it does not matter; we will continue to sacrifice ourselves, as for fifty years we have done, but we will not give our Catholics up to the atheistic teachers, to the neutral school."[31]

The response from the pope badly disappointed the conservatives. In early January of 1893, the pope announced the appointment of Archbishop Satolli to be the first permanent apostolic delegate to the United States. And in May the pope wrote to Gibbons to tell him and the other American archbishops that the Vatican saw no conflict between Satolli's propositions and the mandates of the Third Plenary Council of Baltimore. Tired of conflict, Corrigan and the conservatives accepted the pope's decision with a spirit of resignation. "I trust that the words of Our Lord's Vicar," Corrigan wrote to Gibbons, "will have the consoling effect of His Own when He commanded the wind and the waters and 'there came a great calm.' "[32]

❖

The great Catholic school controversy had ended. But after more than three years of acrimony, the differences between the liberals and conservatives remained. More important, the conservatives felt betrayed. "We are all in a nice pickle thanks to Leo XIII and his delegate," wrote McQuaid to Corrigan. "Just as our arduous work of the last forty years was beginning to bear fruit, they arbitrarily upset the whole. If an enemy had done this! . . . It is only a question of time . . . present Roman legislation having wrought incalculable mischief, that we, school children of the hierarchy, will receive a lesson in our catechism from another Italian sent out to enlighten us."[33] The conservatives feared, with some justification, that Catholic children by the thousands would drift away from parish schools.

But the pope's decision in favor of Satolli's propositions was more than a vindication of Ireland and Bouquillon or a victory for the liberals. The Satolli propositions outlined and emphasized the harmony that existed between the Catholic Church and the American ideals of public education. It was an important day when the pope confirmed that the church had no fundamental disagreements with the principles of public education.

"American Catholics no longer needed to jeopardize their good relations with their neighbors," concluded historian Robert Cross, "in proving their orthodoxy by violent attacks upon the public schools. Instead of being forced to choose between an American culture bent on giving youth the finest possible secular education, and a Church which insisted that an inadequate parochial school, or no school at all, was better than a nonsectarian one, Catholics were free to accept profitable compromises with the state school, even while they worked to develop, under either state or Church offices, a perfect system."[34] It was an extraordinary achievement for the liberals and marked an end to the combative educational policy instituted by John Hughes more than fifty years earlier.

Chapter 7

The Search for Order

OON AFTER the turn of the century, the U.S. Office of Education acknowledged the importance of Catholic parochial schools in the educational life of the nation. "The most impressive religious fact in the United States today," began one chapter in the *Report of the U.S. Commissioner of Education for 1903*, "is the system of Catholic free parochial schools. Not less than one million children are being educated in these schools. This great educational work is being carried out without any financial aid from the state."[1] In a small way, the publication of this chapter in the most widely read government publication on education was a symbolic turning point in the history of Catholic education. For the first time the federal government officially took notice of the nation's second school system. Catholic education had come of age.

But the growth of Catholic parochial education had come at a high price. The rapid increase in the numbers of schools and students over sixty years had been uncoordinated and disjointed at the diocesan level as well as at the national level. This growth underscored the need for organizations and mechanisms to centralize school planning and supervision at the diocesan level. In short, Catholic educators at the turn of the century were searching for order in the development of their schools.[2]

This search for order led many Catholic school advocates to the conclusion that school boards in general and superintendents in particular would be vital to the future success of any diocesan school system in the new century. The 1903 government report noted that "the diocesan superintendent has been a powerful factor in the great progress made in these schools in recent years. It would be well if every diocese had such an officer. Indeed, there can be no perfect organization of the system without him."[3] But at the turn of the century, less than 10 percent of the American dioceses had school superintendents, and it was not clear that bishops would willingly transfer their authority over parochial schools to superintendents.

In an effort to encourage the bishops, Catholic educators sought to clarify the need, aim, and methods of centralized diocesan school supervision. In an influential 1905 address on the subject, E. F. Gibbons, the superintendent of schools in Buffalo, New York, argued that centralized supervision was necessary to facilitate communication among teachers in the diocese, to support the Americanization of ethnic schools, and, most important, to convince skeptical Catholic parents of the uniform quality of parochial education. "What will help convince these Catholic parents and children that their little school is really equal [to public schools]...[and] give them a pride in it and draw other children to it?" asked Gibbons. "The knowledge that their little school is part of a fine diocesan system."[4]

The advice of Gibbons and his colleagues did not fall on deaf ears. By 1910, more than 55 percent of American dioceses had established school boards, and a surprising 17 percent of these dioceses had appointed school superintendents. Writing in 1911 in the recently published *Catholic Encyclopedia*, James A. Burns summarized the progress of the supervision movement. "The board system," he concluded, "represented an important advance in the work of Catholic school organization, and had everywhere a quickening effect. It soon became evident, however, that the system was far from perfect.... There was a need, it was seen, of an executive officer of the central board who would be specifically qualified for the work of inspection and supervision, and who should devote his entire time to the task."[5] Burns and his colleagues urged the bishops of smaller dioceses to follow the example of the archbishops and appoint school superintendents.

It is doubtful that Burns or any other Catholic educator in 1910 could have anticipated how rapidly the bishops would respond to the call to appoint these superintendents. Over the twenty years from 1910 to 1930, the percentage of dioceses with superintendents nearly quadrupled. By the end of the 1920s it was clear to a majority of Catholics that the appointment of school superintendent was vital to insure the continued development of Catholic education in any diocese.[6]

Diocesan school supervision was not without problems, however. There were serious concerns about who was to serve on these school boards and for how long. There also were calls for more extensive training for diocesan school superintendents. Perhaps most explosive of all, however, was a call by a few educators for the centralized control of school funds. There was a wide range of ideas on what should be done, but few Catholic educators were willing to speak openly about their problems; perhaps there was concern that such frank discussion would cause scandal among the laity.[7]

But the laity were not consulted about their schools. The decisions to establish boards and appoint superintendents were made by bishops acting as individuals, and their decisions regarding when to centralize control of their parochial schools were affected by many different factors. This pattern of school board development varied substantially from one region of the country to the next.[8]

In the East, the percentage of dioceses with school boards and superintendents varied from diocese to diocese. At the turn of the century, only 30 percent of the dioceses in New England had school boards and less than 15 percent had superintendents. But a few miles to the south in the mid-Atlantic states, an extraordinary 78 percent of the dioceses had school boards, and 22 percent had superintendents. By 1930, however, the gap between the two regions had narrowed: 74 percent of the New England dioceses had boards and superintendents; the percentage of mid-Atlantic dioceses with boards had increased to 81 percent and those with superintendents to 95 percent.[9]

As was the case in the mid-Atlantic states, the school board movement was very popular in the Midwest at the turn of the century. But unlike the East, enthusiasm for the movement in the Midwest waned as the century progressed. By 1900, for example, a majority of dioceses in the upper Midwest had school boards. Over the next twenty years, however, the percentage of midwestern school boards increased only modestly. By 1930, little more than 70 percent of the midwestern dioceses had boards.

Superintendents were another matter; they were never very popular in the Midwest. Only a handful of bishops had appointed school superintendents by 1900, and few midwestern bishops showed much interest in concentrating educational authority in a single individual. It was not until 1930 that a bare majority of midwestern dioceses reported the appointment of superintendents.[10]

The supervision of the Catholic schools in the South was schizophrenic. In the dioceses of the South Atlantic states, it appeared that the bishops favored the establishment of school boards; by 1910, for example, over half of the bishops had established school boards, and the percentage had jumped to 73 percent by 1920. But in the 1920s, the bishops of these dioceses abandoned their boards in favor of superintendents. By 1930, only 10 percent of the dioceses still had boards, but well over 50 percent had superintendents. In the dioceses of the deep South the supervision movement was slow to take hold, but once it did, bishops in these states strongly favored boards over superintendents. By 1930, fully 80 percent had established boards, but only 20 percent had superintendents.[11]

It is difficult to generalize about the supervision movement in the western United States. In the Southwest, for example, dioceses slowly began to establish school boards about 1910, and over half had boards by 1930; a near majority (46 percent) had appointed superintendents by the latter year. What was unique in the Southwest was the willingness of a significant minority of bishops to appoint lay people to serve on their school boards. Bishops in other sections of the country did not adopt this practice until the late 1950s.

The dioceses of the Pacific states showed little interest in the supervision movement. By 1900 only a third of the bishops had established school boards and none had appointed school superintendents. It took another thirty years for the number of dioceses with boards to increase to 51 percent and those with superintendents to increase to 38 percent.[12]

The varying response to the school board movement across the country underscored the fact that the American church did not move in unison on matters concerning parochial education. Boards and superintendents were appointed early in those dioceses where the local bishops were interested in modern methods of school supervision. In other dioceses, where the local bishops were protective of their control over the schools, school boards and superintendents did not come until much later.

In spite of all the differences, however, there was one common element in the response to the supervision movement. All American bishops sought more order in the administration of the parochial schools in the first three decades of the twentieth century. By 1930, over 60 percent of the bishops in the United States had established school boards and appointed superintendents. The trend toward improving the management of parochial schools was clear.[13]

In addition to supporting centralized management of the parochial schools, Catholic educators at the turn of the century also established national organizations to encourage professional communication among teachers, school administrators, and bishops on the issues affecting parochial schools. The result was two organizations: the Catholic Educational Association founded in 1904 and the Education Department of the

National Catholic Welfare Conference founded in 1919. Even though these organizations shared many goals and many leaders, they served different functions within the parochial school movement.[14]

The Catholic Educational Association — renamed the National Catholic Educational Association in 1928 — was founded in St. Louis in July 1904. The new association was a hybrid organization, the merger of three separate and distinct Catholic educational associations: the Educational Conference of Seminary Faculties, the Association of Catholic Colleges, and the Parish School Conference. After the merger, these associations became departments in the CEA.

The driving force behind the establishment of the CEA was Thomas J. Conaty, the rector of the Catholic University of America. It was Conaty's determination, initiative, and credibility that gave momentum to the efforts of other Catholics to establish a national association devoted to Catholic education. "Many Catholic educators saw the need for a national Catholic educational association that would do for the Catholic schools what the National Education Association was doing for public schools," notes historian Donald Horrigan. "By July of 1902, Conaty had the components for such an organization nearly in place."[15] Yet it would take two more years and extensive negotiation for Conaty to build the basis for a single national Catholic educational association.

The major obstacle faced by Conaty and his colleagues was the fact that Catholic education had traditionally been a parish and diocesan matter. The bishops guarded their independence and autonomy and were wary of a national organization that aspired to speak for them. "They were not inclined toward formal efforts at national unification that might erode their respective positions," adds Horrigan. "Factional rivalries such as those between the Irish and the Germans intensified the distances that separated diocese from diocese, higher education from lower, and college from university."[16] Conaty was enough of a pragmatist to realize that if he was to succeed, he would have to propose a very loose form of organization — a confederation of Catholic educational interests.

Conaty chose the voluntary association as the least threatening organizational model and the most likely to appeal to the largest number of Catholic educators. In a joint meeting of the Association of Catholic Colleges and the Parish School Conference in October 1903, he outlined the rationale for the new organization. "I think the question is really one of a national organization," he noted, "which would include all these subordinate conferences leaving each independent in itself, with its own officers, doing its own work, and yet having a national character."[17] This invitation to join a national association was Conaty's last formal involvement in educational affairs. He had been selected in March to become the bishop of Monterey–Los Angeles. It would remain for others to carry his ideas forward.

Conaty's spirit as well as his ideas were present the following July in St. Louis when the three organizations agreed to become departments of a single educational association. Denis J. O'Connell of the Catholic University of America was elected president, and Francis Howard of Columbus, Ohio, was elected secretary.

The report of that first meeting was full of optimism. The delegates hoped that the new association would "stimulate support and extend Catholic educational activity and afford encouragement to all engaged in the work." These were modest goals, but they were not all that the delegates hoped for. The association could do much more. "It will make us conscious of our power," added the report, "and help us to direct our energy, and to make the most effective use of our resources. It will help in the work of organizing parish schools into unified diocesan systems. It should help to promote harmony and coordination of all Catholic educational interests."[18] No one could say that the membership was not ambitious for the new organization.

The task of implementing Conaty's plan fell to Francis Howard. The new secretary of the CEA was a former chairman of the diocesan school board in his native diocese of Columbus, where he acquired a reputation as a skilled negotiator. For Howard, educational reform was the result and reward for extensive discussion, debate, experimentation, and, finally, widespread implementation.

Experience had taught Howard that change could never be forced on parish schools. It was not surprising, therefore, that Howard resisted efforts by the bishops to take over the new association. The CEA was to be a forum for the exchange of educational methods and ideas, not an episcopal policy-making agency.

Yet Howard was "equally committed to the achievement of national unity in Catholic education. Howard's concern for achieving unity while preserving individual freedom was the hallmark of the guidance he gave the CEA."[19] The depth of Howard's commitment to this goal in general and to the CEA in particular is symbolized by his willingness to serve as secretary for a quarter of a century.

The task for the consensus-oriented Howard was not an easy one. During his tenure as secretary, progressive CEA members clashed with traditional members on a number of educational issues. It was Howard's job to keep the peace, and he sought ways of allowing both sides to be heard. "To achieve a consensus," according to historian Donald Horrigan, "he established an advisory committee modeled after the NEA's national council to study various aspects of controversial issues as they arose and to direct the Association's policy."[20]

In establishing an advisory committee that represented all views on the issues, Howard was able to move disagreements out of the CEA's public meetings into closed committee rooms. "The Catholic Educational Association is an expression of the unity of principle that unites all Catholic educators," wrote Howard in a brief article published in 1911. He had conviction and the influence to give truth to this statement.[21]

One of the major issues facing Howard during the first fifteen years of his tenure was the length and content of the parish school curriculum in an increasingly industrialized society. Beginning in 1908, the Parish School Department began to discuss the implications of vocational instruction and its place in the parish school curriculum.

As with other issues, the progressives squared off against the traditionalists. The progressives saw the need for the introduction of some vocational education in the parish school curriculum, but the traditionalists feared that vocational instruction would undermine the general curriculum. The CEA debated the issue for almost a decade before declaring in 1915 that all of the pupils in parish schools should be drilled in the fundamentals of education before receiving any vocational education.[22]

The 1915 declaration did little to resolve the specific question of the length and differentiation of the parish school curriculum. The Advisory Committee of the CEA was in favor of a six-year curriculum of general education followed by a two-to-four-year secondary education of classical instruction for students going on to college or vocational training.

But in this case, the Advisory Committee ran up against conservative pastors who favored the traditional eight-year elementary curriculum, and from diocesan school superintendents who supported an eight-year elementary curriculum followed by four years of high school. Seeking a middle ground that would placate both of these groups, the CEA Advisory Committee recommended the establishment of a two- or three-year junior high school curriculum and a senior high school curriculum. But with several different curriculum plans being used by parish schools across the country, it was not possible in 1915 to find national unity on the length and differentiation of the parish school curriculum.[23]

The members of the Catholic Educational Association — even its most progressive members — were not very innovative in their approach to elementary education. For example, Catholic educators rejected the so-called Gary Plan of platoon schooling — a program to use the schools year round — even though the plan allowed release time for religious education. Many CEA members believed the plan undermined the natural authority and responsibility of the family and utilized a curriculum cluttered with too many subjects.

Catholic educators also criticized the "Modern School Plan" advocated by progressive educators because the plan rejected traditional subjects, put too much emphasis on science, and gave too much freedom to students in the selection of subjects. In sum, Catholic educators were wary of the educational experimentation advocated by progressive educators because they could not accurately predict the results of their experimentation. Catholics would not gamble with the souls of their children.[24]

Yet Catholic educators could not reject modern educational ideas out of hand without risking the loss of more children to the public schools. The 1920s, a decade of modern ideas, challenged Catholic educators to modernize the Catholic school without abandoning its traditional curriculum.

William F. Lawlor of Newark, speaking at the CEA meeting in 1919, seemed to ask the question of the coming decade: "Are Any Changes Needed in Our Elementary Schools to Meet Post-War Conditions?" Lawlor was cautious.[25] "Deservedly proud of our ability to adjust ourselves quickly and efficiently to any new needs which might arise," Lawlor wrote, "may we go on as heretofore confident that the policy rigorously adhered to in the past has not lost any of its usefulness for the work that lies ahead."[26] As the commentator on Lawlor's paper, Joseph M'Clancy agreed. "The Catholic school system should never desert the cry for fundamentals," noted M'Clancy, "and never indulge in expense to carry out mushroom fads.... We stand for progress, but a progress that is conservative, economical, and Catholic."[27]

Lawlor and M'Clancy were confident of their position. But some educators were uneasy about Catholic education in an increasingly modern age, and at least one CEA speaker responded to these concerns. Just a year after Lawlor and M'Clancy spoke to the CEA, Albert Hollinger acknowledged that Catholic teachers were concerned about the changes in modern educational practice. The Catholic teacher, noted

Hollinger, must ask himself "whether or not his pupils could meet satisfactorily and successfully the various prolific scales, texts, standards, etc., that seem to be the *sine qua non*, the *ne plus ultra*, of modern classroom efficiency."[28]

Yet Hollinger cautioned his colleagues not to be preoccupied with modern pedagogical measures. Catholic students were getting full value out of their education if they were fitted spiritually, intellectually, and socially for American Catholic society. By this Hollinger meant that students should be well versed in the basics of Catholic morality, Catholic literature, and Catholic character formation.

But the confidence of Lawlor, M'Clancy, Hollinger, and their colleagues that traditional Catholic education could withstand the pressures of modern pedagogy was not backed up by results. Catholic leaders continued to feel pressure to improve the quality of Catholic education. In a paper at the 1925 CEA meeting, Francis I. Bredestege advocated the use of scientific procedure in Catholic education. "It is obvious how much advantage there will be," added Bredestege, "in a series of experiments that are unified and coordinated and revolving around a definite aim, because such a series is bound to be exhaustive."[29]

Bredestege also advocated increased cooperation among teachers and new attitudes among educators toward all subjects. "All we can impress on ourselves," he concluded, "is that the work of reform, not in religion only, but in many other school subjects, individually and in correlation, demands our attention and our most serious practical effort. It is part of the big work to which we must be systematically marshaled, and at which we must all work long and hard in cooperation and not merely discuss."[30] Bredestege called for his colleagues to move forward with the times.

But Bredestege and like-minded Catholic educators were never quite sure which modern pedagogical ideas would blend well with the dominant moral tone of the parochial school curriculum. "All Catholic educators agree," noted Father Daniel Feeney at the 1929 CEA meeting, "that Catholic education does not mean secular education plus the recitation of prayers and a knowledge of the Catechism."[31] To be sure, Feeney was right. But Catholic educators could not agree on what *was* a proper secular education for parochial schools. The Catholic educators of the 1920s agreed to disagree and to continue their discussions of the topic at the annual meetings of their national organization, now known as the National Catholic Educational Association.

❊

Just as the NCEA had become the voice of Catholic teachers and educators, so also did the Education Department of the National Catholic Welfare Conference become the voice of the American bishops on education. Both organizations were reflections of a national search for order on the part of the American Catholic community. Beyond this common goal the similarity ends. Whereas the NCEA was established as a national forum for educational ideas, the NCWC's Department of Education was created to defend Catholic schools against increasing government involvement in the Catholic schools and to provide a unified voice on education for the hierarchy.[32]

Education was just one of several concerns of the American bishops when they established the National Catholic Welfare Council in September 1919. The new organization was an outgrowth of the National Catholic War Council, a temporary body formed by the hierarchy in 1917 to address the issues affecting Catholics in wartime. The council worked to provide enough chaplains for Catholics in uniform. It prepared religious literature for distribution to Catholics in the armed forces, and it encouraged the establishment of diocesan war councils to direct local Catholic war work. Yet this temporary national organization also concerned itself with the general welfare of Catholics during the war and became a de facto voice for American Catholicism. In the year following the armistice, the council spent its time on vocational rehabilitation and employment services for Catholic veterans. The Catholic hierarchy agreed that the War Council had been an effective — if temporary — organization.[33]

Many Catholics who were involved with the work of the war council were not so sure that the organization should be temporary. "The creation of the War Council and the involvement of Catholics in war work," notes historian Elizabeth McKeown, "helped to nationalize the outlook of many Catholic leaders and give them a new sense of Catholic strengths in an American political system."[34] With the encouragement of Cardinal Gibbons, council leaders openly discussed the establishment of a permanent organization. "Our diocesan units are well organized," Gibbons wrote to his brother bishops in May. "But the Church in America as a whole has been suffering from a lack of unified force that might be directed to the furthering of those general policies which are vital to all."[35] Council advocates hoped that a majority of the bishops would agree.

The members of the hierarchy gathered in September 1919 to decide the fate of the council. Nearly a hundred bishops met at the Catholic University of America to discuss a plan prepared by council leaders. The plan called for a central administrative committee of seven bishops who would represent the entire hierarchy in the supervision of departments of education, social services, lay activities, Catholic press and literature, and home and foreign missions.

The plan was not uniformly appealing to all of the assembled hierarchy. Conservative bishops objected to the proposed organization as a usurpation of prerogatives that belonged rightfully to the individual bishops. The unwillingness of the conservatives to support the new organization kept the permanence of the NCWC in doubt until Pius XI granted final approval in July 1922. The name was changed to the National Catholic Welfare Conference to reflect the advisorial nature of the organization's work.[36]

The NCWC education department, one of the five mentioned in the original plan, was established in September 1920 with Archbishop Austin Dowling of St. Paul as chairman and James H. Ryan as executive director. The department also had an advisory committee composed of sixteen prominent Catholic educators, including James A. Burns of Notre Dame and Francis Howard of the CEA.

Sensitive to the concerns of the conservative bishops, the directors of the new department emphasized the supportive role of their work. Their statement of purpose referred to the education department as a "clearinghouse of information" and "an advisory agency" in support of Catholic education at all levels. Every effort was made to make the new department as nonthreatening as possible to a skeptical hierarchy.[37]

James H. Ryan emphasized repeatedly that "no effort will be made to control the Catholic schools of the United States." Yet Ryan also emphasized that Catholics should speak with one voice on education. "If our Catholic school system is eventually to reach its natural development and to exert on American public life the influence it should," noted Ryan in one article, "it will be only when every Catholic teacher from New York to San Francisco learns to think, to speak, and to act as a great national Catholic unity."[38] Ryan spoke of ideals, of course. In practice, Ryan hoped to build an effective department without coming in conflict with conservative bishops or stepping on the toes of the Catholic Educational Association.

※

The new department found an important role for itself in responding to federal and state legislation that was believed to be harmful to Catholic educational interests. The NCWC's administrative committee directed the department to conduct a propaganda campaign against such legislation.

But the bishops were careful not to give the department too much freedom. The administrative committee noted that "in defining the Catholic attitude toward measures for state and federal control, Catholics should give the minimum of complaint and of opposition to such movement. They should discriminate between the things they can accept and those they cannot accept — and confine their opposition to the latter."[39] In this regard, the department outlined the NCWC opposition to two major legislative initiatives: federal aid to local public schools and compulsory attendance at public schools.

The first of these initiatives was the Smith-Towner Bill, a proposal introduced in the Congress in 1920 to establish a cabinet-level department of education and provide direct federal aid to local public schools. Even though the NCWC approved of the general goals of the bill — the elimination of illiteracy and improved teacher preparation, for example — it opposed the bill on other grounds. The NCWC thought that such legislation would make the states dependent on the federal government and weaken the autonomy of the states in the control of education.

The NCWC also argued that the appointment of a cabinet level secretary of education would unnecessarily politicize education and make schools subject to partisan interests. Most important, the bishops objected to the bill on financial grounds. The nation could ill afford an additional annual tax burden of $100 million.[40]

Even though they were exercising their constitutional rights in opposing the Smith-Towner bill, the bishops were uneasy about taking public positions on proposed legislation. After issuing public statements on the bill in 1920, the NCWC issued a statement suggesting that the protest be discontinued and "opportunity be given to study the situation developing in Congress." Yet the Smith-Towner protest could not be turned on and off like a faucet; other organizations of Catholics picked up the protest after the NCWC bowed out.

Two Catholic professional associations were vocal in their opposition to Smith-Towner. The Catholic Educational Association opposed the bill "or any other measure which tends to centralize at Washington powers reserved under the Constitution to the respective states or to the people."[41] The German American Central Society, better known as the Central Verein, attacked the bill as "state socialism." The German Americans distributed free pamphlets noting a "grave danger that positive Christianity will not only be ignored but positively combated in the schools." Catholics were united in their opposition to the bill and were pleased by its defeat in 1920 and in subsequent sessions of Congress.

Some Catholics — particularly the bishops — were reluctant to take action against proposed legislation for fear of a backlash against the church. To be sure, the NCWC did oppose proposed legislation on occasion, but for the most part the bishops followed a vow "to make no propaganda" against education bills unless passage seemed imminent. Such a passive stance did not please the most militant bishops such as Cardinal William O'Connell of Boston, who complained that many of his colleagues were surrendering "unknowingly" on the matter of principle.[42]

This reluctance to enter into the debate over proposed federal legislation did not apply to state legislation. In the years after the First World War, the bishops became increasingly concerned about a growing antagonism toward parochial education on the part of many state legislatures. Legislation under consideration in several states threatened the very existence of parish schools, and when the citizens of Oregon passed a referendum calling for compulsory public school attendance, the bishops prepared to swing into action.

The Oregon law, passed in November 1922 to go into effect in September 1926, required parents to send their children between the ages of eight and sixteen to public schools until graduation from grade school. Exceptions were made for children who lived a great distance from a public school, were physically handicapped, or received the county superintendent's permission for private tutoring. Parents who did not comply were subject to fines, imprisonment, or both. The law was a reflection of the persistent fear among many Americans that children in Catholic schools were "being fitted to promote un-American ideals."[43]

At first reluctant to intervene in a state matter, the NCWC preferred that Archbishop Alexander Christie of Portland handle the opposition to the bill. But after the bill passed a statewide referendum, the NCWC agreed in January 1923 to underwrite the cost of a legal appeal and began a nationwide information campaign to inform the public of the benefits of Catholic education. It was this public relations campaign that underscored the value of the NCWC's education department as a national voice for Catholic education.[44]

The campaign elicited results. Courts at all levels — culminating with the U.S. Supreme Court — agreed that the state had no power to force children to attend public schools. Yet the Supreme Court, in a decision known as *Pierce v. Society of School Sisters*, was careful not to proscribe "the power of the state to reasonably regulate all schools." This statement did not come as a shock to the NCWC. In fact, the bishops had expected it and were in support of this carefully defined role for the state in private education. In fact, the NCWC acknowledged that the "general trend of educational legislation is toward standardizing private schools on the same basis as public schools now function, both materially and formally, in regard to the qualification of teachers, courses of study, duration of term, and language of instruction. These things are not objected to."[45]

After the *Pierce* decision in 1925, James H. Ryan reaffirmed the bishops' decision. "The Catholic school," he noted, "has no fear of reasonable supervision on the part of the state. In almost every case it would be welcome."[46] Following the Supreme Court decision, the NCWC devoted its energies to encouraging Catholic schools to bring themselves up to the standards set by the state boards of education.

※

At the turn of the century Catholic education was a patchwork of school experiments held together by a common belief in the value of daily Catholic moral instruction as part of the educational process. Beyond this broad belief, Catholics differed from one parish to the next. There seemed to be little order in Catholic education as it entered the twentieth century.

Out of this chaos came a search for order during the first three decades of the twentieth century. This search was evident in the movement within individual dioceses to establish school boards and appoint superintendents to provide greater uniformity in Catholic schooling from one parish to the next. The search is also evident in the establishment of the Catholic Educational Association and the National Catholic Welfare Conference, two organizations that brought order to Catholic education on the national level. Catholic education in 1930 was more efficient, more structured, and more ordered than it had been thirty years earlier.

Most Catholic educators agreed that the superintendent movement, the CEA, and the NCWC had positive effects on the quality of Catholic education. But educators — particularly those involved with NCWC's education department — had to defend themselves periodically against complaints that the NCWC was "a bureaucratic colossus grasping for a monopoly of ecclesiastical power."[47] To be sure, the NCWC found their own arguments against federal control of education coming back at them. "Catholic leaders in their choice or organizational strategy," notes historian Fayette Veverka, "embraced the social forces they so vigorously sought to restrain in the larger society. Power rather than principle was the real issue as Catholics, more pragmatic than ideological, sought to preserve and protect the interest of Catholic schools."[48]

Chapter 8

Catholic Education and Modern American Society

E DUCATION WAS a matter of concern to all Americans at the turn of the century. Given the rapid change in the American economy, the nation's leaders argued that the substance of formal schooling needed to be more relevant to the promise and the problems of an urban industrial society. Quite naturally, professional educators capitalized on this public concern and established several commissions to study how the quality of instruction might be improved.

These commissions — the Committee of Fifteen to study elementary education and the Committee of Ten to study secondary education — were at the center of an educational revolution known as the progressive education movement. "Progressive education," wrote historian Lawrence Cremin, "began as a vast humanitarian effort to apply the promise of American life — the ideal of government by, of, and for the people — to the puzzling new urban industrial civilization that came into being during the later half of the nineteenth century. The word progressive provides the clue to what it really was: the education phase of American progressivism writ large."[1]

Yet the impact of the progressive education movement was confined almost exclusively to public schools. There is no question that Catholic educators were aware of the changes taking place in public education, but parochial school advocates, for the most part, were suspicious of the progressive education movement.

But Catholic educators did not reject progressive ideas. In

fact, they looked for ways to adopt or co-opt these ideas for their own purpose.[2] The task would not be easy. "In general," notes historian Paul Schuler, "Catholics viewed the American public schools' total adoption of the philosophical supports of progressivism in education as a moral and social disaster. The ideas of these men could not be tempered by Christian teaching in the public school system and Catholics believed they would lead it further down the road to secularism."[3]

There were, however, a few Catholic educators located in the new Department of Education at the Catholic University of America who were willing to cull the work of progressive educators and extract those ideas that were in harmony with Christian teachings. They were particularly sympathetic to the findings of the evolving human sciences of empirical psychology and biology. In fact, these educators were "willing to accept the truth that resided in the findings of these sciences as one means to improve education for the good of Catholic education and American society."[4]

The substantial task of making progressive ideas acceptable to Catholic educators fell largely to two men — Thomas Edward Shields and his student and successor George Johnson.[5] Shields joined the CUA faculty in 1902, and there he pursued his twin passions of education and psychology. Johnson studied under Shields at CUA from 1916 to 1919 and joined the faculty in 1921. These two men led the campaign to bring Catholic education into the twentieth century.

⁂

Shields's efforts to introduce progressive and scientific ideas on education to Catholic audiences are very evident in his 1906 text, *The Psychology of Education*.[6] He wrote the book for use in the correspondence school that he established for Catholic teachers, and it is clear from the text that Shields hoped to introduce progressive ideas to young Catholic teachers. His very choice of words — terms such as "adjustment," "plasticity," and "dynamic" — underscored this emphasis.

More important, Shields used the volume to draw together

in one place the diverse views of scholars such as William James, William Kilpatrick, and James B. Angell, as well as G. Stanley Hall. "Shields' own contribution in this work," notes John Murphy, "was in the order of synthesis and application of the thought of those men for the Catholic teacher."[7]

Shields repeatedly emphasized the need for Catholic educators to be conscious of the child's need to sense and understand the information presented in the classroom if it was to have a lasting effect. The prevailing system of cramming, memorization, and drill was anathema to Shields. "The structure of the mind and the laws of its growth are ignored by this system," noted Shields. "The sacred temple of life is connected into a more or less orderly warehouse for the storage of dead thought and petrified formulae."[8]

Throughout the next fifteen years, Shields reemphasized the points he made in *The Psychology of Education*. Using the pages of his journal, the *Catholic Educational Review*, Shields wrote more than one hundred articles discussing the application of progressive ideas in the Catholic classroom. "It is true that we were done," Shields wrote in 1911, "with the old fallacy which led many well meaning teachers to feed their children's souls on words and word drills at a time when their imaginations and their hearts were famished for want of real food."[9] It was vintage Shields — John Dewey reinterpreted with a theological twist. Shields and his colleagues "drew from the same psychological and democratic sources as did Dewey, but they interpreted them in light of Christian doctrine, denying that social values were superior to individual moral ones." Shields never tired of repeating his message.[10]

Because it was distributed through the correspondence school, *The Psychology of Education* had only limited impact when it was first published. It was not until 1908, when he spoke before the Catholic Educational Association on "The Teaching of Religion," that Catholic educators really heard what he was saying. Shields realized the importance of this forum and prepared a long paper that distilled his ideas on learning and on the new pedagogical sciences and how they could be used in the teaching of the critical subject of religion. He intended the paper to be controversial; in fact, one biographer claimed that Shields had come to the meeting intent on launching a "frontal attack" on the traditional method of teaching religion.[11]

Shields must have known that his progressive ideas would not be popular with his conservative audience. "The large majority of religion teachers and textbook writers," notes Mary C. Bryce, "almost totally ignored advances made by the professors in the sector of public school education. Perhaps the question-and-answer mold of the catechism genre had become so set that any departure from it, if accepted at all, if sufficiently disregarded, would surely go away."[12] But Shields would not go away. Indeed, he was adamant that his new methods were "the only permissible sequence in the presentation of truth to the young and to the undeveloped."[13] For the normally polite and formal CEA meetings, this was a very controversial stance.

Shields had his hour upon the stage to argue several points that he later expanded and published in *The Teaching of Religion*.[14] "The teaching of religion for Shields was centered in the child's experiences," notes John Murphy, "freely developed and related to other areas of learning with respect for the student's feelings, needs and potential; but this freedom was directed toward an unchanging body of truth that would allow no variation or development."[15]

This related closely to a second point made by Shields — that the flexibility of method used in teaching religion did not imply a flexibility of message. Even though he was an innovative educator, Shields was a traditional catechist. He presumed that all students would, without exception, accept the dogma and doctrines of the church. On this one point Shields was in total agreement with traditional teachers of religion.

Shields's controversial paper was not ignored by the educators attending the CEA meeting in 1908. Speaking for traditional educators was Peter C. Yorke, a San Franciscan priest and educator.[16] Yorke's criticism of Shields and his progressive views was respectful, if skeptical. He acknowledged Shields's expertise in biology and psychology, but dismissed modern social science as irrelevant to the religious formation of children.[17] "Catholics have in our own philosophy, in our own practice, in our own experience, a true Catholic pedagogy," he added. "We do not need to go outside our own resources, not only to conserve our system of schools at the highest point of efficiency, but also to give scientific justification for the principles and methods which are the noblest gifts your holy founders gave you brothers and sisters of the Catholic schools."[18] Yorke concluded his remarks with a body-blow to Shields and the progressives. "I feel it my duty to state," noted Yorke, "that the difference between us is a difference of philosophy and in my opinion his system of pedagogy is nothing less than revolutionary."[19]

❖

Shields represented change at a time when the CEA was seeking order and stability, and Yorke and the traditionalists thought it important to separate themselves from Shields and his progressive views. Shields's reputation as a revolutionary stayed with him long after the 1908 meeting. Even though he was the single most influential figure in the professionalization of Catholic education during the first two decades of the century, Shields was never elected to any position of authority within the Catholic Educational Association.

Although he was disheartened by the response to his CEA paper, Shields had no intention of abandoning or changing his views. If his case could not be made on a theoretical level before the membership of the CEA, perhaps it could be made on the practical level in the Catholic classroom. "His ideas were to be realized eventually, he hoped in texts for Catholic schools," noted biographer John Murphy, "the tangible tools for the teacher and the students of the new approach to religion and education."[20]

As with all of his projects, Shields wasted no time in writing and publishing his texts. In spite of other substantial responsibilities, Shields produced his first three textbooks between

1908 and 1910. In this effort, Shields acted not only as author but also as publisher since he owned and operated the Catholic Education Press. It was yet another dimension of Shields's amazing educational enterprise that included a monthly journal and a teachers college as well as the publishing company.[21]

Because Shields considered method to be as important as content, he included in his texts explicit directions on how each book was to be used. In the first book, for example, Shields strictly forbade the use of the book for the first six weeks of the school term and encouraged teachers to have the children teach each other. "The children learn from each other quite as much as they learn from the teachers," Shields noted.[22] The texts and methods were a major break with the past, and Shields hoped that the new volumes would revolutionize the teaching of religion in the Catholic schools.

Unfortunately, it is not possible to determine the popularity of these texts because there are no records for the now defunct Catholic Education Press. Since Shields acted as his own publisher, there was no need to report sales or pay royalties. But one indication of the popularity of the texts is found in a letter from Shields to a colleague written in October 1913. "The books are growing rapidly in popularity," Shields wrote, "and when the series is once completed, they will travel much further. The trouble with all of us, I expect, is the time is not long enough to do half the things that are worth doing."[23]

The popularity of the books was not wishful thinking on Shields's part; several printers and publishers wrote to him expressing interest in taking over the series. But Shields declined, preferring to control the publication of the books himself.

Shields's greatest success with the texts came in the years from 1914 to 1918. In mid-1914, he wrote that there were "some 60,000 children using these books, and a much larger number will come into possession of them during the coming year."[24] Shields was undoubtedly referring to the adoption of the series by the diocese of Pittsburgh. The diocesan superintendent of schools, W. A. Kane, was a student of Shields and an apostle of the Shields method of instruction.

Kane wrote to Shields periodically to detail the implementation of the new series, and Shields often quoted from Kane's letters as evidence of the impact of his teaching methods. When Kane later became superintendent in Cleveland, he introduced Shields's texts there and encouraged an active discussion of their use in Peoria and Milwaukee.[25] By 1918, Shields had seen his texts adopted or considered by diocesan school boards in six states, and he had every reason to hope for continued success. But Shields had suffered a mild heart attack in 1917 and was unable to devote much attention to writing additional volumes or to the promotion of the first three books. Without Shields as the driving force, the books fell into disuse by the end of the 1920s.[26]

Like the prophet Amos in the Old Testament, Thomas Edward Shields was an important but largely isolated voice of reform. For all of Shields's efforts to cajole and persuade his colleagues into using progressive educational methods, Catholic educators refused to abandon their ties to traditional methods of instruction. It would not be until after World War II that a majority of Catholic educators would adopt the principles if not the form of the Shields educational method.

Yet Shields's ideas did not die with him. His intellectual successor was his former student and colleague, George Johnson. Johnson was practical, pragmatic, and self-effacing, yet he also had strong convictions about the purpose of Catholic schooling in a free society. He combined native organizational and political skills with the intellectual drive and educational philosophy of Thomas Shields.[27]

Johnson was never as controversial as his mentor, and his reputation as a conciliator became a great strength for Catholic education. During the years from 1929 until his sudden death in 1944, Johnson reflected the consensus of opinion on parochial education. When he spoke, Catholics and non-Catholics alike knew that Johnson fairly represented the Catholic position on educational issues of the day. Because of this gift,

Johnson served as a Catholic representative on a number of public commissions and at the time of his death was secretary of the American Council of Education. He did all this in addition to serving as the NCEA secretary, head of the education department of the National Catholic Welfare Conference, and professor of education at CUA. There is no question that Father George Johnson was the "organization man" of Catholic education.[28]

Johnson was less of a scholar and more of a pragmatist than Shields. More important, Johnson was a peacemaker, able to convince his colleagues of the value of his ideas without insulting or alienating them. This was a skill that had eluded Shields. Johnson took over many of Shields's classes and for twenty-three years served as an editor the *Catholic Educational Review*.[29]

Johnson's own ideas on education had been influenced by Shields, but not entirely formed by him. Like his mentor, Johnson was receptive to progressive ideas on education, but he was always careful to draw distinctions between his own views and those of his more liberal colleagues. Throughout his career, Johnson was committed to the total integration of Catholic education in a free society. His service on government commissions reflected this commitment. "Committed to the theory that students learn by doing," notes historian Neil McCluskey, "Johnson favored supplementing traditional study and recitation assignments with group discussions, field trips and projects. He also endorsed the use of objective tests and supported educational programs geared to the individual need of the child."[30] Johnson's philosophy was reflected in his 114 articles, two books, and in the laboratory school that he founded at CUA in 1935.

Johnson's abilities as a conciliator were evident soon after he became a professor at CUA. Addressing the controversial issue of standardization, an issue that divided the NCEA membership, Johnson carefully acknowledged the views of both camps. He admitted that there were dangers in the process; standardization might conflict with "individual autonomy" and "reduce everything to dead level uniformity and take from the schools the last vestige of personal initiative and human quality." Yet Johnson also acknowledged that standards had a place in education, in protecting students against "shoddy educational wares" and insuring that "they were not left to the mercy of uneven opportunity that would result with every institution a law unto itself." Johnson also argued that standards were a good defense against those who accused the Catholic schools of providing an inferior education.[31]

Johnson's solution to the standardization issue did not fully satisfy either the conservatives or the progressives, but neither did it alienate either camp. Johnson called for the formation of independent standards for Catholic schools. "It would save us from following a leadership that we rather mistrust," noted Johnson. "It would insure our autonomy and make it possible for us to develop according to our own spirit."[32] Even though he took the middle ground, Johnson could not convince his progressive and conservative colleagues to abandon their positions. Johnson's proposal was never acted on, and efforts to establish formal standards were abandoned. Yet this issue proved that Johnson was a natural mediator — a man at the center of educational issues.

Yet Johnson did not assert himself as a leader even during his tenure as a professor. There is no better example of this side of the man than his 1925 address on the "need for a constructive policy for Catholic education in the United States." Johnson was acutely aware of the criticism that had been leveled at parochial schools. In fact, Johnson was one of those critics who challenged the Catholic tendency to imitate public school practices. He called for the development of a Catholic educational philosophy that would set specific aims and purpose for Christian education, establish adequate machinery at the diocesan level, improve the quality of teacher training, and develop a unique and superior curriculum for the Catholic schools. "If we must be conservative," added Johnson, "at least let us be radical in our conservation. Prove all things, yes; but do not take it for granted that applications of principles valid one hundred years ago are necessarily valid today."[33]

Johnson developed his views on the aims, means, and responsibilities of Catholic education over a twenty-five year career in education. Because he was an unassuming man, his philosophy was not always clear to his many constituents. Yet one can see his views in the positions he took while serving as secretary general of the NCEA, as the head of the NCWC Department of Education, and as a member of several government commissions. His actions spoke louder than his words, but he was always true to his words.

Johnson's philosophy of education was very much reflected in his service as secretary general of the NCEA. The consummate organization man, he moved cautiously but with confidence to wrest control of the organization from conservatives. Almost from his first year as secretary in 1929, he set out to modernize the association in both its thinking and its structure. "Johnson was convinced that a genuine Catholic philosophy of education demanded Catholic educators to be bold and 'experimental' in their search for the most effective methods and procedures for translating 'our fundamental educational philosophy into scholastic practice.' "[34]

Johnson was never reluctant to state his views to the membership. He addressed the NCEA no less than sixteen times during his career — more frequently than any other educator. In almost every speech he prodded his colleagues to consider change. "We should be no more suspicious of 'new fangled' methods in the classroom," he remarked at one meeting, "than we are of 'new fangled' gadgets like radio in preaching the word of God." In his inaugural address as secretary general, he sounded the keynote for his administration. "By open-minded scientific experiment, by constructive thinking, by effective organization and administration we may hope to find the best way of realizing this Catholic ideal of education." As prescient as Johnson was, he could not have anticipated the change that would take place in the NCEA during his tenure.[35]

Many biographers and friends referred to Johnson as the "bridge builder." Indeed, he broke down the barriers that had grown between the NCEA, the NCWC, and the CUA Department of Education. Moreover, he opened the association up to new ties with secular organizations such as the U.S. Office of Education, the National Education Association, and the American Council of Education. "Under Johnson," noted Donald Horrigan, "[NCEA] policy and structure came to embody a spirit of friendly cooperation 'in the service of all American education.' Partnership in American education, not separatism, was the dimension which Johnson gave the Catholic education ministry at the national level."[36]

Johnson's service as a bridge builder gave him many opportunities to consider the place of the Catholic school in American democracy and the proper role of the government in the propagation of education. Certainly the back-to-back crises of economic depression and world war precipitated a general concern about the purpose of education, and Johnson made a significant contribution to the debate.

He was an articulate, thoughtful opponent of federal involvement in education, but a persuasive proponent of the civic responsibilities of Catholic schools. Johnson channeled his views through several mediums — service on two federal committees on education, and speeches and reports at the NCEA meetings were his two major forums.[37]

His ideas were shaped by many factors, particularly by his service on various government commissions and committees. Between 1929 and 1944, Johnson served on President Hoover's Advisory Committee on Education, President Roosevelt's Advisory Committee on Education, the Wartime Commission of the U.S. Office of Education, the Education Advisory Committee of the Coordinator of Inter-American Affairs, and the Advisory Committee on Education of the Joint Army and Navy Committee on Welfare and Recreation.

On most of these committees Johnson was the principal representative of Catholic education, and in this capacity he was often called upon to explain the Catholic position on educational issues. There is no doubt that he was an influential and respected member of these committees. On his death, Congress passed a resolution acknowledging Johnson as "a great public servant who rendered a rich service to the promotion of truly social concepts in and through education."[38]

Johnson also delivered testimony on various Catholic viewpoints — sometimes in an official capacity, sometimes not. In 1934, for example, he took an unpopular position in testimony before the Federal Advisory Committee on Emergency Aid in Education. At the time both the public and parochial schools were nearly bankrupt. The Committee was charged with finding emergency aid for the public schools. Unofficially, Johnson attacked proposals that would provide federal funds to selected public school districts.

To Johnson, such plans unnecessarily involved the federal government in state and local affairs. "The question that every thinking American must answer for himself is this," he told the committee. "How much in terms of liberty am I willing to pay for greater equality? ... An emergency exists for American schools and the temptation is to turn to the Federal Government for help. Whether or not it is the best thing for all concerned to throw the problems into the lap of the Federal Government is open to question; the necessity of the step has yet to be conclusively demonstrated."[39]

Johnson was not so dogmatic that he would not consider aid under any circumstances. He insisted on only two conditions. "We must be extremely cautious," he noted, "lest in our attempts to meet this crisis we depart from our traditional American educational policy and set up mechanisms of Federal control which will become a permanent part of our governmental machinery. Whatever measures we take, we must guarantee that the control of education does not pass into the hands of the Federal Government."[40]

Johnson favored a program that would grant funds to the schools with a minimum of bureaucracy. He also insisted that federal aid should be distributed to all of the schools. "Federal aid should not be extended so as to benefit only those children who are in public schools," concluded Johnson. "It would be contrary to the dictates of justice were a mechanism set up whereby Federal funds would be turned over to the states for the exclusive distribution to tax-supported schools."[41] Johnson encouraged the committee to develop a plan to aid private as well as public schools.

Johnson's views were a reflection of both official and general Catholic opinion, but they did not persuade Congress to distribute public funds to private schools. In fact, the federal government decided to stay out of the thorny thicket of aid to education for the time being. Johnson may have influenced this hands-off policy.

Johnson's patriotism and commitment to American democracy were not contingent on obtaining a share of the public dole. When war came in 1941, Johnson was ready to do his part. "Catholic education has a vital stake in the outcome of this war," he noted in his 1942 report to the NCEA membership. "The forces that are arrayed against our country are the same forces that in other lands are arrayed against the church. ... Our schools and colleges do not exist in a vacuum; they are part and parcel of life and living and were never intended to afford a cloistered refuge from reality. Though they thrive best in peace, they must now gird themselves for war. When freedom was imperiled, their very reason for existence hangs in the balance."[42] Johnson encouraged the NCEA membership to do all that they could as both educators and citizens to support the war effort. Johnson led the way by his service on the National Committee on Education and Defense and the Wartime Commission of the U.S. Office of Education.

Economic depression and world war were the backdrops for the majority of Johnson's statements on education and democracy. But his most substantive and important contribution came through his service on the Commission on American Citizenship established at the Catholic University of America.

Created to encourage Catholic understanding of the responsibilities of citizenship, the commission organized its work into three components. The commission would provide information on civics education to all educators interested in the project; it would develop a curriculum package for use in Catholic classrooms; and it would publish a series of basic textbooks and readers that would shape the ideas of young Catholic students. Not surprisingly, Johnson had a part in shaping and directing all three initiatives.[43]

Johnson was responsible primarily for the educational and curricular aspects of the commission's work. He worked closely with the staff to develop themes of emphasis and then turned specific assignments over to individual staff members. Staff members would, for example, use the themes to develop outlines for textbooks and select a few stories or illustrations to support their claim that the outline would develop the theme. Johnson reviewed each outline, discussed it with his colleagues, and then turned it over to outside curriculum specialists for comment. Johnson's mark was evident on every phase of the project. "He offered ideas to the staff members to work out," notes one biographer, "and then considered neither time, fatigue, nor self sacrifice too great a price to pay in evaluating the results."[44]

The materials prepared by Johnson and his staff had an enormous impact on the content of the Catholic curriculum. The commission began supplying material on citizenship to the Catholic classroom weeklies of their day. In 1938, for example, the commission reported that it was sending citizenship information to classroom weeklies "which reach over 700,000 school children weekly and preparations are underway for the writing and distribution of textbooks and other materials to effectuate the principles of Christian Democracy." The textbooks, published under the general title "Faith and Freedom Series," were enormously popular. By early 1944 the first two volumes were ready, and eventually the eight-volume series was adopted by more than five thousand of the eight thousand Catholic parochial schools in the United States at that time.[45]

The success of the commission was evident long before the sales records on the textbooks were available, however. "It has been the hope of the commission from the beginning," wrote commission member Francis Haas in 1943, "that its work would help to make social education a living moral force and would take Catholic education far toward the goal set for it by the bishops of the United States. It is now our belief that we have accomplished a large part of our work."[46] To no small extent, the success of the curricular elements of the commission's work were a direct result of the efforts and influence of George Johnson.

Johnson also influenced general opinion on Catholic education through his 1943 book, *Better Men for Better Times*. The volume was written for Catholic educators and encouraged them to develop children's basic relationships with themselves and others. Published by the Catholic University of America Press, the volume was aimed at a rather narrow spectrum of Catholic educators. But the book caught the attention of David Lawrence, publisher of *United States News*, who reviewed the book in his popular magazine. *Better Men for Better Times* became a best-seller for the university press and orders came in from thousands of individuals in the armed forces and other organizations. Once again, Johnson's influence extended beyond his expectations.[47]

Johnson's premature death in 1944 came as a shock to all who knew him. He suffered a fatal heart attack while speaking to the graduates of Trinity College in Washington, D.C. It was an untimely death for a man who had done so much for Catholic education, but who had so much more to do. As the consummate organization man, Johnson was the authoritative if unofficial spokesman for America's Catholic schools during the 1930s and 1940s. He was eulogized in many national publications starting with the *Congressional Record*. Long after his death, however, Johnson's ideas continued to live on in his many contributions to Catholic educational organizations.[48]

One of Johnson's eulogists best captured the contributions of this man to American Catholic education. "Convinced of the truth of Catholic philosophy, and of the superiority of American democracy as compared with other forms of government," wrote Edward B. Jordan, "he aimed to prove that there was no conflict between them, and particularly any misgivings on the part of those outside the fold concerning the loyalty and devotion of the members of the Church to our American institutions. If he had no other claim to the gratitude of American educators, his unceasing efforts to bring about harmony and cooperation between public and Catholic school authorities, particularly in the cause of American citizenship, would merit for him recognition as an educational leader of the first rank."[49]

The Catholic response to the ever changing contours of public education in the twentieth century was a mixture of skepticism and cautious modification. To be sure, parochial educators were somewhat reluctant followers of the juggernaut known as progressive education. The names of John Dewey, William Kilpatrick, and other so-called progressive educators did not engender much admiration at the meetings of Catholic educators.

Yet two Catholic educators — mentor and student — saw the clear benefits of progressive education. More important, they realized how progressive ideas could be incorporated into the Catholic school curriculum without compromising the unique qualities of personal education. Thomas Edward Shields and George Johnson served as bridges between Catholic and public education during the first four decades of the twentieth century. They played a vital if largely unappreciated leadership role in parochial education.

Chapter 9

The Making of Sister-Teachers

NO GROUP made greater sacrifices for Catholic parochial education than did women religious. Throughout the nineteenth century, tens of thousands of sister-teachers staffed parish classrooms across the country and devoted themselves to the children of the church. They worked long hours, teaching classes with as many as a hundred students, all for subsistence wages. There is no doubt that the parish school system in this nation could never have grown as large as it did without these sister-teachers. They constituted a "living endowment" that made possible a national system of parochial schools.[1]

The sheer size of the work force dictated the power and influence of sister-teachers. By the end of the nineteenth century, for example, there were more than forty thousand sisters working in dioceses in the United States, the majority in parish classrooms. Elizabeth Seton's Sisters of Charity accounted for close to sixteen hundred of these teachers. The School Sisters of Notre Dame had over twenty-seven hundred nuns in the classrooms of ethnic parishes across the country. The Sisters of Charity of the Blessed Virgin Mary, the School Sisters of St. Francis, and the Felician Sisters were among the 119 communities of women religious sending thousands of sisters into the parish schools of this country by 1900.[2]

The achievement of these nuns is even more extraordinary when one considers the obstacles that they faced. Many of these sisters were born in Europe and were called to the American missions without much preparation. In fact, they often arrived in this country as impoverished as the laity they would serve. Wretchedly housed and poorly fed in their new dioceses, most congregations were forced by necessity to dispense with the most contemplative elements of their religious rule. Theirs was a hard life marked by frequent illness and premature death. Yet it was a life made bearable by the strong religious faith of these women.[3]

As teachers, their lives were made more arduous by the fact that there were few religious or educational traditions within the immigrant Catholic communities in the United States. Most Catholics were not only illiterate; they also were ignorant of the tenets of their faith. To say that sisters faced a challenge is something of an understatement. "Their pupils differed in racial origin, in social standing, and in financial rating, and their pride of country was a rival to their love of the Church."[4]

Yet these women accepted these realities as an opportunity from God. "Wisely the [religious] Communities adapted themselves, their postulants, and their novices to these conditions, which meant very largely dispensing with professional and preservice training in the Novitiate. A course in general methods sometimes initiated the novice into the problems that she could expect to meet in her work; but most of her professional training was acquired by learning to do by doing."[5]

The experiences of sister-teachers varied to some extent from diocese to diocese, and even from decade to decade within a single diocese, depending on the commitment of bishops and parish pastors to the establishment and operation of parish schools. In some dioceses, sister-teachers received support from the church establishment. But in other dioceses, these women religious were on their own.

In fact, many congregations were semi-autonomous, operating independently within each diocese. They conducted direct negotiations with parish pastors, raised their own funds, and established and expanded their own schools. Just as important, these congregations closed schools when support from the parish declined. In the words of historian Edward Kantowicz, it was an "administrative nightmare."[6]

❖

Thus national efforts to better train sister-teachers to serve in parochial school classrooms were struggles against the odds. Even though parochial schools were criticized throughout the nineteenth century for the poor preparation of their teachers, little was done to formalize Catholic teacher training until state legislatures began to require the certification of private school teachers in the 1920s.[7]

The groups responsible for Catholic education — the bishops, communities of women religious, and local parish pastors — showed little interest in a professional teacher corps. To be sure, all three groups paid lip service to the need for better teachers, but none considered teacher preparation a high priority. Year after year in the first two decades of the twentieth century, educators attending the meetings of the Catholic Educational Association would propose new plans for Catholic teacher training, only to have their ideas ignored by those in control of the schools.[8]

The foremost reason for the low priority given to Catholic teacher training was the high priority assigned to the cultivation of religious vocations. "The Communities," notes Sister Bertrande Meyers, "faced with the double task of inducting the young applicant to the religious life and later to the professional, devoted the brief time that they were able to retain the candidate at the Mother House to intensive preparation in the religious life and in community customs, trusting that the vocation which called her to 'come' would, if the foundation of a strong spiritual edifice were laid, enable her to 'do.' "[9] This confidence in the vocation itself and in God's divine assistance led the vast majority of religious orders to give only limited attention to teacher training.

With only a limited amount of time for the education of novices, congregations focused on character formation and general intellectual development; teacher training had a much lower priority. Of greatest importance to every congregation of sisters was to inspire in every novice a sense of community tradition and commitment to the rule of the founder of the order. This is not to say that teacher training was completely neglected. Young novices fresh from the motherhouse were assigned to parishes with high percentages of experienced teachers. It was the veteran sister-teachers who trained the novices in the ways of the Catholic classroom. In the manner of a craft, the master teachers trained their apprentices.[10]

This craft system was the predominant form of sister-teacher training until the teacher certification movement took hold in the 1930s and 1940s. In fact, the craft system lasted long after Catholic educators openly admitted that it was a poor method of teacher training.

It remained popular for several reasons. First, it was economical; it cost the parishes little to have a few novices working in their schools, and often the choice was between a novice and no teacher at all. Second, by assigning the responsibility for teacher training to working sister-teachers, superiors could devote almost all of the novices' time at the motherhouse to the cultivation of the religious vocation and the development of community spirit. Third, the craft system allowed the religious orders to get the nuns into the schools as quickly as possible, thereby meeting the ever-growing demand for teachers to staff the increasing number of parish schools. All of these factors worked against the displacement of the craft system of teacher training by a more sophisticated, school-based program of pedagogical instruction.[11]

It was clear to most Catholic educators that it would be very difficult to end the craft system as long as the demand for sister-teachers remained high. Yet no matter how many novices were sent out each year, the call for more never abated. To be sure, there were never enough vocations to meet the demand for sister-teachers.

Statistics compiled by Mary Oates on the occupational distribution of sisters in the archdiocese of Boston show the impact of this demand for sister-teachers.[12] Throughout the nineteenth century, Boston nuns worked in a variety of occupations including hospital work, social welfare, and teaching. But by the turn of the century the demand for the sister-teachers had taken its toll. In that year the percentage of sisters in the classroom passed the 50 percent mark on its way up to 64 percent by 1930. As Oates points out, "Young women entering church service were encouraged to join teaching communities in order to meet this demand. These communities grew rapidly and were remarkably youthful."[13] The situation in Boston was not unique; the youth and lack of experience of growing numbers of sister-teachers worried Catholic educators across the country.

Catholic education faced a dilemma that was the direct result of contradictory instructions from the Third Plenary Council in 1884. On the one hand, the bishops mandated the establishment of a school in every parish, an instruction that immediately increased the demand for sister-teachers. On the other hand, the council decreed that teachers should be examined periodically to insure the high quality of Catholic instruction and further urged religious congregations to establish normal schools for the training of sister-teachers. These two decrees worked at cross-purposes. It was not possible for the church to expand its school system and at the same time improve the quality of its teachers. Top priority was given to staffing the classrooms.[14]

❖

Solutions to the dilemma of more and better training were not apparent at the turn of the century, but there were educators who were willing to try to fill the void. The institution that became the focal point of this experimentation was the Catholic University of America. As early as 1898, Professor Edward Pace suggested that CUA establish a teacher training program. "A Department of Pedagogy would meet a need that is felt in all the schools," wrote Pace. "The training of teachers is an important function of the University and the most valuable service that it can render to the colleges....Such a pedagogical formation is one of the best means of improving our educational customs in all its grades."[15] It would take Pace several years to convince the CUA trustees to act on his proposal.

Finally in October 1902, with the permission of the trustees, Pace established the Institute of Pedagogy in New York City to provide teacher training to the Catholic teachers of the archdiocese, thereby meeting the requirements of the New York City Board of Education. The success of the institute encouraged the university's president, Thomas Conaty, who speculated that "there are indications that similar work will be called for in other large cities of the country." Conaty underscored "the importance of the University establishing on its own grounds, a fully equipped Department of Pedagogy."[16]

Pace argued that the popularity of the university extension centers indicated a demand for such instruction but that they were a poor response to that demand. It was difficult to obtain local instructors for these institutes and inefficient and expensive to send CUA professors to New York or other cities for several days each week. Not surprisingly, Pace argued for a program centralized on the CUA campus. "A Central Teachers' College located here," he noted, "would prepare men for this outside work in the larger cities of the United States. It would also offer the requisite training to young priests whose Bishops are desirous of appointing competent Superintendents of Catholic Schools." Pace envisioned the CUA Department of Education as a leadership school for *male* Catholic educators only. He offered no solution to the problem of training for sister-teachers.[17]

In November 1902, Pace and CUA had the good fortune to hire the Reverend Thomas E. Shields as an instructor of education and psychology. With strong interests in both psychology and pedagogy, Shields was the perfect choice to begin the new department. In fact, within a few years of his arrival on the CUA campus, Shields supplanted Pace as the driving force behind the campaign for the Department of Education.

Building an education department, teaching hundreds of students each year, and publishing a journal would be enough to keep most individuals very busy, but not Shields. As we saw in the previous chapter, he also established the Catholic Education Press to publish textbooks and other pedagogical publications, and he founded and edited the *Catholic Educational Review,* a practical journal for teachers. Most amazing, Shields financed these operations without assistance from CUA.

In spite of his already hectic schedule in 1910, he added to his agenda the troubling question of the professional education of sister-teachers. Up to that time, CUA admitted only men, thereby excluding the largest and most influential body of educators from pedagogical instruction. This dilemma had bothered Shields for some time. As early as 1907 he wrote that "higher education will prove profitable not only to men, but also to women.... Hence we cannot restrict superior education to either sex."[18] Shields did not fool himself into thinking that he could change university regulations to fit his personal views, so he looked for a way to train nuns in a setting separate from the CUA Department of Education. His answer was the establishment of the Sisters College, a national center for teacher training to be located on property adjacent to the CUA campus.[19]

The Sisters College, of course, did not spring fully formed from Shields's fertile mind. As with all of his programs, the Sisters College emerged over time. Correspondence from the 1890s indicates that he had been thinking about the education of sister-teachers at that time. In 1915, several years after the establishment of the Sisters College, Shields recalled the groundwork that he did for this project. "I traveled through the country for two months each summer since 1895 until the opening of the summer school here in 1911," he remembered, "cultivating the field and preparing for the Sisters College.... In this way, I met some 3,000 sisters each summer, each of whom attended 24 lectures on educational matters and passed an examination at the close of the session."[20] He built upon the momentum of the summer institutes by forming a correspondence school at CUA in 1905 and through this program provided instruction to an additional six thousand teachers. Both programs were successful, but only stop-gap measures. Shields saw the college as the permanent answer.

It was a major step to go from summer institutes and correspondence courses to a national center for the education of sister-teachers, and Shields never forgot the difficulties he faced in making the transition. "The idea was at first ridiculed as the dream of a visionary," he wrote. "In fact, I found it well nigh impossible to get the members of two communities to meet in the same hall to listen to lectures on education. The Church is a very conservative institution and many of the religious communities are still more conservative and it takes time and patience to . . . open up the road to progress."[21] Shields persisted in promoting his dream, knowing that eventually he would succeed.

Shields was correct in his assumption, and he established his college as a summer school. The first session was offered in the summer of 1911 to 255 sisters representing twenty-three orders or congregations. The days were long for the nascent parochial school teachers. Classes ran from eight in the morning to six at night, five days a week.

Yet there were a few noteworthy diversions. The report of the first summer school noted that the sisters visited Mount Vernon and were received at the White House by President William Howard Taft. The sisters also received visits from the Apostolic Delegate and from Cardinal Gibbons. It was a memorable summer for reasons other than pedagogical instruction.[22]

Establishing a summer school did not make the college a reality. To be sure, there was a lot of enthusiasm for the college, but enthusiasm would not pay for buildings and teachers. During the first year of operation (1911–12), classes for twenty-nine full-time students were held at the local Benedictine Convent. Shields quickly moved forward with his plans, however, and purchased fifty-seven acres of land about a mile from the main CUA campus. He received the full approval of the CUA trustees in April 1913. A year later the Sisters College was constituted as an affiliate of the university, making its graduates eligible to win degrees. Finally, in September 1914, Shields was able to move his students to his new campus.[23]

Shields's problems did not end with the construction of the

new campus, however. Operating a school was expensive and funding his college was uncertain. Shields received no subsidy from CUA, and his fund-raising efforts were in competition with the Catholic bishops' campaign to build a national shrine on the CUA campus. But somehow Shields kept the Sisters College afloat. By 1919, he proudly reported that the college had just completed its eighth year and that since it had opened the college had "furnished instruction" to eighteen hundred sisters from 151 congregations.

It was a significant achievement and Shields drew the obvious conclusion. "It will thus be seen," he noted that year, "that the Catholic Sisters College was necessary to safeguard the faith and the religious life of our sisters while they were receiving the instruction in secular branches indispensable to the efficient performance of their duties as teachers in our parochial and secondary schools.... It was necessary to develop unity and cooperation between the diocesan authorities and teaching sisterhoods, no less than the needed unity among the several teaching communities who conduct the work of education in our Catholic schools."[24] Many applauded Shields's enterprise but few believed that the Sisters College was sufficient for the preparation of the thousands of sisters in parish classrooms.

No one challenged the value of the Sisters College for those lucky few who could attend, and Shields was not so bold to claim that the Sisters College could be the primary source of Catholic teacher preparation in the country. Yet Shields did hope that his college, along with the CUA Department of Education, would constitute a national center of teacher preparation by providing direction and leadership for teacher training programs in the dioceses and religious communities.[25]

Other educators devoted their attention and energy to the debate over which of the options for Catholic teacher training would be the most efficient. Should each of the religious communities establish their own teacher training institutes?

Another option was to encourage Catholic colleges across the country to establish teacher training programs similar to the one at CUA. A third option was for each diocese to support teacher institutes to prepare all the Catholic teachers in the diocese regardless of religious community. Each option had its supporters during the first three decades of the century.

The least controversial and most economical option was the teacher training program run by religious communities. Religious superiors supported this option because they remained in control of the education of their own novices. Many bishops also supported this option because it cost the dioceses next to nothing.

The popularity of this option was evident in the fact that by 1910 it was reported that "practically all the teaching orders have them."[26] Even though this option was popular with bishops and superiors, it had few supporters among Catholic educators. "Major difficulties with these establishments," notes historian Mary Oates, "were their variety, the provision of adequate faculty for them, and their dubious status as educational institutions."[27] The community-based teacher training program was the quickest and easiest, but not necessarily the best solution to the teacher training problem.

A second option was the establishment of education departments and teacher training programs at Catholic colleges and universities across the country.[28] This option was popular with bishops and educators but not necessarily with the religious communities that would bear the cost of these programs through tuition payments.

Support for this option emerged early in the debate. Bishop John Lancaster Spalding, the premier Catholic intellectual of his time, proposed such programs in the 1890s. James A. Burns, the well-known Catholic educator, added his support at the turn of the century. "The establishment of Catholic teachers colleges," wrote Burns in a widely circulated pamphlet, "will stimulate the growth of the teacher orders and develop more fully their vast latent pedagogical resources. It will remedy serious defects in their training courses. It will ensure, as nothing else can, the continued growth and progress of the parochial schools."[29] Other educators voiced their support over the next twenty years, and Thomas Shields proved that the option was feasible.

The third option — diocesan teacher institutes and colleges — generated the most controversy. The movement for this option began at the Third Plenary Council in 1884 when the bishops decreed that dioceses should make efforts "for the establishment of normal schools where they do not yet exist and there is a need for them."[30]

There was no doubt that almost every diocese was in need of such a normal school. Educators — particularly those concerned about uniformity from parish to parish — found this option appealing and were very vocal in their support. "A diocesan system," noted Edwin V. O'Hara in 1911, "in which the unity grows up from within, rooted in a recognition of common interests and cultivated by the friendly relations of independent groups will enjoy a more vigorous and fruitful growth."[31]

There were many arguments in favor of these diocesan-level programs, and educators did not tire of repeating them. Diocesan teachers colleges would be economical because they would eliminate the need for duplicate programs run by religious communities in the same diocese. Diocesan-level programs would also foster closer cooperation among various teaching orders within each diocese. Diocesan programs would garner the moral and financial support of the bishops. For all these and other reasons it was difficult to argue that the diocesan teacher training program was not the best option.[32]

But all the arguments and logic were not sufficient to garner the support of the bishops or the superiors of religious orders. Even though the bishops stated their support for diocesan teachers colleges in 1884, they were halfhearted in their commitment. "It would certainly have been possible for each diocese to open a local normal school for parochial school teachers," noted Oates, "financed in part, at least, through tuitions charged the various teaching communities. . . . But this approach was never implanted at the diocesan level. The chief reason was not economic. It was the casual attitude of the hierarchy to the national movement for more professional preparation of elementary school teachers.... The idea of committing time and funds to the education of sisters for elementary grades was considered extravagant and unnecessary by many bishops."[33] The support of the hierarchy did not extend to the elementary school.

The bishops were not alone in their lethargic attitude toward diocesan training programs. They were joined by the superiors of many religious communities who were too competitive to join together in cooperative ventures at the diocesan level. "Each community jealously guarded its traditions, textbooks, and grading system," notes Oates, "and resisted efforts to impose uniform standards on parochial schools. Rather, it maintained that its distinctive teaching methods and curricula were superior to those of other sisterhoods. Community regulations discouraged social as well as professional interchange among members of different congregations and served to reinforce their narrow educational perspectives."[34] For these reasons, religious superiors blocked efforts at diocesan teacher training programs.

Without the support of bishops and religious superiors, the diocesan option was exercised in only a handful of dioceses. In spite of all the discussion, Catholic teacher training did not change much during the first three decades of the twentieth century. To be sure, Shields had established his model college and several Catholic universities had opened departments of education, but these programs could provide training for only a few hundred teachers each year. For the most part, sister-teachers continued to learn their trade through apprenticeships in the classrooms under the guidance of master-teachers. It was the establishment of state certification standards for all teachers in the 1920s and 1930s that ultimately would be responsible for improving the quality of Catholic teacher preparation.[35]

❈

The campaign for state certification gained momentum in state legislatures during the years immediately following World War I. Educators had become aware of the uneven quality of instruction in the schools from one state to the next and even from one community to another. To insure that all children received at least a minimum standard education, many state legislatures passed laws requiring that teachers be certified by state boards of education as being competent to teach. In most states these requirements affected only public schools, but it was clear to Catholic educators that certification of parochial school teachers was just a matter of time.

It is not surprising, therefore, that certification was a prominent topic of discussion at the annual meetings of the Catholic Educational Association throughout the 1920s. In fact, Catholic leaders were quick to respond to the certification question. At the CEA meeting in 1919, the superiors of religious orders and administrators from Catholic women's colleges gathered to share information and devise a response to state certification. All present agreed that state certification of private schools would come over the next decade and all agreed that the religious orders could improve the quality of their community-based teacher training programs and still meet the seemingly insatiable demand for more and more teachers each year.[36]

The recommendation of the conference was an ambitious plan calling for each religious order with a college approved by the North Central Association of Colleges to establish a normal school to prepare and certify teachers of that order. The program at each college would meet all of the requirements of the state but also insure that the orders retained control of the training process. The religious communities that did not have colleges were urged to allow their sisters to attend the normal schools of other religious communities or to establish intensive summer instruction programs so that their members would pass state certification exams.[37]

The recommendation of this ad hoc group of Catholic educators was embraced by other more influential forces within the church. The superintendents section of the CEA agreed "to prevail on the superiors of the different teaching communities to take adequate measures to provide all teachers with certificates either issued or acknowledged by the state."[38] The NCWC, through its recently established education department, also joined in the chorus by taking the position that "raising the standards of the professional education of Catholic teachers was the most important defense that Catholic schools had against further encroachments of the state into private education."[39] With this kind of widespread support, the certification movement was off to an extraordinary start.

Not everyone agreed that Catholic teacher certification was in the best interest of the church and its schools. Two important men, one a journalist and the other an educator, questioned the rush to certify Catholic teachers. Paul Blakely, editor of the influential Jesuit weekly *America,* was outspoken in his criticism. He rejected the theoretical right of the state to certify or support educational practice, but Blakely was enough of a realist to accept the fact that the state had the power to do what it wanted.[40] And George Johnson, the superintendent of schools in Toledo and later secretary of the NCEA, advised Catholics to be careful about moving too far too fast. "Because a few states have signified their intention of certifying religious teachers," noted Johnson, "we should not be in too much of a hurry to commit the whole country to this policy." Johnson, like Blakely, accepted the fact that certification would come eventually, but he worried that the quick acceptance of state standards might "nullify the efforts of the Church to provide her children in the United States with a religious education."[41]

Blakely and Johnson had little impact on their colleagues if the papers presented at the CEA meetings in the 1920s are an accurate estimate of Catholic educational opinion. There seemed to be little doubt in anyone's mind that certification was well worth the effort. "It will serve to maintain and elevate the standard of our schools by providing additional incentive for higher teacher preparation," noted Ralph Hayes, "and will protect our prestige and reputation against the insinuations of those who through ignorance or malice regard our Catholic schools with unfavorable eyes."[42] By the middle of the decade, Edward Jordan of the Catholic University of America could state that "we are apparently all agreed that the minimum requirement for a teacher in the elementary schools should be the completion of a good normal school course after graduation from an accredited high school."[43] No one contradicted Father Jordan.

※

Agreeing that Catholic teachers should meet certification standards was an easy decision compared to an agreement on *how* Catholic teachers should prepare themselves for the classroom. For all the verbal support given to certification efforts, few bishops were forthcoming with the funding or programs needed to accomplish this goal. For the most part the religious communities assumed responsibility for certification. In the mid-1920s, for example, there were over ninety community normal schools with more than seventeen thousand sister-students, a number equivalent to about 25 percent of the teachers in Catholic elementary and high schools at the time.[44]

But community normal schools were a poor solution to the teacher preparation and certification dilemma. "In addition to being educationally weak," notes historian Fayette Veverka, "about half of these community normals were not accredited and unable to help students meet state certification requirements."[45] With the emergence of Catholic teacher colleges, community normal schools became redundant. By the end of the decade the number of community normal schools had dropped to forty-four and the enrollment had dropped by half.

Yet these institutions did not disappear immediately. In fact, community normals would remain an important source of teacher preparation for another twenty years. But by the late 1920s, it was clear to many Catholic leaders that one of the other options would replace the community normal as the prevailing form of Catholic teacher preparation.[46]

A handful of bishops embraced the diocesan teachers college, but few religious superiors had changed their minds in the thirty years since the option had first been suggested. Religious superiors continued to fear the mingling of teaching communities would break down the *esprit de corps* built up during the novitiate. "From experience," noted one superior, "our community does not favor the diocesan teachers college as a type of training for novices. . . . It takes novices away from community life just when they need it most."[47] Without the support of the religious superior, the diocesan teachers college never got beyond the experimental stage.

Having rejected the diocesan teachers college, many religious superiors reluctantly accepted the second option — the establishment of colleges that emphasized teacher education. Even though the costs and the risks were substantial, some orders thought it worth the effort to establish their own colleges not only for the preparation of sister-teachers, but also for the higher education of young Catholic women. Unfortunately, these new Catholic colleges for women did not prove to be the best solution to the sister-teacher certification problem as had been the case for several decades. Religious communities found that the demand for teachers continued to be too great to allow young sisters to study full-time. Thus the newly established colleges focused on the education of young lay women. The preparation of sister-teachers became a secondary activity.[48]

A final option — one never considered in earlier decades — was utilized by a few congregations at the end of the 1920s. The practice of sending young sisters to secular teachers colleges and universities was controversial but effective. "I feel that the experience has been good for the sisters," wrote one liberal-minded superior, "and excellent for those who came in contact with them at the state university."[49]

Few superiors were that confident, however. One survey conducted in 1926 found that only 14 percent of Catholic elementary teachers had received all or part of their education in secular colleges. Even though the vast majority of superiors openly opposed the practice, most admitted that on occasion they permitted sisters to attend secular teachers colleges. "The persistent demand from pastors for more and better qualified teachers," notes Veverka, "in some cases overrode even the strongest reservations about the appropriateness or desirability of certain kinds of education for sisters."[50]

None of the alternatives to the community normal school proved satisfactory to the majority of religious superiors, prelates, or pastors. Yet the campaign to improve the quality of Catholic teacher preparation did have a significant and permanent effect on the education of sister-teachers. Historian Fayette Veverka notes that the number of sisters attending summer normal schools increased 176 percent in the years between 1921 and 1926 and that during that decade nearly three-quarters of the teachers staffing Catholic schools were taking summer school and extension courses of various kinds. These are impressive statistics when one considers the late start of the Catholic educational establishment on the road to formal teacher training.[51]

※

The Catholic response to teacher preparation was a case study of the pressures on parochial education in the twentieth century. If parochial education was to survive, it had to compete with public education on its own terms. To do so meant that Catholic leaders had to better prepare women religious for the classroom. Yet where would the church find the necessary resources to accomplish so large a task?

The answer was a mixture of both faith and ingenuity. Women religious never received the training they might have hoped for. Yet they did receive more instruction and support than many leaders thought possible. As was the case with so many previous Catholic responses to public education, the training of sister-teachers was a compromise.

What was never compromised, however, was the leadership role played by women religious in parochial education from the mid-nineteenth century on. In fact, it would not be difficult to make the case that sister-teachers were the single most important element in the Catholic educational establishment. "If adequate means could be found to measure the relative importance of personal influences," notes Mary Ewens, "it might well be shown that sisters' efforts were far more effective than those of bishops or priests."[52]

As Ewens and others have shown, the responsibilities of sister-teachers for the spiritual and educational life of the American church were extraordinary. They taught successive generations the basic tenets of the faith "and gave them a solid grounding in Christian living and a sense of responsibility for the maintenance of a Christian atmosphere in the homes they would one day run and the religious education of their children."[53] One must attribute the expansion of the Catholic population not only to immigration, but also to the skills of sister-teachers in cultivating a lifelong faith in generation after generation of American-born Catholics.

The Church-State-School Question

W HAT IS the proper relationship between church, state, and school under the Constitution? That question was at the center of a controversy that gripped church-state relations in the decades from 1920 to 1950. The roots of this twentieth-century conflict lay in the unstated intentions of the framers of the Constitution.

Even though the framers believed that church, state, and school should work together to preserve the social order, they failed to define the relationship in the "establishment" clause of the First Amendment. This lack of definition eventually led to social conflict in the mid-nineteenth century, when educators incorporated nonsectarian Protestant values and beliefs into the curricula of the emerging common schools. Catholics were particularly upset by this state of affairs and petitioned state legislatures for funds to support their own schools. The legislative response was to remove Protestant instruction from the public schools and rebuff all efforts to provide public assistance to parochial schools. This answer to the church-state-school question satisfied no one.[1]

Even though Catholics and a few other denominations continued to protest, state legislatures and courts refused to budge. In the fifty years following the Civil War, the policy of specifically prohibiting the distribution of public aid to denominational schools was incorporated into the constitutions of all but three states. Five decades of losing campaigns in more than two dozen states caused many Catholics to abandon all hope of obtaining public assistance for Catholic schools.[2]

The fact that legislatures would not provide public aid did not mean that the states were uninterested in parochial schools. Far from it. In the years following World War I, state legislatures passed numerous child welfare laws affecting the conduct and content of parochial schools. In the six years from 1918 to 1923, for example, state legislatures passed nearly one hundred laws that directly or indirectly affected parochial schools. All of the laws provided for a measure of state control over a variety of private educational activities from record-keeping to compulsory attendance. It was an effort on the part of the state to regulate private schooling; but it was unclear how far the state would go in this effort.[3]

Some legal provisions were related to the state's right to information on the parochial schools. Several states, for example, required parochial schools to obtain state approval for their schools or to register with the state before opening any schools. Other state laws required parochial schools to keep attendance records and report these figures to the state. The most onerous of these information provisions was the right of the state to verify the information through inspection. "The fact that nine statutes containing this provision were enacted during the three or four post-war years when emotion was at high tension," noted one historian, "suggests that anti-parochial school feeling had something to do with this type of legislation."[4]

An additional number of statutes focused on the substantive aspects of education. Almost every state assumed some sort of control over the curriculum of parochial schools. For the most part these provisions established a list of subjects to be taught in all schools. Most states, for example, passed laws requiring parochial schools to teach American history, civics, or related courses that encouraged patriotism. Many states also required that the flag be displayed in every classroom and that teachers take oaths of allegiance to state and country.

In addition to patriotism, legislatures also were concerned about the language of instruction. In fact, of all the various provisions passed by the states, the largest number were those laws requiring that English be the language of instruction in all schools; several states went so far as to specifically limit the use and teaching of foreign languages in both public and parochial classrooms. All of these curriculum provisions were intended to safeguard the American character of the classroom.[5]

Two additional provisions had a similar intent. Laws requiring the certification of teachers by the state were intended to insure that all classroom personnel were citizens, met certain academic and professional standards, and taught their classes in the English language. A second provision common in most states set the age limits of pupils who were required to attend an approved school, set the length of the school term, and in a few states set specific hours of attendance for each school day. Once again, the interest of the state was to insure uniformity in public and private education.[6]

Catholic educators for the most part did not protest these legislative actions. In fact, some churchmen saw in the provisions an opportunity to improve parish schools and make these institutions more competitive with public schools. But certain states passed laws that led to controversy and to the Supreme Court. These controversial cases concerned the abolition of foreign languages from the classroom and the effort to require all children to attend public schools. In two instances these controversies were settled by the Court in what became landmark cases.

The abolition of foreign languages from all classrooms was a direct result of anti-foreign sentiments during and after World War I. In 1919, legislatures in Nebraska, Iowa, and Ohio — states with large German-born populations — passed laws proscribing the use of any foreign language in the classroom, even as a subject, until after the eighth grade. Since German Catholics and Lutherans operated large numbers of parochial schools in those states and used German to teach cultural and religious subjects, it was clear that church and state would eventually clash.[7]

Parents and educators in all three states protested the constitutionality of the laws, but to little avail. The Nebraska Supreme Court upheld the law as necessary to the common good. "The legislature has seen the baneful effects of permitting foreigners who had taken residence in this country to rear and educate their children in the language of their native land," noted the Court. "The result of that condition was found to be inimical to our own safety."[8] In effect the court argued that since the nation was threatened, this interference with individual liberty was reasonable. State courts in Iowa and Ohio handed down decisions that contained similar rationales.

The Lutherans in Nebraska, joined by other religious groups, appealed the Nebraska court decision to the U.S. Supreme Court. In handing down a reversal of the state court decision, the Supreme Court agreed with the Nebraska Lutherans that the law was an unreasonable infringement of the liberties guaranteed by the Fourteenth Amendment. The Court agreed that the Nebraska law, and by inference those in Iowa and Ohio, were arbitrary and unreasonable.[9]

Many Catholics applauded the Court's decision and took it as a sign that the Court would safeguard the personal liberties of Catholic parents. The decision was good news that came at a time when Catholics were fighting to preserve their rights. In Michigan, for example, public school advocates were mounting a campaign to require the attendance of all children in public schools.[10]

The Michigan campaign culminated in a ballot initiative in the fall of 1920. Even though advocates of the measure were vociferous and predicted victory, their confidence was not enough to overcome the opposition of the state's large Catholic population. The proposal to require all children to attend public schools was soundly defeated by a margin of nearly two to one. A second effort in 1924 also went down to defeat. There is little doubt that Michigan Catholics, galvanized by the fearful consequences of such a measure, held the balance of power on this issue.

⠷⠅

But across the country in a state with a small Catholic population, compulsory public education advocates were more successful in passing their legislation. Oregon would seem to be an unlikely state for such a campaign since the state had such a small foreign-born and Catholic population in 1920 and well over 90 percent of all children in the state were enrolled in public schools. In fact, it was because Oregon had so few Catholics that the campaign was viable.[11]

The Oregon campaign emerged out of a strong tradition of nativism in the state. As in other states, the concern over foreigners and the need to reinforce American values intensified in Oregon in the years after World War I. The public school was seen as a bulwark of these values and some advocates twisted this concern into an attack on Catholic schools. In Oregon it was an unholy coalition of the Masons and the Ku Klux Klan that translated this irrational fear into a viable campaign.[12]

The 1922 election campaign was intense, with the Masons and the Klan leading a vociferous and vituperative attack on the Catholic Church as well as its schools. "Speakers sponsored by the Masons, the Klan and other private organizations," notes historian Paul Holsinger, "toured the state emphasizing the evils of private schools, particularly Roman Catholic schools, which became the center of the attack.... All true Americans must see the logic of denying all minority groups, and especially Catholics, the right to have their own schools, the very training ground for later corrupt activities."[13] It was a twisted logic that appealed to the hundreds of thousands of non-Catholics in the state.

Oregon Catholics and other opponents of the bill found themselves defending their patriotism but having little impact on public opinion. On November 7, 1922, the Masons and the Klan won the day. They elected Walter Pierce, a pro-amendment advocate, as governor, they sent pro-amendment legislators to the state house, and, most important, they passed the school initiative by a margin of ten thousand votes.

Compulsory attendance at public schools was to begin in September 1926, but opponents of the measure were determined to test the constitutionality of the new law.[14] They appealed to the U.S. District Court in Portland early in 1923, and in March 1924 the court ruled unanimously that the State of Oregon had exceeded its powers and had unlawfully taken from the schools in question "their constitutional rights and privilege to teach in the grammar grades" as well as deprived them of their property under due process of the law. Newspapers and educators across the country applauded the decision.[15]

Press opinion and district court decisions were not enough to convince Governor Pierce that the law was unconstitutional. In fact, the court decision seemed to make the compulsory public education advocates even more determined. Immediately after the district court decision was announced, Governor Pierce announced the state's decision to appeal the case to the U.S. Supreme Court. One Oregon newspaper captured the fervor of the case: "The people of the United States [will] not stand for any half dozen judges telling them that an overwhelming majority cannot make their own law."[16]

Catholics and opponents of the law were confident of the merits of their case. "The plain implication of the [lower] court decision," noted the *Catholic Sentinel* of Oregon, "is that freedom of education means freedom of education. This liberty of teaching, guaranteed by the Constitution and now formally proclaimed by a federal court is a real liberty, not a pale [example] of liberty as conceived by the Ku Klux Klan."[17] Oregon Catholics were eager to have the Supreme Court settle the matter.

The Supreme Court heard a refinement of the controversy that had been going on in Oregon for the previous three years. The state argued that "only a compulsory system of public school education will encourage the patriotism of its citizens, and train its younger citizens to become more willing and more efficient defenders of the United States in time of public danger."[18] In response, the attorneys for the private school advocates argued that the issue was tyranny versus liberty. "The young minds of the nation should not be cast in any such straight-jacket and their diversification and individual development prevented," stated their brief. "The excess power which results from such a devise clearly serves to maintain despotism and checks the normal evolution of liberty."[19]

On June 1, 1925, the Supreme Court handed down a unanimous decision in favor of parochial education. Known as *Pierce v. Society of School Sisters*, the written opinion noted that the Oregon law was a clear violation of the Fourteenth Amendment to the Constitution. "No question is raised," noted the Court, "concerning the power of the state reasonably to regulate all schools, to inspect, supervise and examine them, their teachers and pupils; to require that all children of proper age attend some school, that teachers shall be of good moral character and patriotic disposition, that certain studies plainly essential to good citizenship must be taught and that nothing be taught which is manifestly inimical to the public welfare."

But the rights of the state did not extend to dictating the *choice* of schools. "The fundamental theory of liberty upon which all governments in this union repose," added the Court, "excludes any general power of the state to standardize its children by forcing them to accept instruction from public teachers only. The child is not the mere creature of the state; those who nurture and direct his destiny have the right, coupled with high duty, to recognize and prepare him for additional obligations." The decision in the Pierce case was widely hailed as the "Magna Carta" of private education.[20]

The decision was greeted with unanimous approval in the secular press. "The need of having some federal tribunal to maintain the rights of citizens when they are invaded by local legislation," noted the *New York Times*, "has never been more evident than in the case of this Oregon school law."[21] Many other papers joined in the chorus. Perhaps the *Portland Oregonian* put it best. "Without a doubt," went the editorial, "a majority of the people of Oregon believe now that the public school is best for their children. But it is not their right to impose their opinion upon those parents who do not believe it so."[22]

The Supreme Court decision was a landmark in constitutional law. "The Oregon decision," noted historian Lloyd Jorgenson, "provided for the non-public schools a protection very similar to that which had been extended to the nonpublic colleges, under different circumstances to be sure, by the *Dartmouth* decision a century earlier."[23]

❖

Just as important, the *Pierce* decision allowed parochial school advocates to return to the issue of public support for nonpublic schools. For the next quarter century, Catholics renewed their legislative efforts to seek, once again, a portion of their tax monies for the support of their own schools.

But this new Catholic campaign for public funding was very different from the bitter rhetorical campaigns of the nineteenth century. Rather than castigating the public schools, Catholic educators focused on the injustice of denying even token assistance to the parochial schools that performed such an important public service.

There is no doubt that this argument was effective. In several small communities, especially those with large Catholic populations, public monies were granted directly to local parochial schools. More common, however, was the distribution of indirect forms of assistance — schoolbooks and bus transportation — to parochial school students, but not to the schools themselves. Not surprisingly, public school advocates protested this use of tax monies, and many cases of direct and indirect aid reached the courts in the years from 1925 to 1950.

The first private school case of any consequence to reach the Supreme Court after *Pierce* was *Cochran v. the Louisiana Board of Education*. In May 1928, the new governor of Louisiana, Huey P. Long, proposed to use state funds to purchase and distribute schoolbooks to children attending both public and private schools. The state school superintendent objected, reminding the governor that practically all the private schools were affiliated with the Catholic Church and that the constitution prohibited the use of public funds to aid religious institutions. The governor was not deterred. "I am a better lawyer than you," Long said to the superintendent, "and books for children go into the act."[24]

Even though the law was passed and implemented with little difficulty, it was clear to many that the new Louisiana law was based on debatable constitutional grounds. Similar laws in other states — most notably New York — had been struck down by the state courts. It is not surprising, therefore, that the opponents of the new Louisiana law challenged it in court even before the program had begun. Beyond the technical and procedural objections, the plaintiffs "alleged that the use of public property for a private purpose was a violation of the due process clause of the Fourteenth Amendment, and that the law had a tendency to destroy the republican form of government guaranteed to the state." The plaintiffs also protested that the new law violated the twelfth article of the state constitution that stipulated that "no public funds shall be used for support of any private or sectarian school."[25]

The Louisiana State Supreme Court disagreed with the plaintiffs, however, by focusing its decision on the aid to the child, not the school. By a vote of four to three, the court decided that the State of Louisiana was not violating the state constitution by lending schoolbooks to children. "The schools," noted the court, "are not the beneficiaries of these appropriations. They obtain nothing from them, nor are they relieved of a single obligation because of them. The school children and the state are alone the beneficiaries."[26] In handing down this decision, the Court set a precedent that has held to this day.

The opponents of free textbooks appealed to the U.S. Supreme Court, but failed to make their case with the justices. Less than two weeks after oral arguments, the Court handed down a decision that the law was constitutional. "The legislature," wrote Hughes for the majority, "does not segregate private schools or their pupils, as its beneficiaries, or attempt to interfere with any matter of exclusively private concern. Its interest is in education broadly; its method comprehensive. Individual interests are aided only as the common interest is safeguarded."[27] With these words, the Court legitimized the concept of indirect aid for private schools.

Even though it was a landmark case, *Cochran v. Louisiana Board of Education* had little impact outside the state. The years following the Court's 1930 decision were years of hardship and economic depression. Few states, even those with large Catholic populations, were able to finance expensive textbook loan programs for private schools. This is not to say that local government leaders were unwilling to work with church leaders to sustain the parochial school system in hard times. In fact, the Depression seemed to foster an outpouring of compromise plans to provide some public assistance to local parochial schools. By the mid-1930s, nearly 350 parochial schools across the country were receiving some form of public aid.[28]

The most publicized example of this local compromise came in Vincennes, Indiana. The hardship of the Depression forced a number of parochial schools in that city to close their doors. Faced with the task of educating hundreds of Catholic students for the first time, the school board took over the former parish schools on an emergency basis and employed members of Catholic religious orders to teach the children assigned to the new public schools.

In most ways the new schools were conducted exactly like other public schools. The course of study and the schoolbooks were the same in all public schools. Religious instruction was prohibited during school hours. All teachers — including the religious — were certified by the state. No rent was paid for the use of the buildings, but the pastor was permitted to instruct the students in religion before the beginning of the school day and the religious pictures and religious dress that distinguish parochial schools and public schools remained the same. All salaries and maintenance costs were paid by the city. It was a compromise that the community could live with.[29]

But not everyone was pleased, and the arrangement was challenged in state court in 1940. After due consideration of the circumstances and the nature of the compromise, the court concluded "that the board of school trustees of the said city, by their course of action, did establish public schools in the buildings formerly occupied by the various parochial schools and that the payment . . . to said teachers of salaries provided by contracts of employment was valid."[30]

Since the cooperative schools had been utilized only on an emergency basis, few argued with the court's decision. Even the editors of the *Christian Century*, a publication noted for its opposition to such plans, was conciliatory in its editorial: "There is no convincing evidence that the whole affair was not conducted in good faith by both sides."[31]

But good faith was not a phrase associated with another controversial school arrangement that dominated the life of a small Cincinnati suburb during the 1940s. The uproar over the incorporation of St. Mary Margaret parochial school into the public school system of North College Hill, Ohio, was national in scope. In fact, the National Education Association referred to the affair as "probably the most serious school situation now current in the nation." The bitterness precipitated by this controversy was one of the important factors in the establishment of "Protestants and Other Americans United for the Separation of Church and State," a militantly anti-Catholic protest group.[32]

The controversy in North College Hill began in 1940 when the public school board with a Catholic majority voted to incorporate the local parochial school into the public school system. This unprecedented arrangement meant the employment of the eight nuns who taught at the school as well as leasing the school building from the archdiocese of Cincinnati. Public outrage over such a partisan arrangement led to the defeat of the Catholic members on the board in the elections of 1941 and the end of the arrangement by the new board. But Catholics won a new majority on the board in the elections of 1945 by arguing that the inclusion of the parochial school in the public system would increase the state subsidy for the North College Hill schools. After the election the board reincorporated the parochial school into the public school system.

The tension over this unusual arrangement did not abate, however. Tension developed into outright hostility in February 1947, when the popular school superintendent refused to follow the board's instructions on the teachers to be hired for the former parochial school. When the board announced that it would not renew the superintendent's contract, students and teachers in the system went on strike. Investigations by the National Education Association were critical of the board, but to little avail; the board would not reconsider its decision and the result was legal action.

The impasse was broken in June when the pressure of local public opinion forced the resignation of the Catholic majority on the board. In the interests of finding an acceptable solution, the other members of the board also resigned. The school system was administered temporarily by a local judge who appointed a new board and rehired the superintendent. The elections of 1947 brought a non-Catholic majority to the board, and St. Mary Margaret's School returned to the rolls of private institutions.[33]

The annual meeting of the National Education Association in July 1947 was a useful forum to reflect on the incident. Archbishop John McNicholas of Cincinnati, chairman of the NCWC education department, hoped to find a common ground with public educators. "We cannot emphasize too strongly our conviction," noted McNicholas, "that the Catholic and public schools are partners in American education. They must work together in the common task of preparing millions of boys and girls for the duties of American citizenship. Catholic school teachers would be greatly encouraged if at this convention the National Education Association were to reiterate our belief that there is a genuine partnership between the two major systems in American education, the Catholic and the public."[34] But the NEA membership did not respond to this overture.

The church-state-school question quandary continued as the NEA opposed any and all public aid to Catholic parochial schools.

⁂

The year 1947 proved to be a time to focus on the church-state-school question. In addition to a number of local controversies over the propriety of public-supported parochial schools, the Supreme Court also entered the fray with a decision that would further refine the debate. In *Everson v. Board of Education*, the Supreme Court permitted the township of Ewing, New Jersey, to provide bus transportation to parochial as well as public school students.

But in approving this aid to parochial school students, the Court also detailed specific conditions for the constitutionality of such aid that limited future efforts to obtain more assistance for parish schools. The *Everson* case was an attempt by the Court to end more than thirty years of wrangling over the constitutional relationship between church, state, and school. Even though the *Everson* decision was considered a landmark decision, it did not completely answer the concerns of either parochial or public school advocates.[35]

The Court agreed to hear the petition of Arch Everson because the question of indirect aid — specifically bus transportation for private school students — was being debated or implemented in several states in the late 1940s. For example, Massachusetts passed a law in 1936 permitting cities and towns to use public funds to transport pupils to private schools. Other states — New York, Kansas, Michigan, Oregon, Louisiana, and Texas — also had adopted transportation laws that benefited parochial school children. It was clear that the Court would have to clarify the legality of this indirect aid in the terms of the First Amendment.[36]

The New Jersey law reached the Supreme Court after a long struggle. Since the state has a large Catholic population, it is surprising that it took New Jersey four years to pass such a modest transportation bill. But politics rather than religion was the problem; after three years of maneuvering, both houses of the legislature passed a bill that was signed by the governor and became law in June 1940. The bill was to take effect July 1, 1941.

Opponents vowed to fight. "We believe that many of the legislators who voted for the bill," noted the New Jersey Taxpayers Association, "did so only because of political expediency even though they knew it was not good legislation." The executive director of the association, Arch Everson, filed suit to stop the implementation of the law. The New Jersey Supreme Court voided the law, but the case was appealed to the Supreme Court.[37]

On February 10, 1947, the Court handed down a five-to-four decision in favor of the defendant. Before explaining the logic of the majority decision, the Court felt compelled to discuss the background and meaning of the First Amendment. "The 'establishment of religion' clause of the First Amendment means at least this," wrote Hugo Black for the majority. "Neither a state nor the Federal government can set up a church. Neither can pass laws which aid one religion, aid all religions, or prefer one religion over another. No tax in any amount, large or small, can be levied to support any religious activities or institutions, whatever they may be called, or whatever form they may adopt to teach or practice religion. In the words of Jefferson, the clause against the establishment of religion by law was intended to erect 'a wall of separation' of church and state."[38] Judging from the thrust of this argument, one might assume that the Court would prohibit publicly supported bus transportation for parochial school students.

But the Court examined the language of the New Jersey law, found no untoward bias toward religious groups, and noted that the state would be in error if it excluded members of any religious faith from receiving the benefits of public welfare legislation. "Measured by these standards," concluded the Court, "we cannot say that the First Amendment prohibits New Jersey from spending tax raised funds to pay bus fares of pupils attending public and other schools.... That amendment requires the state to be neutral in its relations with groups of religious believers and non-believers; it does not require the state to be their adversary. State power is no more to be used so as to handicap religions than it is to favor them.... The First Amendment has erected a wall between church and state. That wall must be kept high and impregnable. We could not approve the slightest break. New Jersey has not breached it here."[39]

It was not a popular decision. "Protestant leaders," notes constitutional historian Richard Morgan, "saw it as onerous that the Court was willing to allow any public money in aid of what they considered a private religious purpose; and Catholic spokesmen, while happy that the constitutionality of state aid for parochial school transportation had been established, saw in the early part of the decision... what they regarded as a very severe reading of the establishment clause."[40]

Other than Catholics, few groups agreed with the majority; public opinion was very much against even indirect aid such as bus transportation. Many newspaper editors speculated that the decision would open the door for more and different kinds of indirect aid to parochial schools. All agreed that it made for bad law and bitter religious controversy. "The fundamental error," noted the *Washington Post* in its February 13 editorial, "lies in the Court's assumption that the intrinsic merit of a private activity, such as financing bus transportation to church schools, may transform it into a public welfare function."[41]

The *Everson* decision exacerbated existing tensions between Catholics and non-Catholics over education. Matters were not helped by Catholic efforts to obtain federal aid for parish schools or by the vitriolic rhetoric of the nation's leading prelate, Cardinal Francis Spellman of New York. In a commencement speech at Fordham University in June 1947, Spellman accused the *Everson* critics of preaching a crusade against the Catholic Church as a social institution. Spellman went on to defend the decision and cast aspersions on its critics. The *Everson* decision, noted Spellman, "gives no preferment to any one religious denomination or to any one school system. It appeals to the fair-minded. It is subject to criticism mainly by the intolerant, who in their failure to win a victory in a court of law seek recourse in the shady corners of bigotry."[42]

Spellman's accusations aroused the ire of many religious leaders. One group of clergymen writing in the *New York Times* disputed Spellman's claims of bigotry but noted the anxiety of millions of Americans over "the political activities of the members of the Roman Catholic hierarchy who, as representatives of a foreign power, have been carrying on increasing propaganda and utilizing continuous and insistent pressure on press and radio and state and federal officials to break down our United States constitutional guarantee of separation of church and state."[43] The *Christian Century* agreed. "If Cardinal Spellman sees fit to consider the resistance to any program initiated by the hierarchy as equivalent to an attack upon the Roman Catholic Church, he is creating an anti-Catholic movement by definition and can easily bring on a real one."[44] Recriminations accomplished nothing, and both sides had the good sense to allow the matter to die in the summer of 1947.

But tension did not abate. In May 1949, a bill to provide federal financial assistance to the states to cover certain costs of public elementary and secondary education was introduced in the House of Representatives by Graham Barden of North Carolina. The bill also prohibited the states from using federal funds to transport parochial school students. Not surprisingly, parochial school advocates opposed the bill, and the NCWC sent Father William McManus to testify against it.

Spellman got into the act in another address at Fordham in which he accused Barden of being a "brewer of bigotry."[45] "The cardinal's rhetoric," notes historian James Hennesey, "tended to be purple and he did not avoid personalities." Indeed he did not as was evidenced by his sharp criticism of Eleanor Roosevelt, a supporter of the Barden bill. Spellman went so far as to accuse the former first lady of a "record of anti-Catholicism [that] stands for all to see, ... documents of discrimination unworthy of an American mother!" Spellman later muted his criticism in a "clarifying statement," but he did more harm than good in defending parochial education.[46] In spite of Spell-man's rhetoric, the bill did not pass.

※

The bitterness over the Barden bill and the *Everson* decision ended three decades of progress in the search for a clarification of the church-state-school question. If Catholics had not achieved their goal — direct public aid to parochial schools — they had obtained a great deal. In the *Pierce* decision the church had an unqualified statement of the right of parish schools to operate without interference. In the *Cochran* decision, the church had a statement that indirect aid in the form of school-books was constitutional. Finally, in the *Everson* decision, the church saw that indirect aid extended to publicly supported bus transportation to parochial schools. There is no doubt that the American church had come a long way in redressing their grievances and obtaining a favorable answer to the church-state-school question.

In 1812, Elizabeth Seton established the Daughters of Charity, an order of sister–teachers who brought order to Catholic educational development in this country by 1830. *(Courtesy: Author's collection.)*

The Daughters of Charity motherhouse in Emmitsburg, Maryland, pictured here in 1834, was the nerve center of a national educational enterprise. *(Courtesy: Author's collection.)*

Bishop John Hughes of New York used a siege mentality to unite the diverse elements of his diocese in support of parish schools during the two decades before the Civil War. *(Courtesy: Author's collection.)*

Non-Catholics were suspicious of Catholic efforts to reform public education. In this 1871 cartoon by Thomas H. Nast, the bishops and the Vatican threaten American children. (*Courtesy: Author's collection.*)

Idealistic to a fault, Archbishop John Ireland of St. Paul precipitated an international school controversy when he proposed a plan to unite the Catholic and public schools. *(Courtesy: Archives of the University of Notre Dame.)*

Teacher certification laws sent thousands of sister–teachers back to school in the 1920s and 1930s. Above is the summer school class of 1929 at Notre Dame. *(Courtesy: Archives of the University of Notre Dame.)*

Cardinal John O'Hara of Philadelphia made it his personal mission to promote Catholic school enrollment and would tolerate no pessimism about the future of Catholic education. *(Courtesy: Archives of the University of Notre Dame.)*

Sister Mario was fortunate to have only 34 students in her class in 1957. Some sister–teachers had more than 50 students per class during the 1950s. *(Courtesy: Archives and Records Center of the Archdiocese of Chicago)*

A sociologist at the National Opinion Research Center and the University of Chicago, Father Andrew M. Greeley has been the foremost authority on American Catholic education for more than 35 years. *(Courtesy: Andrew M. Greeley.)*

Although he was enormously popular with the American people and with Congress, President Reagan could not deliver the tuition tax credits he proposed at the NCEA convention in April, 1982. *(Courtesy: Ronald Reagan Library.)*

Chapter 11 _____

A Generation of Crisis

MERICAN CATHOLIC PAROCHIAL EDUCATION faced innumerable crises throughout its long history. Yet parish schools had survived, even thrived, amid this hardship. There had never been doubts among the American Catholic people that their parochial schools were an important, even vital part of the mission of the American church.

But the three decades from 1950 to 1980 presented Catholic educators with crisis after crisis that shook the very foundations of American Catholic education and caused Catholic educators to question the viability and survival of the parish schools they had worked so hard to preserve.[1]

There was no single cause or event that was responsible for this generation of crisis. The years after the Second World War were a time of enormous change in the American Catholic community. The 1950s, 1960s, and 1970s were years of economic prosperity and educational opportunity as well as years of theological and liturgical development.

American Catholicism in 1980 was a very different denomination than it had been thirty years earlier. The laity had shed the last vestiges of its ghetto mentality and was fully integrated into American society. Through Vatican II, the church radically revised its teaching on religious and theological issues and created a modern liturgy in the vernacular. With these changes, however, came questions about the role and the mission of the parochial school, and the questions never stopped during those three decades.[2]

❖

"For the Catholic community in the United States," notes historian James Hennesey, "World War II was another in a long series of rites of passage."[3] Indeed it was. Young Catholics had distinguished themselves with their bravery and their patriotism and returned home to seek their American dreams with the same determination they had shown at Anzio and Iwo Jima. They returned to college using the GI Bill, married their sweethearts, and had lots and lots of babies. In fact, the Catholic population in the United States nearly doubled from 24 million to 42 million in the years from 1940 to 1960. Most were loyal Catholics; weekly church attendance during these years hovered at about 70 percent. The church as an institution and the Catholic laity as individuals had never been so successful.

Yet even success brought hardship. These loyal young Catholics with their new homes in the suburbs were determined that their millions of children would receive a good Catholic education. In 1949, Catholic elementary and secondary schools had a combined national enrollment of a little more than two million students. By the end of the 1950s, however, the enrollment had more than doubled to 4.2 million and was still rising. Such rapid and ceaseless growth taxed the church mightily. Like the sorcerer's apprentice, the church could not control what it had started. After urging, cajoling, and threatening the laity to establish and support Catholic schools, Catholic leaders found themselves unprepared to meet the tidal wave of demand. It was a crisis of success.[4]

A new generation of "builder bishops" dominated the church in the 1950s. Francis Spellman had succeeded Patrick Hayes in New York and Samuel Stritch had replaced George Mundelein in Chicago, both in 1939. Richard Cushing had succeeded William O'Connell in Boston and Joseph Ritter had replaced Joseph Glennon in St. Louis, both in 1946; and John O'Hara had taken over in Philadelphia in 1951 at the death of Dennis Dougherty. All of these new bishops were determined to meet the demand for more schools. Yet, unlike their predecessors, these men could not quite keep up the pace.[5]

Typical of these problems were those faced by Spellman in New York and Stritch in Chicago. Spellman's numbers were impressive. During the 1950s he built more than two hundred new elementary schools, and by 1960 there was one child in parochial school in New York for every two children in public schools. But Spellman was frustrated. "In spite of the great progress made in expanding the Catholic school system in New York," noted historian Florence Cohalan, "the majority [of Catholic children] were not in it."[6]

Spellman's frustration led him to his outspoken position on federal aid for parochial schools. He was fond of noting the savings to the taxpayers provided by his parochial schools, and at times he was supported in these claims. Lazarus Joseph, city controller of New York, estimated that New York and Brooklyn's parochial schools saved the city $425 million for buildings and $110 million for annual maintenance and operation. "Mr. Joseph thinks [parish schools] are actually a great boon," noted *America*, "which should receive more public encouragement."[7] But that "public encouragement" never came in the form of aid, and try as he might, Spellman never found the funds to build enough schools.

Stritch in Chicago fared little better than his brother bishop in New York even though he was even more vociferous in his determination. At the 1954 NCEA meeting in Chicago, Stritch noted the problems that he and his colleagues faced in parochial education, but he also stressed his commitment to finding a place for every Catholic child who wanted a Catholic education.

Stritch was in trouble almost from the start. In 1953, despite an investment of $12 million for elementary schools alone, Stritch reported "we have not yet met the demands of our people for adequate school opportunities. Four years later, Stritch's Catholic school superintendent complained: "We need more classrooms, more teachers, and more money." By the time

Stritch left Chicago in 1958, he had invested $85 million in seventy-five elementary schools.

It was not enough. "Despite an apparent prosperity," notes historian James Sanders, "the Chicago Catholic educational program at both the elementary and secondary levels had moved into deep trouble by the late 1950s. In a sense it suffered from the weight of its own past success." Like Spellman, Stritch was forced to face the reality of not being able to meet the demand. Yet he remained a committed educator. "We must not only have schools," he noted in 1956, "but we must have excellent schools."[8]

Stritch's colleague in Philadelphia, John O'Hara, did not worry so much about excellence as he did about enrollment. O'Hara's determination to meet the demand for Catholic education approached fanaticism. "From the first to the last," notes historian James Connelly, "the Philadelphia Catholic story of the 1950s is the story of the Catholic schools."[9] In only eight years, O'Hara oversaw the construction of 133 new parochial school buildings with 1,206 classrooms and 20 new diocesan high schools with 213 classrooms. These facilities provided for the total increase in the Catholic school population of over 102,000 pupils.

O'Hara was a strict conservative in all educational matters. He wanted every Catholic child in a Catholic school and every Catholic classroom staffed by a Catholic nun or priest. Dismayed by the failure of the archdiocese to attract sufficient sisters to staff his new schools, O'Hara went so far as to assign diocesan priests to teach in the schools.

But even O'Hara was forced to employ increasing numbers of lay teachers. "The percentage of lay teachers is as heavy as we ever care to have it," wrote Superintendent Edward Reilly in 1960. "In most cases the best lay teachers do not approach the average Religious in performance. Consequently, we feel strongly that the more lay teachers we have, the less effective will be our schools."[10]

In fact, the need for teachers was the critical weakness in the parochial school system.[11] For more than a century, Catholic bishops and educators had relied on underpaid women religious to staff their classrooms. Many went so far as to claim that such women were both morally and educationally superior to their public school counterparts. But beginning in the early 1950s, many Catholic bishops and educators refused to face the fact that parochial education had become increasingly dependent on lay teachers.[12]

Educational traditionalists called for more faith. Their champion, Archbishop O'Hara, was irritated at Catholic clergymen who took a pessimistic view of the future of Catholic education, and on a number of occasions in the 1950s he lashed out at such doomsayers. In July 1954, for example, O'Hara presided at a session on Catholic education at the annual meeting of Serra International. "He was very much disturbed by the paper given by Monsignor William McManus of Chicago who expressed a pessimistic outlook on the ability of Catholic educational institutions to catch up with this task. The archbishop interposed his own ideas in the discussion at considerable length to indicate that the Monsignor was in error in his statistics." O'Hara expected Catholic clergymen to toe the line and follow his lead.[13]

O'Hara was outraged when he discovered that McManus agreed to publish his paper in the December 1954 issue of the *Catholic Mind*. McManus was a realist and argued that the church was never going to have every Catholic child in a Catholic school. He also criticized the overcrowding of Catholic classrooms and argued that parish schools should limit their enrollment. McManus went so far as to suggest that some Catholic children — those from stable religious families — need not attend parochial schools. In fact, McManus hoped that some Catholics would withdraw their children to allow others from less stable families to attend and bolster their Catholic beliefs.

These ideas flew in the face of tradition, and O'Hara was quick to criticize McManus in letters to Stritch and Spellman. Stritch was something of a realist and allowed McManus to continue as assistant director of the NCWC Department of Education.[14]

Two years later McManus published another provocative article that infuriated O'Hara and the traditionalists. "How Good Are Catholic Schools?" McManus asked in the September 8, 1956, issue of *America*, a publication that O'Hara detested. McManus compared Catholic education to an adolescent. "No longer a child," he wrote, "it has a bad case of growing pains, is self-conscious, is misunderstood, and has a bright, if uncertain future."[15]

To prove his point, McManus surveyed twenty-eight dioceses and archdioceses on their school systems. Every one of these dioceses was strained beyond capacity; every diocese turned away applicants. "Our schools' rapid growth also explains the occasional awkwardness of Catholic education," he noted, "overcrowded classrooms, temporary employment of poorly qualified teachers, 'hit or miss' procedures in selecting students, and clumsy supervision." McManus was no pessimist, however. He believed that even though the future was uncertain, it was promising. "Thanks be to God," he concluded, "the youthful Catholic school system is in experienced hands."[16]

O'Hara thought McManus and others who focused on the shortage of space in Catholic schools to be unduly negative. "So far as can be determined in conversation with the Bishops," O'Hara wrote to sociologist Joseph Fichter, "the general feeling is that the Holy Ghost sends us these wonderful babies. He is going to provide the means of giving them a Catholic education of the best type possible." Few other Catholic leaders were willing to entrust the entire Catholic school system to divine intervention.[17]

The dramatic growth of the Catholic school system was made evident in a 1957 article by Joseph Sullivan. "Put briefly," wrote Sullivan, "the rate of Catholic school growth during the previous 57 years was twice that of public schools." Sullivan added that the years from 1950 to 1957 had seen an increase of 50 percent in Catholic school enrollment.

Like McManus, Sullivan was a realist. "The potentiality for any continued rise in Catholic school growth," he concluded, "will be limited only by ability and willingness to solve construction and lay staffing problems. Rising costs of building and salaries will place a heavy strain on the faithful contributors.... The lay staffing problem, among others, raises a serious question as to how soon the Catholic school system will attain full maturity within the church. Is our Catholic population, both clergy and laity, prepared to accept the challenge thus presented?"[18]

As the new decade approached, Catholics had some hope for stability in parochial education. Catholic leaders for the most part were resigned to the fact that lay teachers would be a permanent part of the Catholic educational system. They were also resigned to the fact that there would never be a place for every Catholic child in a parochial school. Perhaps symbolic of the transformation of Catholic educational ideology from the 1950s to the 1960s was the passing of Cardinal O'Hara. His death in 1960 marked the end of the dogmatic, doctrinaire stand on parochial education. Catholic leaders knew that their schools would have to be flexible to meet the challenges of a new decade.

✂

But few Catholics could have predicted the enormity of those challenges. American Catholicism experienced a revolution in the 1960s. For a variety of causes American Catholics came to question their past — including the very need for parochial schools. The changes in doctrine and liturgy mandated by Vatican II seemed to transform Catholicism into a new religion. "Old moorings were cut," notes James Hennesey. "Catholics were more likely than others to move to the suburbs. Parish and school structures had to be altered to fit new needs. A new generation experienced religious training and a cultural environment different from that which their parents had known."[19]

For most Catholics, the crisis in parochial education in the 1960s was almost the same as the 1950s. Shortages of desks and teachers continued; the demand for admission remained high, and most dioceses were falling farther and farther behind. "How Big Is the Crisis for Catholic Schools?" asked the editors of *U.S. News and World Report* in February 1964. The lengthy article underscored the major cause of the crisis: between 1945 and 1962 Catholic school enrollment had increased 129 percent while public school enrollment had increased only 69 percent. The church was now educating one in every eight children enrolled in school and turning away tens of thousands more because of a lack of space, money, and teachers. The system was strained beyond its limits.[20]

Many diocesan school systems began to crack under the strain. In 1962, Cardinal Joseph Ritter of St. Louis called a halt to new school construction until his pastors could organize schools with forty-nine or fewer students per classroom and a ratio of three religious to every lay teacher. Ritter supplemented his limited system with an expanded system of parish schools of religion.

The crisis in St. Louis was not an isolated case. High costs, unsafe classrooms, and a lack of teachers forced the closing of parochial schools in Milwaukee and Green Bay, Wisconsin; Saginaw, Michigan; St. Cloud, Minnesota; Cincinnati, Ohio; and the northern Virginia suburbs of Washington. "The problems arising from the immense increase of the school population are universal throughout the Catholic school system of the United States."[21] Every diocese — including New York and Philadelphia — was feeling the strain.

Catholic education in the early 1960s seemed to have reached a breaking point, unable to cope with the ceaseless legions of Catholic children who sought its services. It was at this point in 1964 that a young housewife had the temerity to publish a small book that asked a big question. *Are Catholic Schools the Answer?* asked Mary Perkins Ryan. Her answer was no. Ryan argued that the Catholic school system was parochial in the pejorative sense of the term and it was an obstacle to the Catholic mission of witnessing the presence of Christ.[22]

Ryan posited that the church would be better served if it shifted its focus from the child to the adult. She asked her readers to consider the impact of reallocating resources to the issues being raised in the Second Vatican Council. It was the home rather than the school that should be the seat of Catholic religious formation.

The book hit the Catholic educational establishment like a brick in the face. Ryan was not a sociologist or educator and her book at times seemed shrill and wrong-headed. Yet like the child questioning the emperor's new clothes, Ryan caused something of a panic. "Mrs. Ryan's little book landed like a stink bomb in the old schoolhouse," wrote one reviewer, and officials from the NCEA attacked the book as "naive and foolish."[23]

Yet Catholic educators could not shake the issues raised by Ryan, and the NCEA annual meeting in 1964 focused on almost nothing else. At a press conference held at the meeting, four Catholic school superintendents predicted that Ryan's book would cause immense harm and confusion. All this from a New Hampshire housewife!

Certainly Ryan's book was a blow to the morale of Catholic educators across the nation.[24] A number of church leaders rushed to defend parochial education. Archbishop Lawrence Sheehan, after noting the solid contributions of parochial education, also saw the value in criticism. "Criticism, on the part of some Catholics, aimed at the elimination of the parochial schools may cause us additional problems," he noted. "It will serve a good purpose, however, if it spurs us to remove as soon as possible every cause of justifiable complaint."[25] The criticism of Ryan and others had given Catholic educators pause for reflection and bolstered their determination to sustain the system.[26]

But all the words of encouragement and positive predictions did nothing to change the volatile demographics of parochial education. In the years up to and including 1962, the demand for parochial education and the enrollment of children in those schools increased each year without fail. But suddenly and without warning, enrollments began to drop. In 1965, Catholic elementary schools enrolled almost 4.5 million children, but three years later the figure had dropped to 3.9 million and would continue to drop each year for the next fifteen years. It was an ironic twist for Catholic educators, who until the mid-1960s had been plagued with overcrowded classrooms and excess demand.[27]

The downturn in enrollments was not uniform in any way. In the suburbs, the demand for parish schools remained high, but limited space forced many Catholics to send their children to public schools. In inner-city areas, enrollments declined as white Catholics abandoned their ethnic neighborhoods for the suburbs. The African Americans who replaced the whites were not Catholic, for the most part, and the end result was that many inner-city parish schools were closed.

A final element in the decline was cost. The scarcity of teaching sisters required parishes to employ lay teachers at competitive salaries, and this cost added significantly to already overburdened parish school budgets. Tuition increased, and many lower- and middle-class Catholics could no longer afford parochial schooling for their children. All of these factors contributed to decline in parish school enrollment.[28]

This shift in the generation of crisis called for action and the NCEA organized a major symposium to address the growing problems of parochial education. It is not surprising that during all these years of crisis, the NCEA thrived. Under the leadership of Frederick Hochwalt from 1946 to 1965, the NCEA grew to new levels of membership and influence. In 1965, for example, the NCEA enrolled over 88 percent of the Catholic schools in the United States as members.[29]

The NCEA was, therefore, the logical forum to address the growing list of problems in parochial education. It was Hochwalt's successor, C. Albert Koob, who was the progenitor of the symposium. "We are in a time of crisis concerning Catholic education," noted Koob in 1967. "Fortunately, we no longer find it embarrassing to discuss this crisis and are willing to admit that funds are short, problems pressing, and planning most difficult. But crisis is not failure. A crisis is a time for careful thinking and positive action. At times of crisis the adrenaline flows more abundantly in the human system and men are strengthened beyond normal. At times of crisis, leadership emerges and forces gather for mutual support to further the common good. So let it be with our educational crisis."[30]

Koob had hopes that the conference would begin the process of "restructuring Catholic education to bring it more in line with the contemporary needs of Church and society." He was certain that such a policy was the best response to the "crisis of confidence" in Catholic education. For seven days in November 1967, 120 Catholic education experts met in Washington and made a number of positive suggestions for the future. They called for more research data on Catholic schools, and this suggestion led to the establishment of the NCEA Data Bank on Catholic Education in 1969.

The symposium also served as a model for regional symposia and workshops that took the NCEA into the field for the first time since the 1930s. "If we were to make any kind of success at all," noted Koob, "we had to give service to the people in the field." Koob could look back on the symposium as a positive contribution to the effort to relieve the crisis of confidence in Catholic education.[31]

But Koob and many other educators had hoped for much more. They had hoped for a common solution to the crisis; what they got was a wide variety of views. It was not possible to come up with a common answer. "When the symposium's statement, drawn up by an editorial committee of thirteen of the participants, was issued over three months later," noted historian John Tracy Ellis, "several who had been present dissociated themselves from it. The latter felt either that the statement did not reflect the urgency of the situation or that it gave undue prominence to higher education and not sufficient emphasis to the diocesan superintendents of schools."[32]

Even the conference participants recognized their failure to reach a consensus. "We recognize the existence of a wide range of options in Christian education," went the symposium statement. "We urge openness in weighing choices among them."[33]

Over the next two years many writers and educators added their voices to the ongoing debate about the future of Catholic education.[34]

Yet ideas were not answers. In 1965, the American church educated almost 47 percent of her school children; by 1970, the percentage had dropped to less than 40 percent. Many dioceses recorded enormous one-year drops in 1968 and 1969 and were forced to close schools that drained limited resources. Milwaukee closed eighteen schools, including the oldest in the archdiocese. St. Cloud, St. Paul, Detroit, and Denver also closed schools in those years. Over all during 1968–69, there were 637 casualties in this war of attrition.[35]

It is no wonder that the decline of Catholic education was big news in 1969. Major publications such at the *New York Times, Time,* and *U.S. News and World Report* did features on the crisis. "The Roman Catholic school system in the United States is in serious even desperate financial trouble," reported *Time* in March 1969. Catholic parents "are caught in a viciously accelerating cycle. As public school taxes and parochial school tuition go up, many parents decide that they cannot afford both. They simply transfer their children to the public school increasing the tax burden as well as the cost per pupil for those remaining in the parochial schools." *U.S. News and World Report* was equally depressing. "A developing crisis that is overtaking the Catholic school system has shown up in many public places this year," noted the editors in September 1969, "bringing anxiety within the Church and financial strain for local governments." It was the Catholic weekly *America,* however, that asked the question that would dominate the debate in the 1970s: "Will Catholic Schools Survive?" asked the editors. No one seemed to have the answer.[36]

The 1960s also had been a decade of general crisis within American Catholicism as a whole. There was a general decline in Catholic participation in church activities of all kinds: weekly attendance at Mass declined, record numbers of women religious and priests petitioned for dispensations from their vows, the number of marriage annulments skyrocketed, the number of young men and women entering the religious life dropped precipitously. Most disturbing, however, was the growing disillusionment among Catholics with the teachings of the church. When Pope Paul VI preached against artificial birth control in *Humanae Vitae,* the majority of the laity ignored or disregarded his advice. In this climate of declining Catholic religiosity, parochial education did not fare well.

The arrival of a new decade encouraged writers and others to look ahead.[37] Calls for reform came from several prominent educators, among them Albert Koob. In a book with the provocative title *S.O.S. for Catholic Schools,* Koob and his colleague Russell Shaw further developed Koob's ideas on new objectives for the Catholic schools. Koob argued that the solution to the Catholic school crisis was not in closing current institutions, but rather in transforming them into "dynamic centers of Christian education with the aim of serving the total community."

These new Catholic schools would no longer be pale imitations of public schools, but elite institutions. "Catholic education should foster an elite based on apostolic commitment," he wrote, "a corps of wholehearted Christians; and this must be its chief goal, not its marginal diffidently hoped for by-product." Koob also argued that Catholic schools should become less child-centered and become "vigorous centers for adult education" directed at both religious and lay people.

Above all, Koob encouraged Catholics not to abandon hope. "With intelligence, imagination and courage," he concluded his book, "the problems of Catholic education can be solved. The present crisis can become an avenue of growth and progress. The opportunity is there and where there is opportunity, there is also duty."[38]

Koob's upbeat message was balanced by a somewhat pessimistic perspective by Andrew M. Greeley. In a book written with William C. Brown entitled *Can Catholic Schools Survive?* Greeley argued that the basic problem faced by Catholic education was a crisis of confidence. "And a crisis of confidence it certainly is," he wrote, "for the basic problem facing Catholic schools in the United States is not a loss of external support, but internal collapse of morale. There is a loss of nerve, a loss of connection, a loss of faith, a loss of enthusiasm. This is the root of the problem of Catholic education."[39]

In the first month of 1971, the editors of *Commonweal*, the influential lay Catholic biweekly, took up the question of school and parish. The editors questioned the American church's preoccupation with the school crisis. What of other aspects of parish life? "If American Catholics have failed to have a truly significant spiritual impact on American life," noted the lead editorial, "surely our long-term preoccupation with the parochial school must be considered as a possible part of the reason.... If many zealous Catholics are prejudiced against the parochial school, it is in part because they see the school as a distracting force that militates against a truly dynamic conception of the parish."[40]

The editors of *Newsweek* agreed in a wide-ranging and extensive assessment of the health of the Catholic Church in the United States. "In religion as in architecture," began the *Newsweek* story, "form tends to follow function and finances. From this perspective, American Catholicism appears to be a school system with churches attached. And indeed, to those students who spend a full sixteen years in them, Catholics schools are the church; from grade school through college — when the system works — students encounter a responsive religious milieu that attempts to integrate Catholicism with expanding intellectual horizons."[41]

If this was so, *Newsweek* saw the future of Catholic education in decentralization, with the laity taking a major leadership role. "Catholic schools may yet turn out to be not only alternatives to public schools," they concluded, "but also centers for encouraging a new kind of pluralism in Catholic thought, morality, and spirituality as well."[42]

Individual dioceses — among them Youngstown, San Francisco, and Chicago — responded by developing new school plans for the 1970s.[43] Yet for all the planning and experimentation, Catholic schools continued to close in record numbers. Who was to blame? What was the cause? Many of the observers of Catholic education had their own opinions, but there was no clear-cut answer. More important, without a clear understanding of the cause of the decline, Catholic educators had no sense of how to stop it.

For Andrew Greeley, the cause of the decline in Catholic schools was weak episcopal leadership, and his answer was to shift control of the schools to the laity. Greeley openly accused the hierarchy of withdrawing their support for Catholic schools — particularly in inner cities — at a time when parental interest in parochial education was on the rise.

Using survey data he compiled through the National Opinion Research Center at the University of Chicago, Greeley discovered that many Catholic parents not only favored the establishment of Catholic schools, but were also willing to pay for them. "The fundamental crisis in Catholic schools is neither financial or organizational," wrote Greeley in a provocative article in the *New York Times Magazine*. "It is theoretical.... Catholic schools will go out of existence mostly because Catholic educators no longer have enough confidence in what they are doing to sustain the momentum and sacrifice that built the world's largest private school system." To Greeley's thinking, Catholic schools were committing suicide.[44]

For Francis Phelan, recriminations such as those put forth by Andrew Greeley served no useful purpose. Indeed, Phelan argued, recriminations and finger-pointing further divided those who supported parochial schools. Phelan noted that there were many causes for the decline of Catholic schooling, so many in fact, that they were difficult to delineate without adding to the confusion. Phelan's plan of action was to encourage Catholic parents and educators to sustain parochial schools that responded to the interests of local communities and neighborhoods. This meant that inner-city parochial schools would become less Catholic and more African American and suburban schools would become more traditionally Catholic. For

Phelan, director of the Education Voucher Project, the strength of the Catholic schools would come through their diversity.[45]

In truth, Phelan had touched on the ray of hope in Catholic education in the 1970s: the important work that these institutions were doing in inner-city parishes. By 1976, it was clear that parochial schools were providing the only educational choice for many African Americans — both Catholic and non-Catholic. "The entire American Catholic community must help to keep these schools open," noted the editors of *America*, "for they constitute one of the primary places where the Catholic Church can give Christian Service."[46]

⁑

No organization felt the impact of the decline in Catholic schooling more than the NCEA. Not only was there a decline in the number of schools during the 1970s, there also was a decline in the NCEA membership. In 1967, for example, the NCEA elementary school membership stood at 9,275; ten years later the number had dropped to 5,832. The answer of the NCEA was to become more responsive to its constituents, to systematically collect data and document trends in Catholic education, to encourage more research in the field, and to build upon the conciliar traditions of Vatican II.

At the NCEA's seventy-fifth anniversary celebration in 1978, the NCEA president reflected on the previous decade of decline and the NCEA's new identity. John F. Meyers emphasized that developing new constituencies was the key to the future. He placed a particular importance on parental involvement. "That's what the NCEA is — the community of all those involved in Catholic education," he wrote. "As long as we can keep them working together and help them to be truly professional, I think we will do a great service to Catholic education."[47]

Meyers's confidence in the future survival of Catholic education — however broadly defined — was not shared in other quarters. To be sure, the rate of decline in the Catholic elementary school population was slowing, but the numbers continued to drop between 1974 and 1980. The continued decline was due in part to a smaller pool of Catholic school children, but that was small comfort. Parents and press alike continued to ask the same question in the late 1970s that they had asked a decade earlier. Could Catholic schools survive?[48]

But Catholic parents and educators had not given up hope. During the last half of the 1970s it was increasingly common for these advocates to ask a different question: will state or federal aid be the salvation of parochial schools? Many of these educators thought so. During these years it was increasingly common to find pastors and parents awash in the sea of paperwork required of grant and public aid applicants. These efforts were buoyed in part by the news that Senator Daniel P. Moynihan would introduce a federal tax credit proposal to further ease the burden of parochial school parents. The Supreme Court also offered some encouraging news in June 1977 in reaffirming earlier rulings that the states could provide textbooks, slides, and other educational materials to parochial schools.[49] Perhaps there was a light at the end of the decade.

Not everyone was pleased with these turns of events. Every hour spent in advocating or applying for or administering public funds was an hour away from the central mission of parochial education. "Sister is a bureaucrat," noted Mary Sherry in the pages of *America*. "The nun who once taught to conjugate verbs and then marched us over to novena had to become an expert in red tape." Is this what Catholic parents wanted? What would be the price of survival? "We have to admit that we have only two choices of action if we really want to have a Catholic school system," added Sherry. "We can put our whole effort into focusing on fighting for our 'rights' and work for a constitutional amendment to permit aid to religious schools. Or we can concentrate on the immediate job of passing on the tradition of our experience of God to the next generation with the resources our parents gave to us."[50]

Not many educators saw Sherry's choices as mutually exclusive. Indeed, many argued that without state aid, the schools would not survive to pass on "the tradition of our experience of God." Although the enrollment decline had leveled off by 1978, parochial education costs continued to rise. "Our continuing problem is maintaining adequate financial support," noted one educator in *U.S. News and World Report.* "Virtually all Catholic schools operate at a deficit with local parishes providing funds to cover expenses not paid by tuition. In some parishes, more than half of the budget is paid by church fees, and there are doubts that such economic aid can continue." Like it or not, most pastors and parents looked to public aid as their salvation.[51]

The champions in the campaign for public aid for parochial schools were an unlikely trio of politicians. Senator Daniel P. Moynihan, Democrat of New York, was joined by Senator Robert Packwood, Republican of Oregon, in proposing legislation to allow Catholic parents a tuition tax credit to partially cover the expense of sending their children to parish schools. They were later joined in their campaign by Ronald Reagan, the conservative former governor of California, who included a tuition tax credit proposal in his 1980 presidential campaign platform. These three men offered hope for many pastors and parents. If Moynihan and Packwood could convince their Senate colleagues to pass a bill and Ronald Reagan could be elected president, perhaps a tuition credit would become a reality. Certainly this was on the minds of Catholic educators as they looked to a new decade.[52]

※

It had been a generation of crisis in Catholic education in the years from 1950 to 1980. First there had been the crisis of growth in the 1950s when demand for parochial education had outstripped the available space. Then came the crisis of confidence in the 1960s when Catholic parents asked themselves if parochial schools were really necessary. Self-doubt in the 1960s was followed by the crisis of decline in the 1970s when devoted pastors and parents asked themselves if Catholic schools would survive. Although the answer by the end of the decade was an unequivocal yes, it was unclear who would pay the high cost of sustaining these schools. In fact, the economic burden of parochial education would be the predominant issue of parochial schooling in the 1980s. Neither pastors nor parents could be sure that the generation of crisis was really over.

Chapter 12

Catholic Schools Observed

W HEN PROFESSOR MYRON LEIBERMAN addressed the annual meeting of the National Catholic Educational Association in 1960, he focused on a major weakness in Catholic education. For all their intensive efforts to establish and sustain their parish schools, Catholic educators knew very little about the impact of the very institutions that they established. Were Catholic schools as effective as public schools in the secular education of children? Were Catholic schools divisive? Did parochial schools preserve religious faith and make their students into devout Catholics?

Leiberman noted that the answers to these questions lay in social science research. If parochial educators were to improve upon the work already accomplished, more scientific and sociological research into the nature of Catholic education was necessary. It was a message that the Catholic educational establishment took to heart. Over the next two decades there was an outpouring of first rate studies on the nature and effectiveness of Catholic schooling.[1]

Efforts to study Catholic education began well before the 1960s. In fact, the tradition went back to the 1930s with the publication of Leonard Koos's study *Private and Public Secondary Education*. On the basis of a state survey of Minnesota high school students, Koos concluded that Catholic high schools were academically inferior to public schools. Not surprisingly, Koos's conclusions were rejected by Catholic educators. Other studies published in the 1940s and the early 1950s show no significant difference in the effects of Catholic versus public education.[2]

The 1950s was a decade of intense American concern about divisions within American society. Among the questions asked by politicians and social critics alike was whether or not the Catholic schools were divisive. Paul Blanshard, one of the most vocal critics of the Catholic Church, argued that such schools were a negative influence on American society, and he was not alone in his beliefs. A conference of distinguished scholars sponsored by the Center for the Study of Democratic Institutions discovered that non-Catholics were deeply concerned that Catholic schools were a divisive force within American society. Yet all of this concern was based on personal opinion and prejudice; there was no sociological research on the impact of Catholic education. Without such studies the debate continued without any prospect of resolution.[3]

The public debate did catch the attention of two sociologists — one a Catholic priest and the other non-Catholic. In the mid-1950s, Joseph Fichter, a Jesuit sociologist, studied one Catholic school intensively and argued from the particular to the general. During his year-long case study of "St. Luke's," Fichter administered personality and intelligence tests to hundreds of sixth-, seventh-, and eighth-graders at the parish school and the same tests to hundreds of similar students from the local public school. In evaluating the tests, Fichter found few differences between the two groups except in the broad area of social concerns. Catholic students appeared to be *more* concerned about issues such as foreign aid, food and housing for the poor, integration, anti-Semitism, and related issues. Fichter concluded that parochial schools developed a deeper social awareness in children than did the public schools. Yet flaws in the research tools, a lack of controls for intelligence and economic status, led many social scientists and educators to reject Fichter's conclusions.[4]

A second study, one directed by Gerhard Lenski of the University of Michigan in 1958, focused on a carefully selected sample of Detroit residents. The Catholic participants in the

survey could be divided into two categories: (1) those who received more than half of their education in Catholic schools,
defined as those with a Catholic education, and (2) those who
received half or less of their education in Catholic schools, who
were defined as having a public education. Thirty-five percent
of the sample fit in category one and 65 percent in category
two.[5]

Before presenting his data and conclusions, Lenski was careful to underscore two "confounding factors" in his study. First
was the fact that particularly devoted Catholic families were
more likely to choose parochial education for their children
than those who were less devout. This factor was important
because it meant that the impact of parochial education on
devotionalism could not be controlled. It could well be a function of family influence rather than education. The second
factor was that devout Catholics frequently raised less devout
children, and in such families religious attitudes changed by
moving toward the norm. Lenski noted that these two factors
tended to cancel each other out and he hoped that simple com-
parisons between his two groups of Catholics would not be
skewed by these two factors.[6]

The first issue that Lenski addressed was the relative effectiveness of parochial schools in inculcating the principles of
the Catholic faith. In short, did Catholic schools make a *religious*
difference? If attendance at Mass was a significant measure, the
answer was a definite yes, but the numbers were not as great
as might be expected. Eighty-six percent of parochial school
graduates attended Mass as compared to only 71 percent of
Catholics with a public school education. The same difference
held for doctrinal orthodoxy. Sixty-eight percent of those with
a Catholic education were doctrinally orthodox compared with
56 percent of Catholics with a public education.[7]

The largest and most significant difference between the two
groups was the question of the Catholic Church being the
one true church. Seventy-eight percent of the parochial school
graduates responded positively to that question while only 61
percent of Catholics with a public school education were in

agreement. "Since so many aspects of Catholic faith and practice result from this doctrine," Lenski concluded, "it would seem from the Catholic standpoint, the successful inculcation of this one doctrine might be sufficient justification for maintaining the Catholic educational system."[8]

The second area explored by Lenski was loyalty to the Catholic subcommunity. In short, were Catholic schools divisive? Lenski's data was ambiguous. It was clear that a Catholic education did strengthen an individual's ties to the Catholic community; those with a Catholic education were one-third more likely to be highly involved in Catholic affairs than those Catholics with a public school education. It also was true that parochial school graduates were more likely to marry Catholics and limit their close friends to other Catholics. It seemed that parochial education built a bond that lasted a lifetime.

Because of such loyalties, Lenski hypothesized that parochial school graduates would be less tolerant of non-Catholics and have more unfavorable images of Protestants, Jews, and blacks. It was commonly believed among social scientists and educators that prejudice flourished in restricted groups. But Lenski found little evidence of prejudice in his study group. "Catholic images of Protestants and Jews are virtually unaffected by the school they attend," concluded Lenski. "The difference between the two categories of Catholics ranged from zero to two percentage points with no consistent directional pattern."[9]

A third area explored by Lenski was the Catholic viewpoint on moral and social issues such as birth control, gambling, divorce, drinking, and Sunday business openings. On many of these issues, the church had taken a strong stand, and Lenski's data showed that Catholic education did shape the views of the laity, particularly on issues related to the family. Sixty-eight percent of parochial school graduates said that it is always or usually wrong from the moral standpoint for married couples to practice birth control. This same group disapproved of divorce by a wide margin. With respect to gambling, drinking, or Sunday business, there were no significant differences between the two groups.[10]

A fourth area — economic behavior — generated some concern about Lenski's findings. Lenski discovered that middle-class Catholics who had a Catholic education rarely had positive attitudes toward work. "Evidently Catholic schools do not generally develop in boys those attitudes, values, beliefs, and intellectual orientation which make it possible for a man to enjoy the more demanding jobs in the modern metropolis."[11]

One final area explored by Lenski was family life. Not surprisingly, Lenski discovered that Catholic education strengthened the family ties of those in attendance. Catholic education also reinforced traditional values in which obedience to authority was more important than independent thinking. What surprised Lenski most was data that showed the families of those who attended parochial schools to be significantly smaller than those who attended public schools. Lenski postulated that parochial school graduates tended to marry later and that the sample was skewed. He predicted that by the end of the child-bearing period, the Catholic-educated families would have more children than their public counterparts.[12]

Both the Fichter and Lenski studies were important efforts to study the impact of Catholic education from different perspectives. Fichter studied a single school and generalized; Lenski surveyed a sample of schools from a major archdiocese. Of the two, Lenski's study had the greater credibility as a research model, but Fichter presented a greater variety of data. Both studies stimulated a general discussion of Catholic schools.

Perhaps the most important point of comparison are the findings of the two studies. Reassuring to both sociologists and others concerned about Catholic education was the fact that these studies led to the same conclusions about Catholic schools. Above all, Fichter and Lenski agreed that parochial schools were not a divisive force within American society. That issue seemed to be the major concern about Catholic education in the 1950s.

❖

For all of the good reviews received by the two books, there was no rush by sociologists to follow up the Fichter and Lenski studies. It was not until four years later — two years after Myron Leiberman criticized Catholic educators for their lack of research — that new studies began under the sponsorship of the University of Notre Dame and the National Opinion Research Center. In 1962, two teams of researchers went into the field to gather data. The first was led by William H. Connolly and Reginald A. Neuwien of the University of Notre Dame, and the second was led by Peter H. Rossi and Andrew M. Greeley of the University of Chicago. The two teams worked independently and approached their subject from different perspectives.[13]

Catholic Schools in Action, the Notre Dame study, was a statistical portrait of the parochial school system.[14] The data was collected nationwide, and thirteen leading dioceses were studied in depth. The authors attempted to be objective and informative, not evaluative, and there was no effort to compare the parochial schools with the public schools. The study focused on the religious and ethical implications of Catholic education as its prime concern and gathered valuable information on admissions policies, tuition costs, organization patterns, size, planned facilities, graduates, financial support, academic achievement, and the training of sister-teachers. Also addressed in an "Inventory of Catholic School Outcomes" was the status of religious instruction and the success of meeting stated goals. Finally, the study dealt with parental characteristics and their expectations for Catholic schooling.

The Notre Dame study was a collection of distinct strengths and weaknesses. Scholars acknowledged that it was a tremendous undertaking that collected data from 92 percent of all Catholic elementary schools, an extraordinary achievement. The ability of one team to collect this data was evidence that parochial schools were open to scholarly study. Second, reviewers acknowledged the cooperation of the hierarchy and the superintendents of schools. It was central to the value of the data. Finally, *Catholic Schools in Action* was valuable as a census or a statistical portrait of Catholic schools in 1962. The data would be useful as a baseline for future studies.[15]

Yet for all its achievement, the Notre Dame study was something of a scholarly flop. First, the four-year delay between the collection of the data and the publication of the study made it less valuable. Second, critics attacked the methods used to measure religious outcomes and student attitudes. Third, critics complained that some data — school visitations and personnel initiatives — were largely excluded from the book. Finally, the major problems facing Catholic education — centralization, financing, and the like — were not identified. The best that could be said of *Catholic Schools in Action* was that it pointed the way for additional studies.[16]

A second sociological study of Catholic education also appeared in 1966 and had a substantially greater impact than *Catholic Schools in Action.* Working through the National Opinion Research Center at the University of Chicago, Peter Rossi and Andrew M. Greeley studied and interviewed a representative national sample of 2,753 American Catholics and sent an additional thousand questionnaires to the homes of other American Catholics. Clearly this was to be a sociohistorical study since the respondents had attended school between 1910 and 1960, but Rossi and Greeley were confident that they could measure the outcomes and attitudes of former Catholic school students. They sought answers to three basic questions: Were Catholic schools effective in shaping the religious beliefs of its students? Were Catholic schools a divisive force in American society? Did Catholic schools impede the economic or occupational advancement of its students? All of these questions had been shaped by the debates of the 1950s.[17]

In response to the first question, Rossi and Greeley argued that Catholic schools had their greatest impact on students from very religious families, but that "those who come from moderately religious families, or non-religious families, are only influenced in a minimal way." Did this mean that Catholic schools were ineffective as religious educators? Not at all, assured Rossi and Greeley. Survey evidence showed that attendance at Mass and the sacraments was significantly higher among moderately religious Catholics if they attended Catholic schools rather than public schools.

The study also revealed that Catholic school students, regardless of their home religious life, were more likely to be informed about church doctrine and accept that doctrine than Catholics who had attended public schools. Given the fact that a stated goal of Catholic schools was to preserve the faith among its congregants, the Catholic schools had done a "reasonably good job." It was hardly a ringing endorsement of Catholic schools as a religious educator, and it was a conclusion that was widely disputed by Catholic educators and critics.[18]

The second question — are Catholic schools divisive? — was a throwback to the earlier work of Fichter and Lenski. It seemed that no matter how hard sociologists tried to inform the public on this matter, the more concerned the general public became that Catholic schools were somehow un-American. Rossi and Greeley confirmed what Fichter and Lenski stated earlier. "We could find no evidence," they wrote, "that the products of such a system were less involved in community activity, less likely to have friends from other religious groups, more intolerant in their attitudes, or less likely to achieve occupationally or academically. On the contrary, we found that they were slightly more successful in the world of study and work, and after the breaking point of college, much more tolerant."[19]

The third question — do Catholic schools impede the economic and occupational achievement of their students? — also elicited a negative response. In fact, among students from the higher socioeconomic groups, Catholic schooling was a distinct asset in academic and career advancement. There was some evidence that even Catholic students from the lowest economic groups were more academically oriented than their counterparts in the public schools. Rossi and Greeley added an interesting observation. "There are apparently two ways by which Catholics can succeed markedly," they wrote, "the path of alienation from the Catholic community and the path of integration into the Catholic subculture. The latter is somewhat more effective."[20] The authors hoped that this evidence would put this old and unfounded concern to rest.

Unlike the authors of the Notre Dame study, Rossi and Greeley were willing to speculate on the meaning of their data. Certainly, they argued, Catholic schools were "neither as bad as their most severe critics portray them, nor as good as they might be."[21] It was also true that Catholic education was not the most important element in the value formation and religious attitudes of Catholic children. The religiousness of parents and socioeconomic class were clearly more important. Furthermore, the authors added, "there is no evidence that Catholic schools have been necessary for the survival of American Catholicism."[22] Yet on balance, the schools seemed to have been worth the effort, and they concluded that these schools would continue and might even thrive.

The impact of the Rossi and Greeley study was far greater than the Notre Dame study. The book was widely reviewed and generated a variety of responses. The Catholic press hailed the book as evidence of the value and worth of Catholic schools. But the *New York Times* picked up only the negative implications of the study and claimed that the study proved that Catholic education was "wasted" on a quarter of its students. Daniel Callahan writing in *Commentary* disagreed with the study on the future of Catholic education. "Sooner or later," wrote Callahan, "it is bound to dawn on more Catholics that the much desired reform of the Church cannot take place as long as so much of its money is channeled into education."

Perhaps the most balanced and useful review appeared in the *Harvard Educational Review* in the summer of 1967. Even though the reviewer was disappointed that the authors qualified their conclusions "so as not to claim too much for their data or for the Catholic school system," he found the book to be "by far the most useful study that has ever been attempted in the area of American Catholic education."[23]

⁎

The publicity generated by the Rossi and Greeley study, as well as growing interest in the study of Catholic education, led to a gathering of 120 specialists at "Blueprint for the Future: The Washington Symposium on Catholic Education." The end result of the conference was a call for "well-designed programs of research and experiment aimed at obtaining reliable data to guide decisions about the most productive use of resources."[24] In 1967, the bishops acknowledged a need for more research "to evaluate our present endeavors, to project our future responsibilities, and to make a thorough inventory of our resources in personnel and finances. In 1969, the NCEA announced the establishment of a national data bank on Catholic elementary and secondary schools; the end result would be annual statistical summaries of Catholic education. The sociological observation of Catholic education became more frequent and accurate.[25]

The NCEA staff played a distinctive role in taking the pulse of Catholic education during the early 1970s. At annual meetings the staff and the membership joined in placing a special emphasis on the concept of community and how it could help to redefine the identity of Catholic schools. No longer "parochial" or parish-based, these new Catholic schools included larger communities of people — non-Catholics as well as Catholics.

As part of this search for a new identity, the former NCEA director of research, George Elford, published *The Catholic School in Theory and Practice,* a manual that emphasized the self-study process. "Elford's method," noted one review, "preserves the uniqueness of the particular school and at the same time the qualities which should characterize Catholic schools."[26] Not surprisingly, Elford placed a heavy emphasis on redefining the community for each school. Using Elford's method and its new data bank, the NCEA continued to monitor the vital signs of parochial education during the troubling years of enrollment decline in the 1970s.

The NCEA also served as a showcase for and promoted the controversial results of Andrew Greeley's follow-up study of Catholic education. Joined in this effort by colleagues Kathleen McCourt and William C. McCready, Greeley set out to determine the state of Catholic parochial education in 1974, ten years after the study he did with Peter Rossi. The results of Greeley's study, published in 1976 as *Catholic Schools in a Declining Church,* were widely discussed in both the Catholic and secular press as well as at a NCEA symposium called to discuss the book.

Greeley and his colleagues had both bad and good news to share with Catholic educators. Certainly the bad news was obvious. Enrollment at Catholic schools was in a state of decline and had been so since 1965. Greeley and his colleagues could not specifically pinpoint a single cause for the decline. "Some of the decline in elementary school enrollment may be due to changing patterns of family size and child spacing," they concluded. "Some of it is also the result of the disinclination of bishops and school administrators to replace inner-city parochial schools from which Catholic families have moved to new suburban schools. Finally, some of the decline may result from a conscious repudiation by Catholics of the idea of parochial schools or a decision that in one's own community, the public schools simply offer better opportunities."[27]

Greeley and his colleagues set out to learn more by asking a number of questions. One series had to do with the effectiveness of Catholic education. Does a Catholic education predispose Catholics to accept the changes that had taken place in the church since Vatican II? Has the effectiveness of parochial education on adult religious behavior changed since 1963? Are there still differences in the adult religious practices of Catholic children educated in parochial versus public schools? What will be the impact on the attitudes of parochial school graduates of the separation between popular Catholic practice and official church teaching?

Greeley and his colleagues also wanted to measure the changing attitudes of the laity toward Catholic schools. What is the nature of the change in Catholic commitment to and understanding of Catholic schools in the last decade? What financial commitment are American Catholics willing to make to sustain their commitment to parochial schools? What social classes are most likely to support parochial schools? It was a long list of questions, but Greeley had to have information before he and his colleagues could speculate on the cause or causes of the decline in Catholic school enrollment.

The answers that Greeley uncovered presented something of a paradox. The Catholic schools of 1974 were in a state of decline, yet they were held in uniformly high regard. How could this be so? Greeley and his colleagues dissected this dichotomy.

The measure of the decline was evident in the enrollment numbers. In 1964, Greeley and Rossi determined that 44 percent of Catholic children had been enrolled in parochial schools, but by 1974 the number had dropped to only 29 percent. "A school system originally intended to provide for the spiritual and secular education of all Catholic children," noted Greeley sadly, "is today living up to that promise for little more than one-quarter of its children."[28]

Which families were most likely to support parish schools? In general, the parents of parochial school students were in their forties and had themselves received a Catholic education. When asked why they sent their children to parish schools, these parents emphasized the quality of the secular education over religious instruction by a nearly two-to-one margin. This percentage was even higher for parents with some college education.

If college-educated parents believed that parochial schools offered superior secular education, why then were attendance levels declining? The answer, it seemed, had to do with availability. "More than selected background characteristics or particular attitude or value," noted Greeley, "the availability and cost of Catholic education seems to determine who uses the schools."[29]

Simply stated, Greeley and his associates discovered that

parish schools were not available to a substantial percentage of Catholic families. In the decade between his two studies, Greeley found that an increasingly large number of upwardly mobile Catholics had joined an earlier generation in moving to the suburbs. The parishes they established or moved to in the years after Vatican II had no parish schools. "The failure to build new schools," noted Greeley and his associates, "accounts for two-thirds of the decline in Catholic school attendance — almost all of this in the suburbs."[30]

Greeley was quick to admit that it did not necessarily follow that these suburban Catholic families would have sent their children to parish schools even if they were available. Are parents who send their children to parish schools more inclined to support such schools than parents who send their children to public schools? No, Greeley discovered. There was a high level of support for parish schools among all segments of the American Catholic population. Over two-thirds of all Catholics surveyed also believed that parents who sent their children to parish schools should receive a tax refund or credit for their tuition payments.

In their conclusion, Greeley and his colleagues underscored three points. First, Catholics across the board had high regard for parish schools. Among those families that used the schools, the high quality of the instruction was most important. Among those Catholic families who didn't use the parish schools, religious instruction was most important. In spite of this high regard, however, attendance figures continued to decline.

Their second and third points were interrelated and pointed to the reasons for the continuing decline. The reasons for the decline had nothing to do with the quality of Catholic schooling, he noted. The decline came because of high costs and inaccessibility. "We see Catholic school attendance in cities dropping because urban residents cannot afford the increasing tuition," he concluded, "and we see Catholic attendance in the suburbs dropping because parochial schools have not been built to keep up with the shift of the Catholic population from city to suburbs."[31]

In a critical, powerful, and personal afterword, Greeley assigned the responsibility for the decline in Catholic education to a failure in the leadership of the American church. Quite bluntly, Greeley called on the American bishops to "get out of the Catholic education business and turn the funding and the administration over to the laity." Greeley was not so naive as to think that the bishops would take such an action voluntarily. "To proceed on such a path," Greeley added, "would involve a substantial surrender of power by the bishops and by the parish clergy. No one likes to surrender power; no one likes to think of money, especially 'Catholic money' being spent without having much to say about how it is spent."[32]

Greeley was not optimistic about the fate of Catholic schooling in the next century. "Catholic schools, an extraordinarily powerful asset of the American Church, will go down the drain with hardly a voice raised in protest because the decision making system of the American Church has permitted a policy to evolve concerning the schools which virtually guarantees their continued decline. It is not a question of malice, but of systematic ignorance, that is to say built into the decision-making system."[33]

Greeley also was pessimistic that his report would do much to change the course or direction of this decline. He thought that it would receive some publicity in the press and become the focus of debate at religious sociological meetings, but that it would have little impact on the bishops, the ultimate decision-makers.

Greeley was right on target regarding the impact of the book. The results were discussed in the pages of the *New York Times* and other newspapers, and the book was widely and favorably reviewed in both secular and religious periodicals. Not surprisingly, the NCEA used the book as the focal point for several sessions at its 1976 meeting. Even though Greeley reiterated his findings in a more popular book in 1977, the bishops took little notice of his conclusions. As the end of the decade approached, schools in urban parishes were closed, but few new ones were built in the suburbs.[34]

※

Greeley's pessimistic assessment notwithstanding, other sociologists found some reasons to be proud of the parochial school
system. The northern and eastern European Catholics who had
fled urban parishes for new ones in the suburbs had been replaced by Hispanic and African American Catholic families.
Children of color were now sitting behind the desks of urban Catholic schools. Even non-Catholics in the ghetto were
sending their children to parish schools. In fact the majority of
children in the schools of many parishes were non-Catholics!

Responding to this trend, several sociologists assessed the
impact of parochial schools on American minorities. In a study
of Mexican American children in San Antonio, Philip Lampe
measured the effects of parish schooling on acculturation.
Based on surveys with seven hundred students conducted
over two years, Lampe found that parish school students were
substantially more acculturated than their public school counterparts. He also found that parish school students were more
likely to have non-Hispanic friends, were more willing to date
and marry outside their own ethnic group, were more willing
to identify with the WASP value system, showed significantly
less prejudice against other ethnic groups, and were more willing to fulfill their civic duties such as voting, military service,
and obedience to the law. In short, Hispanics in the parish
schools were more assimilated into the larger society of San
Antonio than those who attended public schools.[35]

Social scientists also assessed the impact of parish school-
ing on African American children. A team of researchers from
Marquette University focused on fifty-four schools in six cities:
Washington, D.C., New Orleans, Chicago, Milwaukee, New
York, and Los Angeles. Each school had to have at least 70
percent minority enrollment to be included in the study.[36]

The study revealed some startling information. First, the
Marquette team confirmed Greeley's earlier finding that the
escalating cost of tuition was an enormous burden on minority families. Average tuition at these schools in 1978–79 was

only $400, but fully half of the families had an annual income of less than $10,000. "The ability and willingness of genuinely poor families to meet the cost of tuition at private inner-city schools is one of the remarkable findings of the study," noted the team.[37]

The authors also explored the reasons for the extraordinary parental demand for private schools. In almost every case, the authors found, the parents believed that private and parochial schools offered a superior education to the education offered in inner-city public schools. In short, "the inner-city private schools have become a functional alternative to quality suburban schools."[38]

The authors further found that a substantial majority of the parents (78 percent) agreed that religious classes were important, and almost all parents (94 percent) agreed that learning moral values was essential to a good education. Both, of course, were offered only in private and parochial schools.

Yet these parochial school children were not necessarily devout Catholics or even came from Catholic families. Of the families in the survey, a full third claimed to be Protestant (31 percent) or had no religion (2 percent). Among African American families with children in parochial schools, a majority (53 percent) were Protestant. Even among Catholic families, religion was of only modest importance with only 54 percent reporting that they attended Mass each week. Clearly the desire for parochial education had more to do with the quality of the secular instruction than it did with religious indoctrination.

Parents also were drawn to parochial schools because they were more responsive to their interests and concerns. "The requirement in many schools of active parental participation and involvement in school activities also appears to foster among parents an exceptional loyalty to the school and a willingness to make extraordinary sacrifices on its behalf."[39] Parents identified with parochial schools as their school whether they were Catholic or not.

What about the charge that private schools — even inner-city parochial schools — were elitist, selecting only the best students and rejecting those with discipline or learning difficulties? The Marquette team found little evidence of this elitism. To be sure, these schools were distinctive, placing heavy emphasis on moral values and discipline. But there was no evidence that these schools rejected students because of their personal problems. "The data of our study indicates that parental motivation is the criterion foremost in the minds of school officials, both for first time enrollees and public school transfers." Indeed, the team found that 80 percent of the schools in the survey had accepted public school transfers and 56 percent of those schools had accepted transfer students with discipline problems.[40]

Most important, parochial schooling had a distinctly positive impact on the behavior and academic achievement of its students. "The data indicates that school factors appear to compensate for family background deficits," noted the Marquette team. "For example, the data shows that the school has the greatest impact on improving behavior for children from poor homes, with rather less impact on those from middle-class backgrounds."[41]

On academic achievement, the results were less clear. In fact, after converting the diversity of testing instruments used in these schools to a common scale, the team found a wide range of performance as measured by standardized tests. The range, the authors speculated, was due in large part to the diverse family backgrounds of these students. It was clear that private inner-city schools had a significant impact on the behavior, if not the achievement, of all of its students.

The Marquette researchers were very pessimistic about the future of inner-city parochial education. They identified three threats to the continued existence of these schools. First was the declining availability of teachers due to the salary differential between private and public schools. Second was the deteriorating physical condition of the private school buildings in inner cities. Finally, the authors saw the failure of government at all levels to provide financial relief as the major threat.

Without a major infusion of funds, these schools would soon close, thereby cutting off the only viable alternative to public education in most major cities.[42]

Yet the Marquette team underestimated the tenacity of Catholic parents in general and inner-city parents in particular. Statistics for the last three years of the 1970s showed a modest but significant increase in the numbers of students enrolled in Catholic elementary schools. Even more interesting was the increase in the percentage of minority children in these schools, a trend that continued to increase over the decade. To be sure, the decade showed a substantial decline, especially in the years from 1970 to 1974, but the decline abated in the last few years of the decade. Perhaps sociologists and others observing Catholic schools had identified a new trend. A few educators were cautiously optimistic about the future.[43]

The formal and systematic evaluation of parochial education was a reflection of many factors. First among these was the general trend among all educators to scientifically measure the impact of education in the postwar years. It was not enough for Catholic educators to teach reading, writing, and religion. Were Catholic schools providing an educational experience as good as that offered in the public schools? Parents, pastors, and educators wanted to know, and they encouraged social scientists to find the answers.

A second reason for the number of sociological studies of Catholic schools during the years from 1950 to 1980 was the rapid rise and decline of enrollment figures over three decades. During the 1950s and the first half of the 1960s, sociologists wanted to know how parochial schools were coping with the influx of millions of students. In the years that followed these social scientists examined how the schools coped with the flight of millions of students. Catholic schooling was anything but static, and this rapid change appealed to sociologists as a subject of study.

Overall, the range of studies of Catholic education was a

recognition by social scientists of the significance of this alternative to public schooling. A social movement that educated more than 10 percent of the children in the United States and was funded completely by private funds was worthy of serious study. It was a recognition that was long overdue.

Chapter 13 _____

The Church-State-School Question Revisited

_____

T HE STRUGGLE over public funding for parochial schools in the postwar decades was calm and orderly compared with the previous three decades. Gone were the accusations that parish schooling was un-American and therefore unworthy of community support. Also gone, however, were the local government efforts to support parish schools through the travails of the Great Depression.

The conflict over public funding for parochial schools in the years from 1920 to 1950 had come to a dramatic climax in the landmark Supreme Court case *Everson v. Board of Education*. In that decision the Court had hoped to end all of the controversy and define the constitutional limits of public aid to parochial schools.

The Court proposed a three-part test to determine the constitutionality of any particular type of aid. To be constitutional, such public aid could not directly support or promote a religious denomination, it could not entangle the state in the regulation of religion, and the activity to be funded must have a direct benefit to the state. With these three provisions, the Court hoped to still the cacophony of voices for and against public aid to parochial schools.[1]

But the *Everson* decision had almost the opposite effect. Over the next four decades advocates and opponents of state aid argued among themselves, with state legislatures, and with the courts over the application of the *Everson* provisos. The Court had not prohibited public aid. In fact, the *Everson* decision specifically permitted states to provide bus transportation for parochial school students. Not surprisingly, the question in the mind of parochial school advocates was whether or not there were any other types of aid that also were constitutional. The next forty years would be consumed by legislative and legal efforts to specifically define the limits of the Everson decision.[2]

※

Throughout the 1950s, the states and local communities struggled to work within the confines of the *Everson* decision. In Oregon, the state courts allowed special education classes at public expense to children attending parochial schools.[3] In Illinois, the state attorney general ruled that parochial schools were entitled to public nursing services. In New York and Illinois, state legislatures passed legislation to include parochial schools in publicly supported driver education programs. In California, the state argued over whether or not public truant officers could enforce state compulsory education laws to return truants to parochial schools. The number of variations on the *Everson* decision seemed endless.[4]

One constant, however, was a gradual and sustained decline in hostility between Catholics and non-Catholics over the question of public aid to parochial schools. Beginning in the mid-1950s and continuing through the election of John F. Kennedy as president in 1960, a climate of mutual respect grew in both the Catholic and the non-Catholic press. By the end of the 1950s, the old order of hate and hostility as fostered by Protestants and Other Americans United (POAU) and other groups at the end of the 1940s was gone. The stage was set for a renewed discussion of public aid for parochial schools as part of the election campaign of 1960.[5]

As the election season of 1960 approached it became increasingly likely that the Democratic candidate would be the Catholic senator from Massachusetts, John F. Kennedy. On a political balance sheet, Kennedy had a long list of pluses — he was young, vigorous, charismatic, and rich. He was an effective public speaker with good ideas who presented a striking contrast to the grandfatherly figure of Dwight D. Eisenhower.

But Kennedy also had a long list of negatives. His youth and lack of experience also worked against him in some circles. And then there was his religion; no Catholic had ever been elected president. Could Kennedy be trusted? Would he be subservient to the pope? Many Americans were uneasy about this young man.[6]

As a candidate, Kennedy used every opportunity to address the concerns of non-Catholics. He took their fears seriously and responded directly. In March of 1959 — more than fifteen months before the Democratic national convention — Kennedy gave an interview to *Look* magazine and declared himself a champion of the separation of church and state. "Whatever one's religion in private life may be," Kennedy told the reporter, "for an office holder, nothing takes precedence over the oath to uphold the Constitution and all its parts — including the First Amendment and the strict separation of church and state." It was a clear, unequivocal statement, far more direct than one given by the previous Catholic candidate, Alfred E. Smith, in 1928.[7]

Later in the interview, Kennedy addressed the question of public aid for parochial schools, an issue that had not come up in the campaign of 1928. "There can be no question of Federal funds being used for support of parochial or private schools," Kennedy stated bluntly. "It is unconstitutional under the First Amendment as interpreted by the Supreme Court. I am opposed to the Federal Government's extending support to sustain any church or schools. As for such fringe matters as busses, lunches, and other services, the issue is primarily social and economic and not religious."[8] With this one bold statement, Kennedy dashed the hopes of millions of Catholics who had prayed that one of their own would champion public aid for parochial schools.

The Catholic press responded to the *Look* interview with dismay. "It is humiliating for Catholics," noted the editors of *America*, "that even a man with the brilliant war record of Senator Kennedy thought himself obliged to answer questions that everyone knows are the remnants of the bad old days of Know-Nothingism."[9] *America* went on to criticize Kennedy for not standing up for parochial schools — "an elementary question of equal treatment under the law." The editors of the *Catholic World* agreed, noting that Kennedy "will find few Catholics in agreement with his views. To refuse to grant a Catholic parent his proper share of tax funds seems to strike down a precious right guaranteed by the First Amendment."[10] The Kennedy statement was a bitter blow, but parochial school advocates were not about to give up.

The battle over public aid to parochial education was rejoined shortly after Kennedy was inaugurated in January 1961. Just after his election, Kennedy appointed a distinguished panel of educators to recommend major legislative proposals on education, and among the panel's recommendations was a general aid program for public schools, but nothing for private schools. The report received little attention in the press and was generally ignored in the administration. But Catholic leaders — particularly Cardinal Francis Spellman — took this report as an ominous sign. Once again Catholic schools were to be shut out of the government's aid package.[11]

Spellman could not let yet another example of government injustice go by without a comment. Not quite two weeks after the report was released and three days before the inauguration, Spellman let forth with a bombastic salvo that reverberated throughout the country. "I believe and I state that these recommendations are unfair to most parents of the nation's 6,800,000 parochial and private school children," thundered Spellman.[12]

The administration had no comment on the Spellman controversy. Certainly the cardinal's views had no effect on the president's education proposal, and on February 20 Kennedy outlined his proposal in a special message to Congress. The message made mention of parochial schools only to exclude them from the program. "In accordance with the clear prohibition of the Constitution," Kennedy noted, "no elementary or secondary school funds are allocated for constructing church schools or paying church school teachers' salaries and thus non-public school children are rightfully not counted in determining the funds each state will receive for public schools."[13] The president clearly articulated the position opposite that of Spellman and the parochial school leadership.

The passage of this legislative package was not a foregone conclusion, however. To ease the bill's passage, the administration linked the public school assistance provisions with the renewal of a popular program of aid for areas that educated the children of military servicemen.[14] But the bill was blasted in the pages of the diocesan press, and congressional representatives, especially those from the big cities of the Northeast, began to receive large quantities of mail opposing the bill.[15] Catholics — who made up 25 percent of the nation — seemed to be united in the opposition to the first major legislative package of the first Catholic president of the United States.

At first Kennedy tried to ignore or dismiss the Catholic opposition. At a press conference on March 1, he turned aside questions about aid for parochial schools, and he was criticized in the press for not addressing the issue. At his March 8 press conference, however, the president expressed great sympathy for parents who bore the "heavy burden" of supporting parochial schools. But he reemphasized his belief that such aid was clearly unconstitutional, as underscored in the Everson case.[16]

In retrospect it is not surprising that Kennedy would hold a position so at odds with the Catholic community. The president was a millionaire's son who had gone to private preparatory schools and then on to Harvard. He had never attended parochial or Catholic schools and had only a few friends who were Catholic. "He was not a product of expressly Catholic institutions and culture who had gone into politics," noted Hugh D. Price in one contemporary account of the conflict. "Rather he was a politician who happened — privately to his advantage — to be Catholic."[17]

The hearings on the education bill were tense and promised

to reopen old interdenominational wounds. Protestants who testified before the Senate flatly opposed any consideration of aid for parochial schools and accused Cardinal Spellman of "compelling" non-Catholics to support a wholly controlled function of the Roman Catholic Church. The Catholic community, as represented by Monsignor Frederick Hochwalt of the NCEA, called for a balanced approach — aid for both public and parochial schools.[18]

As is often the case in legislative conflict, Congress looked for a compromise. Congressman John McCormack of Massachusetts and Senator Wayne Morse of Oregon queried constitutional scholars on the limits of aid to parochial schools. What about low-interest loans to aid in the construction of parochial schools? What about grants to all schools — public and private — to assist in the construction of mathematics, science, and modern foreign language classrooms? The administration seemed willing to go along with the idea of loans for the construction of special purpose classrooms. The outstanding issue was how to thread such a bill through the Congress.[19]

What happened surprised everyone. As the education bills moved through the appropriate committees, public opinion on all aid to education shifted from pro to con. Congress began to receive mail from constituents opposing aid for public as well as parochial schools. The final blow came in the House Rules Committee on July 18 when all three education bills were tabled. Speaker of the House Sam Rayburn told the president that the education bills were "as dead as slavery."[20]

The failure of the school aid package to pass the Congress brought recriminations of all sorts. Many — including Senator Morse — blamed the Catholic community. Others argued that the Catholic resistance was inevitable. "The one point on which all could agree was the lack of Presidential leadership," added Price. "The President was simply not prepared to jeopardize his whole legislative program — and perhaps his chances for reelection — by a bitter fight to the death for aid to education."[21] Aid to both public and private schools seemed dead not only for that legislative session, but also for the decade.

❖

The death of the 1961 education bill did not stanch the interest in finding some sort of answer to the church-state-school question. Early in 1962, the president tried once again to introduce a public education aid bill; once again, the Catholic community opposed it, and the bill went nowhere. Congress had no interest in repeating the debacle of the previous session.

The landslide election of Lyndon Johnson in 1964 set the stage for the next effort to provide aid to parochial schools. In addition to his own overwhelming election victory, Johnson won substantial majorities in both houses of Congress. Just as important, Johnson was a creature of Congress and a man determined to succeed where his predecessors had failed; he would pass an education bill.

Yet Johnson was shrewd; he would not try to ram through a bill opposed by either side of this conflict. He carefully crafted a bill that would satisfy both the National Education Association and the U.S. Catholic Conference. The focus of the bill was to help impoverished school children, no matter where they enrolled. The program would be administered by the public schools for the benefit of all children including those enrolled in parochial schools. This is not to say that the bill did not have opponents. Indeed, a few Democrats were uncertain of its value.[22]

What assured victory for the Elementary and Secondary Education Act of 1965 was the unprecedented support of an unlikely coalition of private groups. Some groups, such as the National Education Association and the National Council of Churches, supported the bill for fear that they would be excluded from the congressional decision-making process if they remained rigidly opposed to any assistance to parochial school students. Other groups, such as the U.S. Catholic Conference, had hoped for more general aid to parochial schools, but had no objection to the bill. After the debacle in 1961 both sides were ready for compromise. Both sides knew as well that they were dealing with a different president in a different time.

"The overwhelming victory of the president and the party in 1964," noted one Johnson aide, "had the effect of forcing the pressure groups to come to terms with each other."[23] With a diverse coalition of private groups in support of the bill, it passed on April 9, 1965, only eighty-seven days after it had been introduced in the Congress. "For nearly one hundred years," notes historian Diane Ravitch, "attempts to pass federal aid to education had failed. Approval was made possible at last because of the broad consensus on the necessity of improving the educational opportunities of poor children."[24] It was a historic first step in providing aid to parochial school children, but not to the school themselves.

It also was to be the only federal support for parochial school students in the postwar decades. No other aid package for private or parochial schools was able to muster the support needed for passage. The ESEA proved to be a symbolic but hollow victory for those who hoped that this historic legislation was only the beginning of an expanded aid program.[25]

❈

Catholic activists eventually shifted their attention away from the federal government toward state legislatures. The most organized and powerful lobby within the states were the hundreds of chapters of a relatively new organization known as Citizens for Educational Freedom. Founded in 1959, CEF was a group of parents and educators "dedicated to the cause of securing freedom and equality in education." The group was remarkably successful at making their case in state capitals across the Midwest and Northeast, the states with very large Catholic populations. CEF, for example, was instrumental in the passage of "Fair Bus Laws" in Michigan, Ohio, Pennsylvania, and Wisconsin in the middle 1960s. Later in the decade CEF forces succeeded in winning various forms of state aid to parochial schools in Pennsylvania, Ohio, Rhode Island, Connecticut, and New York.[26]

The efforts of the CEF and other Catholic lobbying efforts were not without opposition. Groups such as Protestants and

Other Americans United, the American Jewish Congress, and the American Civil Liberties Union argued that such state aid violated the First Amendment of the U.S. Constitution and vowed to fight these programs all the way to the Supreme Court. Little did either side realize at the time how much of a battleground the Court would become over the next decade.

The first of the church-state-school cases to reach the high court was *Flast v. Cohen* (1968). A coalition of organizations from New York sued the U.S. Department of Health, Education, and Welfare, arguing that taxpayers regardless of religious faith had legal standing to sue the federal government over the use of federal funds for religious schools. More specifically, the question to be answered was whether or not a taxpayer could challenge the constitutionality of legislation such as the ESEA even if the plaintiffs were not personally affected by the law. In an eight-to-one decision, the Court agreed with the plaintiffs thereby setting the stage for fractious litigation over the church-state-school issues. It had been more than twenty years since the *Everson* case had supposedly ended the debate.[27]

The Court decided a second school aid case that same session in favor of parochial schools, a decision that surprised the legal community and the nation. In *Board of Education v. Allen*, the Court affirmed the constitutionality of a New York program that required local school districts to furnish textbooks from state-approved lists to private and parochial schools within their districts. Technically, the books remained the property of the local school districts, but the books would remain in the private schools until they were no longer usable. The program had been eagerly passed by the legislature as a way of pleasing New York's large and powerful Catholic community.[28]

At the end of the 1968 term, Court watchers on church-state issues must have been perplexed. The Court had opened the door for more taxpayers to sue their governmental agencies over the use of tax funds for parochial schools. At the same time, the Court seemed to approve of at least some form of aid — certainly textbooks and maybe more. *Flast v. Cohen* and *Board of Education v. Allen* led to numerous new state aid programs followed by numerous lawsuits.

⁂

Many Court watchers saw in the *Allen* decision the harbinger of other pro-church decisions to come. With a new Chief Justice in Warren Burger and a second case accommodating religion, many feared that aid to private schools could well be constitutional by the next Court term. But these fears were unwarranted. In retrospect it is clear that the Court was not willing to go much farther than schoolbooks and bus transportation. Cases decided by the Court over the next seven years would further *restrict* — not expand — the types of aid open to parochial schools.

The first of these cases was known as *Lemon v. Kurtzman*, an amalgamation of three separate cases concerning the "purchase" of parochial schoolteacher services by the states of Pennsylvania and Rhode Island. In simple terms, the legislatures of these heavily Catholic states were seeking a legal way to supplement the salaries of underpaid parochial schoolteachers. Both legislatures had high hopes that the new Burger Court would look favorably on these programs.[29]

But the Catholic education community was in for a shock. Speaking for a majority of the Court, Burger outlined three conditions that must be met for a school aid program to be constitutional. Burger noted that all such programs must have an adequate secular purpose, that the programs could neither advance nor inhibit religion, and that the programs could not excessively entangle the government with religious institutions. Burger and his majority noted that the Pennsylvania and Rhode Island programs met the first two conditions, but failed the third. These programs were, therefore, unconstitutional.[30]

The Court did not accept any school aid cases in 1972, but 1973 was another story. The Court accepted no less than half a dozen church-state cases, five of which had direct implications for aid to parochial schools. The first of these cases, a reprise from 1971, also was known as *Lemon v. Kurtzman*, but was called "Lemon II" to distinguish it from the 1971 case. Speaking again for the majority, Burger allowed the Pennsylvania and Rhode Island parochial schools to keep the funds that they had received from the states between the establishment of the programs and the Court decision of 1971. It was an accommodationist decision that gave the champions of those schools the hope that the decisions to follow would reflect the same spirit.[31]

Once again supporters of parochial schools were disappointed. In the next case, *Levitt v. Committee for Public Education and Religious Liberty*, the Court held that it was unconstitutional for the state of New York to reimburse private and parochial schools for the cost of administering state-mandated services such as compulsory attendance laws, the compilation of health records, and the proctoring of Regents examinations and other mandated pupil evaluation tests. Once again the Court ruled that the program excessively entangled the government in the operation of parochial schools. In addition, the Court was critical of the fact that the compensation did not specifically exclude teacher-prepared tests and that compensation for all services were entangled. New York would have to do a better job of segregating the aid to be provided for truly secular services.[32]

In this decision the Chief Justice and his majority shifted positions. Their concern about aid to parochial schools was more than a matter of excessive entanglement; the Court also was concerned about the other two conditions noted in the *Lemon* test: most specifically direct aid to religious activities. States must be exceedingly careful, the Court implied, to insure that any public funds granted to the schools could not be used for parochial schools. Once again, the accommodationists' hopes of a bond between church, state, and school were dashed.[33]

Two other cases were handed down on the same day as the Levitt decision. Each of these cases further clarified the Lemon test. In *Committee for Public Education and Religious Liberty v. Ny-*

quist, the Court ruled that it was clearly unconstitutional for the State of New York to provide monies for the maintenance and repairs of facilities and equipment in nonpublic schools with concentrations of impoverished students. It was direct aid to the schools, and there were no restrictions on how the equipment or facilities could be used. Although Burger would have allowed two other provisions in the New York law — tuition grants and tax deductions — he could not persuade a majority of the Court. The majority found all three of the provisions of the New York law to be unconstitutional.[34]

This majority also held in a second case handed down that day. In *Sloan v. Lemon,* the Court struck down a Pennsylvania law that provided tuition relief to parents of parochial school students. The Court was not persuaded by the reasoning of the Pennsylvania legislature that the bill had the effect of assisting the state in reducing the rising cost of public education, that the rising cost of education threatened parents' constitutional rights to choose nonpublic education for their children, and that nonpublic schools were an asset to the state in preventing higher education costs. To the Court, the Pennsylvania program was nothing more than a conduit for funds to be passed to parochial schools.[35]

The decision made it clear to all but the most committed parochial school advocates that the Court would not consider any accommodationist plans beyond textbooks and bus transportation as outlined in the *Allen* and *Everson* decisions. The Court emphasized once again that the test to be applied was the one articulated in the first *Lemon* decision. Most justices applied this three-part test very strictly.

The 1973 Court term dealt a severe blow to parochial school advocates. "Hardly any Catholic educator," reported *Newsweek,* "denied that last week's decision by the Supreme Court to forbid virtually all public aid to parochial schools was a shuddering blow to the very existence of parochial schools."[36] The depression within the Catholic community was pandemic. "I have been working on school aid for fifteen years, "wrote Father Charles Whelan in the pages of *America,* and now there is

an almost impenetrable barrier to almost any new form of substantial assistance for education in non-public schools. Maybe
I should find something better to do than die in the citadel."[37]
It was the lowest point in the long struggle for accommodation
between church, state, and school.

⁂

And yet parochial school advocates were not about to give up
on their schools or their campaign for public aid. As definitive
as the Court's decisions seemed to be, Catholics had not lost
their faith that an accommodationist perspective would prevail. "We started this school system 100 years ago," remarked
one school superintendent, "and it's not going to disappear today."[38] Indeed it would not, but the Court decisions of 1973
made it clear that Catholics would have to pay for their schools
without meaningful public assistance. "People have been expecting someone else to bail us out," said one priest. "Now we
realize that we will have to do it on our own."[39]

The slim glimmer of hope for accommodation came in the
form of voucher plans. Under such arrangements all children
in a district would be issued "vouchers" to be applied for education at the school of the parents' choosing, either public
or private. Participating schools would need to meet certain
standards for facilities, teacher certification, and curricula and
would have to insure that there was no racial discrimination
in admission. Since the plan was not in existence — indeed
it was only a concept — it was not clear if the Court would
find it acceptable using the Lemon test. But it was an idea that
gave Catholics hope. "I may not live to see the day of victory,"
concluded Father Whelan, "but I am not going to give up."[40]

The unwillingness of the Catholic community to abandon
its cause was evident in the number of church-state-school
cases filed with the Court during the rest of the decade. Legislatures in Pennsylvania, New York, and Ohio persisted in
passing legislation that granted goods and services to parochial school students; and in many cases, the Court passed
judgment on the constitutionality of these services. In *Meck v.*

Pittenger (1975), the Court reaffirmed the loan of textbooks to parochial schools, but outlawed the loan of other types of instructional materials and forbade the donation of counseling and testing services.

Two years later in *Wolman v. Walter* (1977), the Court allowed Ohio to provide standardized testing, diagnostic services, therapeutic work, and remedial instruction to parochial school students if these services were provided away from school grounds. But the *Wolman* decision also reaffirmed the ban on the loan of instructional materials other than textbooks and limited the use of public bus transportation to trips to and from school.

Finally, in *Committee for Public Education and Religious Liberty v. Regan* (1980), the Court reconsidered the right of New York State to pay nonpublic schools for costs incurred in complying with some state-mandated requirements such as testing, reporting, and record keeping.[41]

The Court decisions of the last half of the 1970s were an effort on behalf of a working majority of justices to apply the *Lemon* test to specific types of aid and services to nonpublic schools. What was clear to both sides in the litigation was that there would be no accommodation on substantial programs of public aid for parochial schools. There could and would be some accommodation at the edges, however, as was evident in the *Meck, Wolman,* and *Regan* decisions.

Yet three decades of Court decisions and struggle had meant little. "The Court has continued to be stingier than the Constitution requires or sound educational policy would suggest," wrote the editors of *America* at the end of the 1970s. "In particular, the Court's distinctions between textbooks and instructional materials and between publicly funded teachers in mobile vans and the same teachers in special classrooms in parochial schools makes neither logical nor practical sense. As a result, the efforts to expand categories of legitimate assistance should be continued."[42] Indeed, they would as Catholics took hope in the promises of Ronald Reagan to press their causes for tuition assistance in the 1980s.

❖

Reagan's landslide victory, made possible in part by Catholic votes, did not insure greater aid for parochial education. The new president's support for tuition tax credits was half-hearted, and little was done until late in 1982. Many Catholics were disheartened; others were cynical.

All Catholics were given hope, however, by a decision by the Supreme Court late in 1983 to address the legality of tuition tax deductions. Even though tax deductions were not the same as tax credits, it was clear to all involved that the high court's decision would have a significant impact on the future of tuition tax credits. If the courts ruled that deductions for private school tuition were unconstitutional, there was no chance for tuition tax credits. But if the court upheld such deductions, the tuition tax credit campaign would receive an enormous boost.

Catholics were heartened by the decision. "It is the first time that the Court has approved any program of substantial tuition relief for the parents of private school students," noted the *Washington Post*.[43] Tuition tax advocates claimed victory and public school advocates feared a loss of resources. Yet the specific language of the opinion revealed that neither side was quite right.

In upholding the Minnesota law in *Mueller v. Allen*, the Court did not break with the church-state principles laid down in previous decisions. Specifically, the majority agreed that the Minnesota law had not violated the three-part test articulated in *Lemon v. Kurtzman* in 1971, nor did the law parallel the abuses the Court outlined in its *Nyquist* decision. In short, the *Mueller* decision was not to be the basis for a wholesale reordering of the church-state-school issue.[44]

The Court singled out two provisions of the Minnesota law that, on its face, made it different from previous tuition aid programs. First was the fact that the tuition tax deduction was only one of many tax deductions in the state code. The Court noted it had always allowed the states broad latitude depending on local conditions to redistribute the tax burden. Second, the Court noted that the deduction for educational expenses was available to all parents — those who sent their children to public schools as well as those sending their children to private or parochial schools.

Even though Catholics were pleased with the Court's decision in the *Mueller* case, few were willing to predict that federal aid was a foregone conclusion. The editors of *America* would only go so far as to say there is "the slightest hint that a voucher system might be acceptable." Others noted that sharp divisions over the issue remained in both the Court and the Congress. The most likely impact of the decision, noted Jim Castelli, "will be that as many as half the states — particularly those with heavy Catholic populations in the Northeast and Midwest — which have been frustrated in previous efforts to help private schools — may simply pass local versions of the Minnesota law. If that happened, it could take the steam out of the push for a federal law."[45]

This muted optimism also came from Capitol Hill. Tuition tax credit supporters such as Robert Dole and Daniel Patrick Moynihan stated the obvious — that the decision did not hurt the chances for tuition tax credits and may have helped. The *Mueller* decision, added Moynihan, "is not as such a decision for or against tuition tax credits. It is simply a statement that this is an issue that may be decided free of any constitutional constraint."[46]

But two years later, Catholics faced two more Court decisions that undermined the cause for tuition tax credits. The two cases were similar in nature; both involved cities where teachers paid with tax monies were sent into private schools to provide educational services. In Grand Rapids, the school board hired teachers to provide physical education, art, music, language, remedial reading, and other special courses in Catholic and Lutheran schools. The board argued that such courses were supplementary to the state-required curriculum. In New York City, the school board sent teachers into parochial schools to provide federally funded and mandated remedial reading programs for disadvantaged children.

Were either or both efforts constitutional? Certainly the Catholic community thought so. But a careful count of how the justices would divide on the issue revealed a narrow majority, either for or against. It would be close. The Court heard oral arguments in early December 1984 with the promise of a decision by the middle of the summer.[47]

The two decisions — *Grand Rapids v. Ball* and *Aguilar v. Felton* — came down like thunder on the first day of July. In a word, the Court said no to any direct aid to parochial schools. A narrow five to four majority rejected the claim that such aid performed a public service. "Any proposal to extend direct governmental aid to parochial schools alone," wrote the Court in the *Aguilar* decision, "is likely to spark political disagreement from taxpayers who support public schools." Furthermore, the majority agreed that "aid to parochial schools necessarily required a degree of government involvement that is apt to lead to the breaking point." This same majority rejected the Grand Rapids program as a clear violation of the First Amendment.[48]

The reaction among Catholic leaders and other supporters was anger. "In the plain language of the poor," wrote Bishop William McManus, "once again we've been shafted." What angered McManus and other Catholics was the fact that the Court was utterly unimpressed by fifteen years of evidence that their fears about what might happen to church-state relations had not in fact occurred.[49] Somehow, a way had to be found to provide these vital services to the poor. "Depriving the Church of these programs isn't hurting the Church," noted one teacher. "It's depriving children of services they're entitled to."[50]

The beginning of the new school year was a time of reassessment for Catholics. "In some ways we're back to square one after twenty years of trying to make this thing work," noted an assistant superintendent of the St. Louis parochial schools. Indeed, the *Aguilar* and *Felton* decisions had cut off any possibility of direct aid to parochial schools. If Catholic schools were to receive aid, it would necessarily be indirect aid. "We've tried a lot of options," noted one official. "We know of things that have worked and things that haven't worked. Now were back to the drawing board to try to negotiate a new plan."[51]

But a new plan was not forthcoming in 1985 or during the rest of the decade. To be sure, Catholic leaders discussed the possibility of building satellite classrooms on public sites and have children walk back and forth between the satellite and the parish school. The Reagan administration mused about the possibility of direct grants or vouchers to families with children in need of special services. But neither idea had much support and both were dismissed as unworkable, unconstitutional, or both.

Public aid to parochial schools was a dead issue on Capitol Hill at the end of the decade, but Catholic leaders were unwilling to give up on finding a plan. "We have to realize legislative efforts take a long time." noted Father Thomas Gallagher, the education secretary of the U.S. Catholic Conference, "It's difficult to mobilize Catholic school parents. We made no real dent on the legislative front because all too often we've been a house divided among itself."[52]

Looking back over the thirty-seven years between the *Everson* decision and the *Felton* and *Aguilar* decisions, Court watchers would find relatively little change in the Court's position on the church-state-school question. In fact, the principal forms of aid in 1990 were much the same as they were in 1950 — schoolbooks and bus transportation. The Court also narrowly validated tuition tax deductions on the state level, but the impact of the decision was minimal. The Court had changed its membership, but its views on aid to nonpublic schools had not shifted. The *Everson* and *Lemon* decisions continued as the answers to the church-state-school question.

A Decade of Doubt and Resolve

T HE EARLY YEARS of a new decade always bring predictions for the future, and Catholic educators certainly could not resist the temptation in 1980. Parochial education — most particularly Catholic institutions — had suffered through fifteen years of decline. Indeed, the Catholic school population had plummeted more than two million students between 1965 and 1980. Catholic educators prayed and predicted that the 1980s would bring change. Yet these predictions of a brighter future were laced with doubt. The 1980s was a decade of hope but not certainty for Catholic education.

Certainly "hope" was the operative word early in the decade. "The mood of the annual convention of the National Catholic Educational Association," noted the *New York Times* in April 1981, "was markedly different from that of the past few years. Gone were the unhappy faces and expressions of frustration. For the first time in about a decade, principals and teachers in Catholic schools were facing the future with optimism."[1] This optimism was based on a number of trends, including a growing disenchantment with the quality of public education, a sharp rise in interest in the teaching of values, and, perhaps most important, a renewed campaign for aid to private schools led by a very popular president of the United States.

"There has been an awesome turnaround," proclaimed Michael O'Neill at the 1981 NCEA meeting. Even though he was considered a thoughtful commentator on the future of education, not everyone was quite as confident as Father O'Neill. Throughout the 1980s, Catholic educators shifted from hope to despair and back to hope again depending on the education news of the day. No one — even the most pessimistic commentators — expected the Catholic schools to continue to decline at the disastrous rate of the 1970s. Yet neither did the most optimistic commentators expect the 1980s to usher in years of growth like the 1950s and 1960s. In fact, Catholic educators throughout the decade focused on the uncertainty of the future.

❖

Even the upbeat articles on Catholic education contained elements of doubt. Many of these essays, in fact, seemed as if their purpose was to shore up the sagging spirits of parents and educators who were losing hope for parish schools. Throughout the decade, journalists called their readers to arms in essays entitled "Let's Support Catholic Schools at Any Price," "Can Catholic Schools Survive the Economic Crunch of the 1980s?" "Catholic Grade Schools: An Idea Whose Time Has Passed?" "Stop Killing Catholic Schools," and "Keeping Catholic Schools Open Is a Family Affair."[2]

Among the first and most revealing of these essays was one by William McCready, a social scientist at the National Opinion Research Center of the University of Chicago. Using a variety of sociological tools, McCready came to the unqualified conclusion that "the schools are very effective at influencing people to remain close to the Church and in these times, that is no little achievement." McCready also discovered that most Catholics were willing to support the construction of new Catholic schools and increase their contributions in support of existing schools.[3]

Yet this seemingly positive picture was balanced by the fact that parish schools continued to close and enrollments continued to decline. It seemed that Catholics were willing to support the idea and concept of Catholic schools, but somewhat reluctant to come up with the cash to underwrite a school in their own parish.

This pattern was evident in the response to McCready's

article in *U.S. Catholic*. Many readers, of course, agreed whole-heartedly with McCready's call to support Catholic schools at any price, but there were many other subscribers who challenged this position. "Catholic schools are important, but not at any price," wrote Father Robert Streveler. "I am the pastor of two rural parishes. Neither has a school. Financially and logistically, I cannot see us paying the price to run a school here." A chorus of lay people echoed Father Streveler's sentiments. "I really believe in our religion," concluded Margaret Quilty, "and there are more paths to heaven than just Catholic schooling."[4]

Yet the most ardent supporters of parish schools could not be dissuaded or dismayed by their fellow Catholics. Year after year these advocates hammered away at the value of parish schools. "The real economies of Catholic education," noted the tireless Father O'Neill, "lie in such intangibles as vision, hopes, spirit, conviction, morale, program quality, staff satisfaction, personal relationships between school, staff, clients, public image, feelings of involvement in decision-making, openness and trust."[5] Other articles reinforced O'Neill's theme with case studies of schools across Catholic America.[6]

One source of optimism for Catholic school advocates was the election of Ronald Reagan as president in 1980. He alone of all the candidates of either party had endorsed the concept of tuition tax credits. Catholic school advocates had worked hard for Reagan's victory and expected him to keep his promise to support aid to private schools. Such aid would go a long way toward securing the future of parochial education.

After several false starts, Reagan finally delivered on his promise in the spring of 1982. In mid-April, the president appeared before the annual meeting of the National Catholic Educational Association. In clear, unequivocal language, Reagan promised to honor his campaign pledge. "Our bill will be aimed at the middle- and lower-income working families who now bear the double burden of taxes and tuition, while still paying local taxes to support public schools."[7] His promise was greeted by applause.

But the president's support was not enough to enact a law, and Congress had little interest in tuition tax credits. In fact, there were some Catholics who were downright cynical about Reagan's support. "I think it was a con job," commented one priest after the speech. "There is no way tuition tax credits can pass. He served up apple pie and ice cream and that's all."[8]

Even the most optimistic supporters of tuition tax credits knew it would be a battle. Throughout the summer, supporters saw their chances of a law go from slim to none. Even though a compromise bill did reach the floor of the Senate, it was dead on arrival. There would be no tuition tax credit law in 1982.[9]

Without any prospect of public aid, it was not clear if Catholic parish schools would prevail in the next century. The decline in the number of parish schools and students had leveled off in the mid-1980s, and this ebb gave advocates the luxury to ask themselves more questions about the future of their schools.[10]

That Catholic leaders were disappointed at the lack of progress on tuition tax credits was obvious. Indeed, some Catholics saw the root of this failure within the Catholic community itself. "American Catholic school parents are chumps, patsies, dopes, and born-a-minute suckers," wrote Virgil C. Blum, the founder of the Catholic League for Religious and Civil Rights. "They are political pygmies. And everyone in Washington knows it, from President Reagan down to the lowliest page." Catholics "weren't even noticed because they had not organized into an interest group to represent their proper interests in the White House and on Capitol Hill." Blum proposed the establishment of an aggressive "parents interests group" funded by voluntary contributions. If tuition tax credits were to be a reality, Catholic parents would have to organize and pressure their elected representatives.[11]

Blum's call to arms did not generate much of a response from the nation's more than 50 million Catholics. To be sure, the president continued to support tuition tax credits and made a major effort to persuade Congress to join the cause.[12] But even the Great Communicator, as Reagan was often called, could not persuade the Congress to pass the tax credit bill, and it was tabled in November 1983.[13] Halfhearted efforts to revise the plan and introduce legislation in 1984 and 1985 went nowhere.[14]

※

The future of Catholic education, most journalists concluded by mid-decade, would be determined by the resolve of the Catholic people — bishops and pastors as well as parents. All of these groups came in for criticism from Catholic school advocates. "When you get down to it," concluded one beleaguered school principal, "it really becomes a question of priorities. What would you do if you didn't spend money on schools? Spend the money on yet another program? Buy new stained glass windows? What could you spend the money on that would prove more effective?"[15] These tough questions often were met with embarrassed silence, or worse, indifference.

Parents were the focus of a lot of the criticism. Catholic school advocates refused to listen to complaints about the cost of parish schools or the limited quality of the facilities and programs of parish schools. This was all a smoke screen as far as the advocates were concerned. "I am tired of hearing the melodramatic cries about the cost of Catholic education," noted Sister Mary Ann Walsh. "Whether a parent chooses Catholic school education reflects less on his financial system and more on his value system. People pay for what they want." This theme was repeated in story after story in the Catholic press.[16]

Other less passionate analysts dissected the lethargy among Catholic parents. Some writers attributed the school closings and the enrollment declines to demographics. "Catholics moved to the suburbs in the 1960s and 1970s, had fewer children, and, often finding no Catholic school, sent their youngsters to public school. One consequence was that the urban Catholic school diminished."[17] The reasons why suburban Catholics failed to build new parish schools were clear. Most commentators concluded that the laity had a lack of leadership, a change in priorities, and a lack of will. Although many

Catholics were willing to send their children to existing Catholic schools, they were unwilling to make the major financial commitment to build new ones.[18]

Catholic parents were not the sole target for blame, however. A number of commentators attributed much of the decline in Catholic schools to a change in priorities within the American church establishment. "The maintenance of Catholic culture among traditionally identified American Catholics, while still important, and even the chief function of many a parish, is no longer the prime issue it once was," noted David O'Rourke. "A dozen years ago, the Catholic bishops devoted a significant part of their annual meeting to the question of federal funds for Catholic schools. Today the schools are almost a minor issue. The focus is on armaments and social order."[19]

O'Rourke and other commentators saw this change in priorities as a root cause of the malaise that had overcome the laity in regard to parochial schools. If the bishops were no longer concerned about parish schools, why should parents care? Many bishops saw the shift away from the schools to the more relevant issues of war, peace, and economics as a form of church renewal. Few of these leaders, however, saw the downside to this renewal. "Sadly it is this renewal that is the root of the alienation of the people from the Church," added O'Rourke. "The experience of conversion and commitment that is common on the leadership level of the Church is simply not part of the experience of many Catholic people. After having seen the Church changed under their feet without even having been asked about it, they now see it walk away from them leaving them behind."[20] In short, the people in the pews were not sure anymore what it meant to be a Catholic, let alone if they should support Catholic schools.

In a typically provocative essay published in *America* at the end of the decade, Andrew M. Greeley asked if Catholic schools were facing a "golden twilight." A widely published and respected sociologist, Greeley concurred with those commentators who pointed to demographics as a major cause of the decline. "The Catholic population," Greeley noted, "gradually moved away from the places where the existing schools are. Enrollment has declined because of the lower birthrates in the last two decades. . . . Catholic schools seem to be entering a twilight — not facing immediate extinction, perhaps, but slipping slowly into darkness."[21]

Yet Greeley more than most commentators argued that the demise of Catholic schools was unnecessary, even tragic. "The system that the church leadership sent quietly into that good night," added Greeley, "was abandoned at the height of its success." He pointed to new data showing conclusively that Catholic schools "have produced a substantial impact on the educational, political, moral, religious, sexual, and financial behavior of its students." Few institutions, Greeley added, could claim that kind of impact.

Greeley's essay was tinged with sadness. The words he used were those of eulogy. Gone were the indignant phrases attacking the bishops and others who had abandoned parish schools; there was just a sense of loss. Greeley had little hope that his data or any other data would change the attitudes of bishops and pastors who could not "afford" Catholic schools or parents who were "too sophisticated" to send their children to parochial schools.

But Greeley, a tireless advocate of parochial schools, would not join this group. "God willing," Greeley concluded, "I will continue to purchase space for the church school question in the General Social Survey so that the splendid twilight of the Catholic schools can be recorded for posterity. Thus historians of the future can marvel at how foolish we were to give up because of loss of nerve and loss of faith what have been our best resources. Catholic schools, after all, were the answer."[22]

❈

It was not all gloom and doom in the Catholic press in the 1980s. Parish schools were effective in providing an educational alternative for about two million children each year. More important, parish schools provided a value-based curriculum that was forbidden in public institutions. "A lot of people are concerned now about moral and ethical issues," the president of the NCEA told the *New York Times*, "and so we see a great surge in the numbers who want not only a good academic education, but also want to see their children in schools where the values of the home will be respected."[23]

Thus "parish schools make a difference because they are different" was an important subtext of the Catholic debate over the future of their schools. Indeed, there was a fairly steady concern by parents and educators alike about both religious and moral education in parish schools. Was it enough for Catholic schools to teach a value-based curriculum? Were Catholic educators doing enough to insure that their students had specifically Catholic values? Although there was a lot of disagreement over the content and the approach to religious instruction, everyone — liberal and conservative, parent and educator — could agree that the current program was less than perfect.

It was not clear where Catholic education was going in the 1980s. A 1981 survey conducted by the National Opinion Research Center and funded by the Knights of Columbus indicated that Catholic education did have a positive effect on some elements of a Catholic's moral life — attendance at Mass, the consideration of religious vocations, and the opposition to abortion. But the Knights, at least, were dismayed to learn that attendance at Catholic school had no effect on student attitudes toward prayer and sexual morality. This caused some school advocates to question the status quo. "We've got a captive audience for values education," noted one educator. "It seems that we ought to be doing more with it."[24]

Conservatives pointed to this data — and other anecdotal evidence — to call for a return to old-fashioned moral instruction. But the parish school establishment, especially the NCEA, argued that such an approach was simplistic. "There is no returning to the Church or the religion of a bygone time," noted one educator in *America*. "Controversy comes," added a superintendent, "when people see a different methodology and think that the content has changed. Not using the *Baltimore Catechism*, for example, is a change in method, not in the content of the Faith."[25] Educators asked these conservatives to concentrate on substance, not on form.

But many Catholics were not willing to let matters be. Dissatisfaction was aptly summarized in a January 1983 article in *U.S. Catholic.* "What are Catholic schools teaching kids about religion?" asked James Emswiler. As a parent, Emswiler was perplexed because there were so many opinions about what constituted a solid Catholic religious education. "As far as religious education is concerned," wrote Emswiler, "there is no such thing as 'Catholic schools.' In the past, parents would say, 'I send my children to Catholic school,' and others would know exactly what was meant. Today, parents may be asked, 'which one?' "[26] To say that there was a lot of confusion in the Catholic educational establishment over its religious curriculum was something of a truism.

This confusion was dramatically evident when progressive and traditional Catholics talked past each other in promoting specific changes in Catholic school religious instruction. Responding to the Catholic bishops' pastoral letter on war and peace, progressive educators pushed for a religious education that centered on issues of war and peace, social justice, and the environment. Cardinal Joseph Bernardin of Chicago, one of the authors of the peace pastoral, urged Catholic educators to seize the day. Those who heard Bernardin speak at the NCEA meeting in Washington were impressed. "The movement is fledgling in the schools," noted one educator. "What we are endeavoring to do is to make [social justice issues] central [in the curriculum] and the bishops' pastoral letter will give it a big impetus."[27]

Other educators sought specific ways to incorporate the peace pastoral into the Catholic school curriculum. "The Challenge of Peace: A Call to Educators" was a conference that brought together three hundred people from twenty-eight states and several foreign countries to develop strategies for presenting the complicated document to children. "Though the pastoral must necessarily be presented in different ways for pupils of different ages," noted one educator, "even children in the elementary grades will learn about it." Conference participants fortified themselves with workshops and prayer and prepared themselves for the school year about to start in a few weeks.[28]

Not surprisingly, traditionalists were little concerned about incorporating the peace pastoral into the Catholic school curriculum. They were more concerned about the general decline in the quality and quantity of religious instruction. "It is my opinion that today's Catholic school students are receiving a watered down version of Church doctrine and there are many parents who agree with me," wrote Jerry Becan in *America*.[29]

In fact, the term "religious illiteracy" popped up in the Catholic press throughout 1983. What concerned Becan and other traditionalists was that "the immediate result is that today's Catholic education does not foster the firm commitment to the faith that students in previous generations had. The long-term result will be that Catholic school graduates will drift away from their church."[30] It was a chilling thought for devout Catholic parents who sacrificed to send their children to parish schools.

Becan's solution was a simple one: bring back the *Baltimore Catechism*. Becan asked, "What was wrong with the *Baltimore Catechism?*" Nothing, as far as he was concerned. "Anything can be improved," he noted, "and the Catechism was no exception. But if it had to be replaced, it should have been replaced by something better." To Becan's thinking, this was not the case. "I do not know why the depth of the Catechism was exchanged for the shallowness of today's approach," he concluded. "But can't we stop and reflect and try to give our children the education we had: a thorough grounding in the principles of a faith that could become for them a force influencing every aspect of their lives?"[31]

The response to Becan's questions came from William Odell in the pages of *Our Sunday Visitor*, a weekly paper that went out to millions of subscribers. Odell conceded that Becan had raised "important questions in his article, but I think we err when we draw the battle lines between the *Baltimore Catechism* and modern methods of religious education."[32]

Odell argued that the concern over religious education in the 1980s should not be counterbalanced with nostalgia for the past or recrimination about the present. "The 1980s seem to be developing into a period of serious reappraisal of the challenges before us," Odell wrote. He dismissed the idea of returning to the *Baltimore Catechism*, but expressed a dissatisfaction with the present as well. "We very definitely need to reverse the trend of religious illiteracy," he concluded. "We need faith development that is deeply rooted spiritually, not culturally. It is not our society that we want molding our faith. Rather, it is our faith we want transforming our society."[33]

Everyone in the Catholic community seemed to agree that change was needed, but no one was quite sure what was to be done to improve the church's "religious literacy quotient." In fact, religious educators took to heart the federal government's 1983 report on public education entitled *A Nation at Risk*. For Catholic educators, it was denomination at risk. Thus it was no surprise that William D. Kelly, the executive director of the NCEA religious education department, recommended specific changes in the religious education curriculum.

Kelly recommended a curriculum and a program that would extend over twelve years to prevent the mistakes of "too much too soon or too little too late." He called for those responsible for teacher training to redouble their efforts to insure that their teachers know precisely what content they are responsible for transmitting. Kelly further encouraged the direct involvement of parents in the catechetical process, and he called for teachers to do more testing of students' knowledge of religious content. Finally, Kelly concluded, "religious teachers and catechists should be more courageous and enterprising in challenging their students to deepen their intellectual understanding of the faith." It was an ambitious program, but also a vital one. "Meeting this challenge," Kelly added, "will determine in good measure the degree to which we will have intelligent, articulate Catholics capable of being effective witnesses and evangelizers in the church of the next millennium."[34]

⁂

In spite of all these challenges, many Catholic parents remained deeply committed to their parish schools. Whatever problems these institutions had, parents were attracted to the religious environment of parish schools. Throughout the decade, Catholic parents would repeat their point over and over again. "Religion is more caught than taught," noted one principal. "This should be an operating principle in any Catholic school. Religion and spirituality are to be lived and not relegated to the academic time period during which religion is taught." Parents, whatever their overt complaints, seemed to understand this point.[35]

These parents also agreed that a large part of the environment was determined by teachers. Even the Vatican recognized the critical importance of teachers, the vast majority of whom were lay people. In a document released in October 1982, the Sacred Congregation for Catholic Education praised the contributions of the lay men and women working in parish schools. "This document's main purpose," noted *America*, "is to highlight the value of teaching so as to brace up lay people already engaged in this hard but essential business and to recruit young lay Catholics for work in the schools and particularly in Catholic schools."[36] Perhaps most important in this document was the fact that the Congregation called for teachers to receive "an adequate salary, guaranteed by a well-defined contract and authentic responsibility." Interpreting this mandate on a school-by-school basis became an issue of concern for educators in the 1980s.

Salaries were a constant problem for school administrators. The typical Catholic school teacher was a young unmarried woman with a deep commitment to her Catholic faith. She was paid a sum that few considered adequate — as little as half the salary of public school teachers in the same area. Not surprisingly, the attrition rate among teachers was very high. It seemed that no one — not even the most dedicated teachers — could afford to make a career of teaching in parish schools.[37]

This point was underscored by a casual comment made by a Chicago social scientist who regularly studied the Catholic schools. In an interview in *U.S. Catholic,* William McCready of the National Opinion Research Center referred to parish school teachers as a "religious order." "These young people had the same dedication and commitment to the schools that the nuns of an earlier era had," noted McCready. "The difference was that they didn't envision that as their life forever."[38] It was a mild shock to many Catholic parents to think that the young women teaching their children were taking virtual vows of poverty when they signed their teaching contracts.

Yet year after year these dedicated young women entered the parish school classroom. "Rugged dedication" was the term used by one journalist to describe this phenomenon. "Nuns they are not; dedicated they are," wrote Barbara Mahany. "A burning commitment to Catholic education, regardless of pay, seems to be stoking the vocations of lay teachers around the country."[39] The teachers themselves also described their work in terms often used for religious vocations. "It's a feeling of just total dedication," concluded one second grade teacher, "not to the school, but to the children. I feel like it is a religious calling."[40]

But parish school administrators could not count on an endless supply of these selfless women willing to work for minimum wages. Many in the Catholic school establishment were concerned. "Although most teachers interviewed said they were willing to put up with low pay and heavy extracurricular loads," noted Mahany, "saying intangibles more than made up for the shortage of cash, all sadly told tales of colleagues who dropped off the Catholic school payrolls when the money squeeze became a strangle."[41] Everyone agreed that lay teachers were the strength of parish schools and that more had to be done to retain these wonderful people. But where would the money come from and how should the schools be reformed? These were unresolved questions throughout the 1980s.[42]

⁂

The impact of these teachers and parish schools generally was most evident and dramatic in inner-city parishes. In fact, parish education was one of the few bright spots in an otherwise bleak educational picture in the largely impoverished neighborhoods of America's largest cities. Many residents of these largely black neighborhoods saw their parish schools as a way out of the ghetto, so it was no surprise that black enrollment in parochial schools jumped nearly 25 percent between 1971 and 1981.[43]

Social scientists — most notably James Coleman and Andrew M. Greeley — noted the positive results of this trend. In fact, Coleman went so far as to claim that "Catholic schools in general do less for students from the most advantaged backgrounds." Greeley reaffirmed Coleman's claims in a separate study. "Something seems to be happening in the Catholic schools that is not happening in the public schools," he concluded. "It leads me to conclude that the Catholic schools, which were set up to help poor immigrants, now do the same for minorities."[44] It was an extraordinary success story, and the Catholic press took every opportunity to get the word out.

A variety of factors were involved in this success. Certainly the black children who attended parochial schools generally came from smaller, more stable, and higher income families than their public school counterparts. Certainly black parents of children in parochial schools generally were more involved in their children's education than the parents of children in public schools.

Yet just as important was the environment in which these children were educated. Catholic schools had deeply committed teachers and orderly classrooms. Most important, parochial schools set high standards and expected results from their students. "The important thing is to make children believe in themselves," noted one Catholic teacher, "but you can't do it by coddling them. . . . It's important to them to see that they can compete. And the idea that black children can't do the work is baloney. I see red every time I hear it."[45]

Although the cost of maintaining these schools was very high, many Catholics saw them as an opportunity to reach out to the African American community. Many of these inner-city parish schools encouraged their families to attend Mass together on Sundays, and virtually all of these schools required all pupils — non-Catholic as well as Catholic — to receive and participate in religious education classes. "A school system is an effective and legitimate means toward evangelization," added one superintendent. "In fact, that's the chief purpose of any Catholic school." The Catholic school in the inner city was visible evidence of the church's commitment to the African American community. Many blacks responded by joining the church.[46]

Throughout the 1980s, therefore, the press continued to highlight the extraordinary achievement of the church in providing top quality education for minorities. Case studies appeared on black Catholic schools in Los Angeles, Chicago, Milwaukee, New York, and Washington in publications as diverse as Chicago, Our Sunday Visitor, America, and the Washington Post.[47]

By the middle of the decade, the director of planning for the Office of Educational Research and Improvement of the U.S. Department of Education provided statistical support for all of the anecdotal evidence. In an essay on how Catholic schools have served minority interests, Bruno V. Manno reported that minority enrollment in Catholic schools had jumped from a little under 10 percent in 1970 to over 20 percent by 1984. In fact, Manno noted, the minority enrollment in the largest archdioceses often exceeded the average. In cities such as Chicago (43.9), New York (55.2), Los Angeles (65.2), Newark (74.1), Detroit (58), and Brooklyn (40.2) the figures were more than double the national average.[48]

Manno went on to criticize educational policy makers and the media for their unwillingness to abandon the stereotype of parish schools as the bastion of the white and the wealthy. "These groups must recognize that Catholic schools are not havens for whites fleeing public education or for an elite avoiding social responsibility," concluded Manno. "They have less internal racial and economic segregation than do public schools."[49]

Manno went on to explain that Catholic schools embodied two basic notions common to public schools. First, Catholic schools were based in neighborhoods; parish schools were, in fact, community schools run by and for the members of the community. Second, Catholic schools were committed to serving a mixture of different ethnic and racial groups that make up the neighborhoods where they are located. "Catholic schools are not perfect," Manno concluded, "but the data indicate they serve a larger public composed of differing religious, racial, ethnic, economic, and academic groups. This is a valuable role that should be taken into account and fostered in setting public policy."[50]

The 1980s were years of uncertainty, but out of that uncertainty came a new identity. Once a haven of white immigrant children making the transition from Europe to America, the Catholic schools of the 1980s had become visible symbols of the commitment of some parents — both Catholic and non-Catholic — to the education of their children. To be sure, many Catholic parishes had closed their schools, and other parishes were unwilling to open new schools. But just as important were the many parishes in the inner cities as well as in the affluent suburbs that made great sacrifices to sustain their schools. As Andrew Greeley and others had articulated it in the Catholic press, the future of Catholic education rested on the foundation of parental commitment.

Conclusion

T HE FUTURE of American Catholic parochial education is uncertain. Thirty years ago there were more than 5.7 million children enrolled in Catholic schools, but by 1994 the enrollment had slipped to less than 2.5 million, a plunge of 56 percent. Even though the rate of decline has abated, hardly a year goes by without a net loss in the number of Catholic schools and students.

"Ironically," notes one report, "this all comes at a time when Catholic schools appear to be at a peak academically and spiritually."[1] Independent studies by a brigade of social scientists underscore that point. Students in parish schools outperform their friends in public schools on virtually all standardized tests. Even public school officials agree that some of the elements of Catholic education might well be adopted in public schools to improve student performance generally.[2]

It is a sad state of affairs, therefore, that just when parish schools are doing so well, they are closing their doors. "At the very time Catholic school graduates are being celebrated for leaving their public school counterparts in the chalk dust," notes Peter Daly in the *Washington Post*, "the Catholic school itself is disappearing."[3]

The salient question is why are these schools closing if they are doing such a good job? The answer is complex, intertangled with changing social values, changes in family structure, changes in the forms and content of public education, and the rising cost of private education relative to other living expenses. All of these factors have contributed to the decline over the past thirty years, and all of these factors will continue to affect parochial schools in the next century.

The beginning of the decline of Catholic parochial education can be traced to the drastic drop in religious vocations in the late 1960s. For more than a century, orders of priests and nuns staffed Catholic classrooms at minimal cost. But in the years after the end of the Second Vatican Council in 1965, tens of thousands of these men and women abandoned or were excused from their religious vows, and many others shifted to different ministries, forcing parish pastors and principals to hire lay teachers and pay them a living wage. Many school administrators found this task to be economically unfeasible and closed their schools.

A second factor affecting parish schools is the changing structure of the American family. Where once the typical American Catholic family consisted of two parents and a gaggle of kids, the new American Catholic family is often a single parent with one or two children. Even in two-parent households, both parents work and are in need of day-care facilities and after-school programs. In short, Catholic families no longer have the time or energy to contribute to the operation and maintenance of a private parish school.

Related to the change in the structure of the typical Catholic family over the past thirty years has been a correlate change in American values. "We as a nation," notes William J. Byron, former president of the Catholic University of America, "are now more than ever possessed by our possessions. Wisdom leads the list of casualties in a conflict of values where greed, promoted by popular culture, is on the rise and sacrifice, proclaimed as a value by the Catholic tradition, is on the decline."[4]

In such an environment, with so many social pressures to buy a bigger house, another car, a video cassette recorder, or a personal computer, Catholic parents find that they have no money left to pay parochial school tuition, let alone the resources needed to build a new school.

Another factor is the changing nature of public education. As late as the 1950s, especially in rural areas of the country, public schools taught a form of nonsectarian Protestantism as part of the curriculum. Catholics in those areas and even in the big cities did not always feel welcome. But a 1961 decision by the Supreme Court stripped all public schools of any references to religion. Students of all faiths came to be treated equally.

Catholic parents are also attracted to public schools by the quality of the facilities, teachers, and courses. The principal concern of all parents — Catholic as well as non-Catholic — is the future careers and economic security of their children. Unlike their parents and grandparents, Catholic parents today do not value the spiritual development of their children as highly as their career development.

But the most powerful reason that Catholic parents do not support parish schools is that there is no pressure to do so. "There is nothing like the presence of an external enemy," notes Father Byron, "to solidify a community in shared identity and mutual support. Catholics are more comfortable in the United States today. They are less rigid about their religious practice."[5] Their grandparents and parents saw parish schools as a form of protection and security for their children against a frequently hostile American society. In an increasingly pluralistic, ecumenical world, discrimination against Catholics is a distant memory.

When Catholic leaders first established parish schools — especially in the century between 1830 and 1930 — their stated goal was to serve both their faith and their nation. "The fact is," noted David J. O'Brien nearly thirty years ago, "that the hierarchy, clergy, and the laity, all wished to be both American and Catholic and their attempt to reconcile the two, to mediate between religious and social roles, lies at the heart of the American experience."[6] By all accounts and measures, parish schools did an extraordinary job of meeting those stated goals.

But if these goals have been met, is there a continuing need for parish schools? Public education is no longer a threat to Catholic children. Catholics as a group have blended into American society without the loss of their religious faith. Indeed, recent studies by the Educational Testing Service indicated that out-of-school religious education programs do an

effective job — almost as effective as parish school programs —
of passing on the faith.[7] It is not clear why Catholics should
put an increasing percentage of their resources into institutions
that have already fulfilled their stated goals.

Catholic educators respond that these schools should be supported precisely because they have been so effective in meeting
those stated goals. Stated simply, Catholic schools are both a
model and an alternative to public education. Where Catholic schools had once followed every innovation introduced in
public education, the roles have been reversed. Catholic schools
are now laboratories for the development of effective tools in
reaching a broad cross-section of children.

What can public education learn from parish schools? In a
recent study entitled *Catholic Schools and the Common Good,* three
social scientists outlined the successful hallmarks of Catholic
education, hallmarks that could be adapted by public schools.[8]

Foremost among the qualities of parish-based education is
decentralization. To be sure, all parochial schools are nominally controlled by superintendents and diocesan boards of
education. But for the most part, parish schools are administered at the local level. Funding for the schools comes from
the community, and teachers are hired by principals without
interference. Parents have a greater involvement and effectiveness in the education process because they are working with a
single institution in their neighborhood rather than a faceless
bureaucracy downtown.

A second quality related to the first is the fact that parents, students, and faculty share a broad set of beliefs that
give each school a moral purpose. Achieving this unanimity
in a public institution may not be easy. But if our nation's
motto means anything, then public institutions must do more
to achieve "one out of many." Shared values are possible if
parents, students, and faculty care about education.

This care is also reflected in a shared code of conduct that
stresses "human dignity and the belief that human reason can
discern ethical truth."[9] This code need not be religious, but neither can it be arbitrary. More important, the case must stress a

good greater than individual achievement or gratification. "It is difficult to envision," wrote the authors of *Catholic Schools and the Common Good*, "how unleashing self-interest becomes a compelling force toward human caring."[10]

Another hallmark of parochial schools worthy of emulation is size. The small size of most parish schools promotes interaction between students, parents, and staff. Because teachers serve in many different roles during the school day — disciplinarians, counselors, and friends as well as specialists in one or more academic disciplines — they become mentors and role models. The small size of most parish schools insures that parents and teachers know one another and their children well. In short, small size facilitates communication.

Finally, parish schools place a special emphasis on academics. Small size and limited resources necessarily require administrators to concentrate on basics. The end result is a student body well grounded in the mathematical and literary skills so necessary for success at future educational levels. Large schools with cafeteria-style curricula may very well meet short-term demands for relevant instruction, but there is little evidence that courses in industrial management and family living are as valuable as literacy and mathematical skills in a constantly changing society.

But in spite of these qualities, parish schools face a troubled future. The cost of parish education has been high — much higher than the spreadsheets reveal. In spite of belt-tightening and other economies, few parishes can raise the funds necessary to maintain their own schools. This is particularly true in the inner-city neighborhoods of America's largest cities. Poverty is an obstacle that has been almost insurmountable, even for the most dedicated Catholic educator.[11]

As is the case in public education, money — or lack of it — will determine the future of parish education. Church leaders have come to the realization that they must take extraordinary measures to raise the cash to propel their schools into the next century.

Increasing tuition is the most logical way to raise additional income for these schools. In fact, there is a built-in advantage for parish schools when the families they serve have a significant financial interest in their survival. "Kids know that their parents think education is important," notes Peter J. Daly, "because they pay money for it and give time to the school."[12]

It is not clear how much parents can afford to give to their parish school without limiting their families in other ways. Many suburban, affluent Catholic families can and will pay thousands of dollars to keep their children in parish schools. But the rising cost of parish schooling is a burden on inner-city families who must struggle to come up with a few hundred dollars to cover basic costs. If their schools are to survive, they must find other sources of income. Without other resources, parish schools run the danger of becoming elite institutions available only to wealthy Catholics.

Not even the most optimistic Catholic believes that parents will ever be able to pay the entire cost of their children's parochial education, and few parish pastors or diocesan administrators have the financial resources to supplement the tuition paid by parents. It is no surprise, therefore, that Catholic educators across the country are spending increasing amounts of time in the pursuit of funds from the business and financial community and using scarce funds to mount advertising campaigns. The goal of these efforts is to increase the awareness of the value of Catholic education both inside and outside the Catholic community.

A final source of income is public aid. Republican presidents over the past twenty-five years have advocated such support, but to little avail. Congress, bowing to public opinion, has resisted efforts to pass such a bill. In some states, state legislatures have passed laws allowing parents to deduct unreimbursed school expenses from their state income tax returns. Even though the dollar value per family is small, the symbolism of this support is great. Just as important, the Supreme Court found the deduction to be constitutional.

With little prospect for public aid and only a modest prospect of outside funds, it is clear that the future of Catholic parochial education will be determined by the parents of the children who are educated in these schools. More than two centuries ago, the parents and pastor of St. Mary's parish in Philadelphia established the first parochial school in this country. And as long as there are parents and pastors interested in parochial education, these schools will survive. Even though American Catholic parochial education will never again attain the position of influence it had in the mid-twentieth century, parish schools will remain important education laboratories for some time to come.

Guide to Further Reading and Research

ATHOLICISM is one of the oldest traditions in North America. Beginning with the establishment of the parish of St. Augustine in the Spanish colony of Florida in 1565, the church has nurtured both the spiritual and material welfare of millions of Americans. The church is fast approaching the anniversary of 450 years of continuous service in the territory that now forms the continental United States.

It is unfortunate, therefore, that until recently American Catholics in general, and the church establishment in particular, have done so little to document and tell the story of that service, particularly its extraordinary educational enterprise. In fact it was not until a century ago, with the establishment of the U.S. Catholic Historical Society in New York, the American Catholic Historical Society in Philadelphia, and the Catholic Archives of America at the University of Notre Dame, that Catholic scholars began to preserve and write the unique and important history of their church. For these initial efforts, we must thank John Gilmary Shea, Martin I. J. Griffin, and James F. Edwards — men who dedicated their lives to preserving the contributions of Catholicism to the American experience.

As part of their effort, these men documented the attitudes of the Catholic community toward education. Yet the impact of these historians on the general development of American educational historiography has not been very significant. Catholics have been the "invisible" contributors to the history of American schooling. The reasons for this lack of influence can be traced to a severe limitation on the quantity and quality of historical source materials on Catholic education, as well as to a tradition of filiopietism among Catholic educational historians.

The source materials on Catholic schooling are as varied as the educational experiences themselves. For some archdioceses, the record is quite complete, but for other dioceses there are few materials. It is somewhat ironic that a denomination with a reputation for bureaucracy and standardization would do such an uneven job of preserving the documentation of its work.

This is not to say that all Catholic bishops were insensitive to the value of archives and records. Many bishops directed their pastors to prepare annual reports describing both the spiritual and financial condition of their parishes. Yet the orders of bishops were not always obeyed, and the quantity and quality of records vary substantially from parish to parish.

The variations in documentation are also due to the attitudes of the bishops and the administrative structures that they developed. The quality of record keeping in the nineteenth century was an extension of each bishop's personal habits. Some bishops were avid record keepers, but just as many left almost no documentation. The uneven nature of documentation for the study of American Catholicism in the nineteenth century is a source of real frustration for scholars.

The builder bishops of the twentieth century did a better job than their predecessors in documenting the parish school movement. Concerned about efficiency and uniformity, these bishops centralized control over all church operations in their respective dioceses. They required pastors to submit regular reports on school operations as well as weekly collections. The volume of records on Catholic parochial education in the twentieth century is extraordinary, especially in comparison to those available for the nineteenth century.

Yet it does scholars little good if these records and documents are unavailable. And that was the case in most dioceses until the 1970s. Made aware of the Catholic contributions to American culture by the forthcoming bicentennial of American independence, the National Conference of Catholic Bishops

called for "a nationwide effort to preserve and organize existing records and papers that can be found in chancery offices,
general and provincial houses of religious orders, and institutions of our country."

As part of this effort, the NCCB recommended that each
residential bishop appoint a properly qualified individual to
serve as diocesan archivist and expressed the hope that the
bishops would grant access to diocesan archival materials to
qualified researchers. The bishops reminded all Catholics "of
their obligation to hand down to posterity the record of those
accomplishments for the Church and the nation."

This brief, forthright document was the stimulus for the establishment of many new diocesan archival programs. In fact,
the number of Catholic archives more than doubled in the
four years after the dissemination of the NCCB statement, and
the number of diocesan and religious archivists has grown
large enough to justify the compilation and publication of the
Catholic Archives Newsletter.

Catholic diocesan archival programs were not the only repositories to be refurbished during the 1970s. Religious congregations of women also joined in the effort to preserve and make
available the archival materials that document their substantial service to the church. Under the auspices of the Leadership
Conference of Women Religious, Evangeline Thomas, C.S.J.,
directed a program that trained 375 archivists representing
hundreds of congregations across the country, surveyed the
archival holdings of those congregations, and published the in-
valuable *Women Religious History Sources: A Guide to Repositories
in the United States.* No other volume brings together as much
information on the history of women religious congregations
in the United States.

Both the quantity and the quality of the published historical literature on Catholic education in the United States has
been very poor. Starting with James A. Burns's two volumes,
The Catholic School System: Its Principles, Origin, and Establishment
(New York, 1908) and *The Growth and Development of the Catholic School System in the United States* (New York, 1912), there

have been only marginal efforts to write a balanced history of Catholic schooling in this country.

For the most part these efforts were defensive and filiopietistic, more apologetics than history. Most followed the "seed to fruition" thesis lain down by Burns. The best of these traditional histories are Harold A. Buetow, *Of Singular Benefit: The Story of U.S. Catholic Education* (New York, 1970) and Glen Gabert, Jr., *In Hoc Signo? A Brief History of Catholic Parochial Schools in the United States* (Port Washington, N.Y., 1973).

Catholic educational historiography in the United States was dominated by Burns until the mid-1960s. This extraordinary hegemony has been analyzed by Vincent P. Lannie in his aptly titled essay, "Church and School Triumphant: The Sources of American Catholic Historiography," in *History of Education Quarterly* 16 (Summer 1976): 131–45. Burns's influence waned during the 1960s in the midst of the changes brought on by Vatican II. This new era of freedom and self-examination within the church encouraged scholars to explore the history of Catholic schooling in an unbiased fashion.

Two scholars made substantial contributions to the professionalization of Catholic historiography. Neil G. McCluskey published three books and numerous essays that helped to reshape the scholarly approach to Catholic education. McCluskey penetrated the defensive shell around the parochial school historiography of the Burns school. Although his work is dated today, it has yet to be superseded. See Neil G. McCluskey, *The Catholic Viewpoint on Education* (Garden City, N.Y., 1959); *Catholic Education in America: A Documentary History* (New York, 1964); and *Catholic Education Faces Its Future* (Garden City, N.Y., 1969).

A second scholar who helped to break the filiopietism of the past was Vincent P. Lannie. Lannie's major contribution was to provide solid and balanced narratives of important turning points in the history of Catholic education. See his *Public Money and Parochial Education: Bishop Hughes, Governor Seward and the New York School Controversy* (Cleveland, 1968); Lannie and Bernard Diethorn, "For the Honor and Glory of God: The

Philadelphia Bible Riots of 1844," *History of Education Quarterly* 8 (Spring 1968): 44–106; and Lannie, "Alienation in America: The American Catholic Immigrant in Pre–Civil War America," *Review of Politics* 32 (September 1970): 503–21.

Lannie also made a substantial contribution to the historiography of Catholic education as the director of a number of first-rate doctoral dissertations and as the editor of the short-lived *Notre Dame Journal of Education* (1970–76). The spring 1976 issue included several essays by Lannie and his students. See Lannie, "Sunlight and Twilight: Unlocking the Catholic Educational Past," and the other essays in that issue.

McCluskey and Lannie were not alone in their efforts to professionalize Catholic educational history. Essays and chapters by a number of other scholars have contributed to the portrait. Foremost of these essays is Robert D. Cross, "The Origins of the Catholic Parochial Schools in America," *American Benedictine Review* 16 (June 1965): 194–209. Researchers also will benefit from reading his book *The Emergence of Liberal Catholicism in America* (Cambridge, 1958). The many essays of Timothy L. Smith are also required reading. Most useful for the story of Catholic education are "Parochial Education and American Culture," in Paul Nash, ed., *History and Education* (New York, 1970), 192–211; "Protestant Schooling and American Nationality, 1800–1850," *Journal of American History* 53 (March 1967): 679–96; and "Religion and Ethnicity in America," *American Historical Review* 83(1978): 1155–85.

Several other scholars deserve a special mention. John Tracy Ellis published a number of studies that have illuminated selected aspects of American Catholic educational history. The revised edition of his classic volume *American Catholicism* (Chicago, 1969) contains much that will benefit historians of education. Also of significant value are his *Documents of American Catholic History* (Milwaukee, 1956) and his two-volume biography of Cardinal James Gibbons, noted below. A useful companion to Ellis's compilation of documents is Hugh J. Nolan's edition, *Pastoral Letters of the American Catholic Hierarchy*, 4 vols. (Huntington, Ind., 1971). Finally, no scholar or student should overlook James Hennesey's masterful study *American Catholics: A History of the Roman Catholic Community in the United States* (New York, 1981), an excellent chronological history of the American church and its people.

Several Notre Dame scholars also have made important contributions to the study of Catholic schooling. Thomas T. McAvoy published "Public Schools versus Catholic Schools and James McMaster," in *Review of Politics* 28 (January 1966): 19–46. Also of value is McAvoy's general history, *A History of the Catholic Church in the United States* (Notre Dame, Ind., 1969).

McAvoy's principal student, Philip Gleason, published "Immigration and American Catholic Intellectual Life," *Review of Politics* 26 (April 1964): 147–73. Gleason's book *Keeping the Faith: American Catholicism Past and Present* (Notre Dame, Ind., 1987) includes the best overview of the educational decrees of the Third Plenary Council of Baltimore.

Gleason's colleague at Notre Dame, Jay P. Dolan, discusses parochial education in his masterful volumes, *The Immigrant Church: New York's Irish and German Catholics, 1815–1865* (Baltimore, 1975) and *The American Catholic Experience: From Colonial Times to the Present* (Garden City, N.Y., 1985). The latter book includes an excellent chapter on parochial education.

Also of value are Howard Weisz, "Irish American Attitudes and the Americanization of the English Language Parochial School," *New York History* 53 (April 1972): 151–77; and two studies by Mary J. Oates: "Organized Volunteerism: The Catholic Sisters in Massachusetts, 1870–1940," *American Quarterly* 30 (Winter 1978): 652–80, and "Learning to Teach: The Professional Preparation of Massachusetts Parochial School Faculty, 1870–1940," *Cushwa Center Working Papers* (Notre Dame, Ind., 1981).

Jay Dolan also served as the editor of an important collection of reprints and original titles under the series title "The American Catholic Tradition." The series includes a variety of books on diverse aspects of American Catholicism. The story of Catholic parochial education and parish life was prominent among them. Of particular value to the historiography of parochial education are three titles in the series: Robert Emmett Curran, *Michael Augustine Corrigan and the Shaping of Conservative Catholicism in America, 1878–1902* (New York, 1978); Mary Ewens, *The Role of the Nun in Nineteenth-Century America* (New York, 1978); and Bernard Julius Meiring, *Educational Aspects of the Legislation of the Councils of Baltimore, 1829–1884* (New York, 1978). In addition, several other titles in the series touch on educational topics, and the entire series is worthy of consideration by any scholar interested in the history of Catholicism.

A companion series to Dolan's "American Catholic Tradition" appeared in 1988. A number of volumes in "The Heritage of American Catholicism" focus on Catholic schools. Of particular note are Robert N. Barger, *John Lancaster Spalding: Catholic Educator and Social Emissary*; Norlene M. Kunkel, *Bishop Bernard McQuaid and Catholic Education*; James M. McDonnell, *Orestes Brownson and Nineteenth-Century Education*; Barbara Misner, *"Highly Respectable and Accomplished Ladies": Catholic Women Religious in America, 1790–1850*; David L. Salvaterra, *American Catholicism and the Intellectual Life, 1880–1920*; Fayette B. Veverka, *"For God and Country": Catholic Schooling in the 1920s*; and Timothy Walch, *The Diverse Origins of American Catholic Education: Chicago, Milwaukee, and the Nation*. All of the studies appeared in 1988.

Of greatest interest and value among the books in that series is F. Michael Perko's *Enlightening the Next Generation: Catholics and Their Schools, 1830–1980*. In this one volume, Perko has gathered many of the classic essays on the history of American Catholic schools. Essays by Vincent Lannie, Robert Cross, Thomas McAvoy, Howard Weisz, and Philip Gleason, all cited above, are included in this very handy compilation.

The volume and variety of books on Catholic education in the colonial period is slim indeed. The best among the small lot is John Tracy Ellis's *Catholics in Colonial America* (Baltimore, 1964). Also of value is Charles H. Lippy et al., *Christianity Comes to the Americas* (New York, 1992); Mary A. Ray's *American Opinion of Roman Catholicism* (New York, 1936) is dated but still useful for its research into a range of primary sources.

Carl Kaestle's *Evolution of an Urban School System: New York City, 1750–1850* (Cambridge, 1973) is an excellent case study that includes valuable information on the origins of parochial as well as public education in that city. Patrick Carey, in his *People, Priests, and Prelates* (Notre Dame, Ind., 1986), analyzes the trustee controversy that plagued the American Catholic Church until the 1820s. Finally, Timothy Walch's compilation, *Early American Catholicism, 1634–1820: Selected Historical Essays* (New York, 1988), brings together the best of the articles that have appeared on Catholic education in the colonial period.

Catholic education emerged as an important social movement in the decades before the Civil War. The fuel for this emergence was the massive immigration of Irish and German Catholics during those years. Thomas Archdeacon's *Becoming American* (New York, 1983) and Roger Daniel's *Coming to America* (New York, 1990) are valuable surveys of this migration and resettlement. Reaction to the foreign-born by the native population is discussed in Ray Allen Billington's *The Protestant Crusade* (New York, 1938) and Michael Feldberg's *The Philadelphia Bible Riots of 1844: A Study of Ethnic Conflict* (Westport, Conn., 1975). On the establishment of parish schools as alternatives to Protestant-oriented public schools, readers should consult the work of Vincent Lannie, Jay P. Dolan, Timothy Walch, and Timothy L. Smith cited above.

Some of the major players in the establishment of antebellum parish schools are discussed in Charles Fanning's *The Irish Voice in America* (Lexington, Ky., 1990), especially his chapter on Mary Anne Sadlier, and Paul Messbarger's *Fiction with a Parochial Purpose* (Boston, 1971). Biographies of note are Hugh J. Nolan's *The Most Reverend Francis Patrick Kenrick: Third Bishop of Philadelphia, 1830–1851* (Philadelphia, 1948), Richard V. Shaw, *Dagger John: The Unquiet Life and Times of Life of Archbishop John Hughes of New York* (New York, 1977), and James McDonnell, *Orestes Brownson and Nineteenth-Century Education* (New York, 1988).

The decades following the Civil War saw renewed growth and expansion of Catholic schools, particularly among immigrant Catholics. Colman Barry's *The Catholic Church and German Americans* (Milwaukee, 1953), Richard M. Linkh's *American Catholicism and European Immigrants* (New York, 1975), and Charles Shanabruch's *Chicago's Catholics: The Evolution of an American Identity* (Notre Dame, Ind., 1981) tell much of the story. Brian Mitchell's collection, *Building the American Catholic City: Parishes and Institutions* (New York, 1988), includes a number of valuable essays on parish schools.

These decades were dominated by a range of extraordinary individuals. Interested researchers should start with the work of Robert Cross, Norlene M. Kunkel, Robert Emmett Curran, and John Tracy Ellis cited above. Also of great value is Marvin R. O'Connell's *John Ireland and the American Catholic Church* (Minneapolis, 1988).

Studies of the first two decades of the twentieth century are, for the most part, unpublished doctoral dissertations. Of note are William Scanlon, "The Development of the American Catholic Diocesan Board of Education, 1884–1966," Ed.D. dissertation, New York University, 1967, Edgar M. McCarren, "The Origins and Early Years of the Catholic Educational Association," Ph.D. dissertation, Catholic University of America, 1966, Paul J. Schuler, "Reaction of American Catholics to the Foundations and Early Practices of Progressive Education in the United States, 1892–1917," Ph.D. dissertation, University of Notre Dame, 1970, and John F. Murphy, "Thomas E. Shields, Religious Educator," Ph.D. dissertation, Columbia University, 1971. Also of great value are two recently published dissertations: Elizabeth McKeown, *War and Welfare: American Catholicism and World War I* (New York, 1988), and Fayette Breaux Veverka, *For God and Country: Catholic Schooling in the 1920s* (New York, 1988).

The middle decades of the current century have received more attention from scholars than the first two decades. The church-state-school question has been addressed by a number of historical and legal scholars. Readers are encouraged to start with Richard Morgan's *The Supreme Court and Religion* (New York, 1972), a clearly written summary of the thicket of court cases from the 1920s to the 1970s. Also of value is Edward Drouin's massive dissertation, "The U.S. Supreme Court and Religious Freedom in American Education in Its Decisions Affecting Church-Related Elementary and Secondary Schools during the First Three Quarters of the Twentieth Century," Ph.D. dissertation, Catholic University of America, 1980. The most recent account is William G. Ross, *Forging New Freedoms: Nativism, Education, and the Constitution, 1917–1927* (Lincoln, Neb., 1994).

The preparation of women religious for life in the classroom is analyzed in Sister Bertrande Meyers's still valuable *Education of Sisters* (New York, 1941), in the work of Fayette Veverka and Mary Oates cited above, in John Murphy's essay, "Catholic Teacher Preparation in the Nineteen Hundreds," in F. Michael Perko, ed., *Enlightening the Next Generation* (New York, 1988), and in Patricia Byrne's chapter, "Saving Souls," in Jay P. Dolan et al., *Transforming Parish Ministry* (New York, 1989).

These few studies are hardly sufficient, however, given the relative importance of sister-teachers to the history of parochial education. Why has this topic been ignored? The reason for this historiographical neglect is multifaceted. Certainly the prejudices of earlier generations of Catholic historians led them to concentrate almost exclusively on the hierarchy. As a result, the history of priests, parishes, and women religious were almost completely ignored.

It is also true that religious orders themselves were reluctant to have their stories told. Only recently have most religious orders of women organized their archives and made their historical materials available for research. Whatever the cause, it is clear that historians of Catholicism can no longer ignore the extraordinary contributions of sister-teachers to the life of parochial education.

Urban Catholicism has fared much better. Edward R. Kantowicz has written the definitive biography of George Cardinal Mundelein, the archbishop of Chicago, in *Corporation Sole: Cardinal Mundelein and Chicago Catholicism* (Notre Dame, Ind., 1983). Kantowicz's study is matched by James W. Sanders's

Education of an Urban Minority: Catholics in Chicago, 1833–1965 (New York, 1977), which concentrates on the archdiocese's greatest period of growth from 1915 to 1965.

Boston also has received attention of late. James O'Toole has written *Militant and Triumphant: William Henry O'Connell and the Catholic Church in Boston, 1859–1944* (Notre Dame, Ind., 1993), a masterful study of this important churchman. Paula Kane's recent book, *Separation and Subculture: Boston Catholicism, 1900–1920* (Chapel Hill, 1994), is an important new volume that dissects the layers of society in this New England metropolis. Scholars can only hope that other cities will receive more scholarly attention.

The historical literature on the history of Catholic schooling in the decades after World War II is slim indeed. Interested readers should start with Jay P. Dolan et al., *Transforming Parish Ministry: The Changing Roles of Catholic Clergy, Laity, and Women Religious* (New York, 1989). Also of value is Diane Ravitch's *Troubled Crusade: American Education, 1945–1980* (New York, 1983), Lerond Curry, *Protestant-Catholic Relations in America: World War I to Vatican II* (Lexington, Ky., 1972), and the two surveys cited at the beginning of this essay: James Hennesey's *American Catholics* (New York, 1983) and Jay P. Dolan's *The American Catholic Experience* (Garden City, N.Y., 1985).

The study of this period is woefully short on biographies. An excellent start is a collective biography of Chicago's Catholic leadership. Steven V. Avella's *This Confident Church: Catholic Leadership and Life in Chicago, 1940–1965* (Notre Dame, Ind., 1992) is both a starting point and a model for other diocesan studies. Also of note is Charles Dahm's *Power and Authority in the Catholic Church: Cardinal Cody in Chicago* (Notre Dame, Ind., 1981), a journalistic portrait of this controversial churchman.

Three other biographical studies merit a mention. Thomas T. McAvoy's *Father O'Hara of Notre Dame: The Cardinal-Archbishop of Philadelphia* (Notre Dame, Ind., 1967) is a sympathetic but scholarly biography of the cardinal archbishop of Philadelphia. Robert Gannon had the burden of writing *The Cardinal Spellman Story* (Garden City, N.Y., 1962) while his subject was still

alive. To his credit, Gannon did not pull his punches, and the
book remains a useful study of the man who dominated the
American church in the 1950s and 1960s. Finally, John Kotre's
*The Best of Times, The Worst of Times: Andrew Greeley and American
Catholicism, 1950–1975* (Chicago, 1978) is a valuable overview of
this prolific social scientist who has done so much over the past
thirty-five years to monitor the health of parochial education.

Sociologists have done as much as or more than historians
in telling the story of Catholic education in the postwar years.
Joseph Fichter's *Parochial School: A Sociological Study* (Notre
Dame, Ind., 1958), Gerhard Lenski's *The Religious Factor* (Garden City, N.Y., 1963), and Peter G. Rossi and Andrew M. Greeley's *The Education of Catholic Americans* (Chicago, 1966) all add
to our understanding of Catholic schools in the 1950s. Greeley
and colleagues Kathleen McCourt and William C. McCready
update the story through the early 1970s in their book, *Catholic Schools in a Declining Church* (Kansas City, 1976). Finally,
James Cibulka, Timothy O'Brien, and Donald Zewe concentrate
on the important role played by Catholic schools in inner-
city parishes. Their book, *Inner City Private Elementary Schools:
A Study* (Milwaukee, 1982), has not received the attention it
deserves.

In addition to the books noted above, researchers should be
aware of other resources of great value to the study of Catholic education. The establishment of the Cushwa Center for
the Study of American Catholicism at the University of Notre
Dame has given momentum to Catholic historical research
through the publication of a newsletter, a working paper series,
and an annual book competition, as well as through a substantial research grant program. The *U.S. Catholic Historian*, the
lively quarterly sponsored by the U.S. Catholic Historical Society, has provided yet another outlet for the fruits of Catholic
historical scholarship.

Researchers interested in learning more about what has been
published in the field can consult two helpful bibliographies:
James Hennesey's "American Catholic Bibliography, 1970–
1982," 2 parts, *Cushwa Center Working Papers* (Notre Dame, Ind.,

1982–83), and John Tracy Ellis and Robert Trisco, eds., *A Guide to American Catholic History*, 2d ed. (Santa Barbara, Calif., 1982). The tremendous growth in the literature in the past dozen years more than justified new editions of both of these works.

"We stand on the verge of a major expansion of our understanding of the history of the Catholics in this country," wrote James O'Toole more than a decade ago, "and the continued cooperation among archivists and historians will make that expansion possible." The work produced over the past twenty-five years is more than evidence of this cooperation.

Yet Catholic scholars must guard against a feeling of satisfaction. "American Catholic historiography," notes James Hennesey, "if it remains fairly set in its ways and preoccupations, likewise remains heavily parochial in regard to the publishers and the journals it employs." Hennesey is quite correct; witness the fact that not a single study of American Catholicism is cited in the American Historical Association's most recent assessment of historical scholarship, *The Past Before Us: Contemporary Historical Writing in the United States* (Ithaca, N.Y., 1980). The mission of Catholic historians remains the integration of their historical research and writing into the mainstream of American historiography.

Notes

Chapter 1: The Origins of Catholic Education

1. Parkman, as cited in Charles H. Lippy, Robert Choquette, and Stafford Poole, *Christianity Comes to the Americas* (New York, 1992), 166–67. For a general background on Catholic mission enterprises in the New World, see Jay Dolan, *The American Catholic Experience* (Garden City, N.Y., 1985), 15–68; John Tracy Ellis, *Catholics in Colonial America* (Baltimore, 1965); Charles Gibson, *Spain in America* (New York, 1954); John Francis Bannon, *The Spanish Borderlands Frontier, 1513–1821* (New York, 1970), in addition to *Christianity Comes to America*.

2. Dolan, *American Catholic Experience*, 44–51; Bannon, *Spanish Borderlands Frontier*, 68–71; Lippy et al., *Christianity Comes to the Americas*, 37–50, 185–87.

3. Bolton, as cited in Dolan, *American Catholic Experience*, 25; see also Lippy et al., *Christianity Comes to the Americas*, 37–38, 120–29; Dolan, *American Catholic Experience*, 44–51; Gibson, *Spain in America*, 68–89.

4. Ellis, *Catholics in Colonial America*, 40–45, 54–67, 75–105.

5. Herbert E. Bolton, *The Rim of Christendom: A Biography of Eusebio Francisco Kino* (New York, 1936); Ellis, *Catholics in Colonial America*, 67–74; Dolan, *American Catholic Experience*, 27–28; Lippy et al., *Christianity Comes to the Americas*, 73–75; Sherburne Cook, *The Conflict between the California Indians and the White Civilization* (Berkeley, Calif., 1976).

6. Ellis, *Catholics in Colonial America*, 107–22; Dolan, *American Catholic Experience*, 29–30; Lippy et al., *Christianity Comes to the Americas*, 117–20.

7. Ellis, *Catholics in Colonial America*, 134–45, 164–67, 211–29; Dolan, *American Catholic Experience*, 31–42; Lippy et al., *Christianity Comes to the Americas*, 158–213.

8. Dolan, *American Catholic Experience*, 52.

9. Joseph Donnelly, *Jean de Brebeuf, 1593–1649* (Chicago, 1975); William V. Bangert, *A History of the Society of Jesus* (St. Louis, 1972); James Hennesey, *American Catholics* (New York, 1981), 25–26; Dolan, *American Catholic Experience*, 36–37; Lippy et al., *Christianity Comes to the Americas*, 160–65.

10. Ellis, *Catholics in Colonial America*, 225–29, 269–73; Lippy et al., *Christianity Comes to the Americas*, 213–15; Dolan, *American Catholic Experience*, 41–42; Joseph Donnelly, *Jacques Marquette, 1637–1675* (Chicago, 1968).

11. Ellis, *Catholics in Colonial America,* 19–20; Hennesey, *American Catholics,* 36–55; Dolan, *American Catholic Experience,* 69–97; Timothy Walch, *Catholicism in America* (Melbourne, Fla., 1989), 19–24.

12. Mary A. Ray, *American Opinion of Roman Catholicism* (New York, 1936), 120–23, 394–96, and passim; Arthur J. Riley, *Catholicism in New England to 1788* (Washington, D.C., 1936), 30–33; 256–60; Timothy Walch, ed., *Early American Catholicism, 1634–1820* (New York, 1988), 155–243.

13. Francis X. Curran, *Catholics in Colonial Law* (Chicago, 1963), 1–109; Ellis, *Catholics in Colonial America,* 338–46; Riley, *Catholicism in New England,* 259–60; Walch, *Early American Catholicism,* 155–243.

14. Charles Carroll of Annapolis to his son Charles Carroll of Carrollton in 1760 as quoted in Mary Carthy, *English Influences on Early American Catholicism* (Washington, D.C., 1959), 14; See also Ronald Hoffman, "Marylando Hibernus: Charles Carroll, the Settler, 1660–1720," in Walch, ed., *Early American Catholicism,* 155–84.

15. Harold A. Buetow, *Of Singular Benefit: The Story of U.S. Catholic Education* (New York, 1970), 27–29; Ray, *American Opinion of Roman Catholicism,* 158–63.

16. Buetow, *Of Singular Benefit,* 29–31; Ray, *American Opinion of Roman Catholicism,* 157–63.

17. Buetow, *Of Singular Benefit,* 31–35; Ellis, *Catholics in Colonial America,* 370; Joseph Kirlin, *Catholicity in Philadelphia* (Philadelphia, 1909), 23–29; Ray, *American Opinion of Roman Catholicism,* 162–64.

18. Charles H. Metzger, *Catholics in the American Revolution* (Chicago, 1962), passim; Hennesey, *American Catholics,* 55–68; Dolan, *American Catholic Experience,* 96–97; Curran, *Catholics in Colonial Law,* 109–22; Walch, *Catholicism in America,* 24–26.

19. Neil G. McCluskey, ed., *Catholic Education in America: A Documentary History* (New York, 1964), 47.

20. Patrick W. Carey, *People, Priests, and Prelates: Ecclesiastical Democracy and the Tensions of Trusteeism* (Notre Dame, Ind., 1986); Dolan, *American Catholic Experience,* 110–24; Walch, ed., *Early American Catholicism,* 363–96.

21. Thomas J. Donaghy, *Philadelphia's Finest: A History of Catholic Education in the Catholic Archdiocese, 1692–1970* (Philadelphia, 1972), 1–29; Kirlin, *Catholicity in Philadelphia,* 110–11; Buetow, *Of Singular Benefit,* 34–36.

22. Donaghy, *Philadelphia's Finest,* 26–27; Burns, *Catholic School System,* 138; Buetow, *Of Singular Benefit,* 88–91.

23. Donaghy, *Philadelphia's Finest,* 28; Burns, *Catholic School System,* 140–41.

24. Buetow, *Of Singular Benefit,* 90–91; Burns, *Catholic School System,* 142–43.

25. Buetow, *Of Singular Benefit,* 86–88; Francis Cohalan, *A Popular History of the Archdiocese of New York* (New York, 1983), 9–37; Carl Kaestle, *The Evolution of an Urban School System: New York City, 1750–1850* (Cambridge, 1973), 145–48.

26. Buetow, *Of Singular Benefit*, 88; Walch, *Catholicism in America*, 32; Hennesey, *American Catholics*, 90–92.

27. Kaestle, *Evolution of an Urban School System*, 145–46.

28. Ibid., 146; Vincent Lannie, *Public Money and Parochial Education* (Cleveland, 1968), 29–41.

29. Matignon to Carroll, November 6, 1808, as quoted in Robert H. Lord et al., *A History of the Archdiocese of Boston*, 3 vols. (New York, 1944), 1:599; Walch, *Catholicism in America*, 32.

30. The best available biographies of Elizabeth Seton are Joseph I. Irvin, *Mrs. Seton: Foundress of the American Sisters of Charity* (New York, 1962), and Anabelle Melville, *Elizabeth Bayley Seton, 1744–1821* (New York, 1951). See also Barbara Misner, *"Highly Respectable and Accomplished Ladies": Catholic Women Religious in America, 1790–1850* (New York, 1988).

31. Melville, *Elizabeth Bayley Seton*, 253–59; Misner, *"Highly Respectable and Accomplished Ladies,"* 191–203; Buetow, *Of Singular Benefit*, 60–63.

Chapter 2: Strangers in the Land

1. The best general history of immigration and ethnicity is Thomas J. Archdeacon, *Becoming American* (New York, 1983); see in particular 57–84. Other useful works are Roger Daniels, *Coming to America* (New York, 1990), Oscar Handlin, *The Uprooted* (Boston, 1951), and Maldwyn Jones, *American Immigration* (New York, 1960).

2. Archdeacon, *Becoming American*, 27–56; Jones, *American Immigration*, 147–76; Handlin, *The Uprooted*, 63–93.

3. Alexis de Tocqueville, "On American Catholics in Relation to Democracy, 1835," as cited in John Tracy Ellis, *Documents of American Catholic History* (Milwaukee, 1956), 239.

4. The most complete study of the Charlestown riot is Ray Allen Billington, *The Protestant Crusade, 1800–1860: A Study of the Origins of American Nativism* (New York, 1938), 68–91; on the Philadelphia riots, see Michael Feldberg, *The Philadelphia Bible Riots of 1844: A Study of Ethnic Conflict* (Westport, Conn., 1975), and Vincent P. Lannie and Bernard Diethorn, "For the Honor and Glory of God: The Philadelphia Bible Riots of 1844," *History of Education Quarterly* 8 (Spring 1968): 44–106; on Boston, see also Thomas H. O'Connor, *Fitzpatrick's Boston, 1846–1866: John Bernard Fitzpatrick, Third Bishop of Boston* (Boston, 1984); on Philadelphia, see Sam Bass Warner, *The Private City: Philadelphia at Three Stages of Growth* (Philadelphia, 1968), 137–53.

5. Billington, *Protestant Crusade*, 87–90.

6. Feldberg, *The Philadelphia Bible Riots of 1844*, 162–94; Lannie and Diethorn, "For the Honor and Glory of God," 93–95.

7. Billington, *Protestant Crusade*, 68–91; William K. Dunn, *What Ever Happened to Religious Education?: The Decline of Religious Teaching in the Public Elementary School, 1776–1861* (Baltimore, 1958).

8. Carl Kaestle, *The Evolution of an Urban School System: New York City, 1750–1850* (Cambridge, 1973), 158.

9. Lawrence Cremin, *American Education: The National Experience* (New York, 1980), 376–88; David B. Tyack, *The One Best System: A History of Urban Education* (Cambridge, 1974), 104–9; Robert L. Church and Michael W. Sedlak, *Education in the United States: An Interpretive History* (New York, 1976), 55–83.

10. Timothy L. Smith, "Protestant Schooling and American Nationality, 1800–1850," *Journal of American History* 53 (March 1967): 695.

11. Kaestle, *Evolution of an Urban School System,* 151–55; Vincent P. Lannie, *Public Money and Parochial Education* (Cleveland, 1968), 75–118.

12. Dunn, *What Ever Happened to Religious Education?* 262–72; Neil G. McCluskey, ed., *Catholic Education in America: A Documentary History* (New York, 1964), 51–64; Lannie, *Public Money and Parochial Education,* 29–102.

13. Timothy Walch, *The Diverse Origins of American Catholic Education: Chicago, Milwaukee, and the Nation* (New York, 1988), 101–4; Paul J. Foik, *Pioneer Catholic Journalism* (New York, 1930); Robert F. Hueston, *The Catholic Press and Nativism, 1840–1860* (New York, 1976).

14. Hugh J. Nolan, ed., *Pastoral Letters of the American Catholic Hierarchy, 1792–1970* (Huntington, Ind., 1971), 17–126; McCluskey, *Catholic Education in America,* 51–64; Walch, *Diverse Origins of American Catholic Education,* 101–4; Hueston, *Catholic Press and Nativism.*

15. McCluskey, *Catholic Education in America,* 54–55; Nolan, *Pastoral Letters,* 25.

16. Nolan, *Pastoral Letters,* 17–126.

17. McCluskey, *Catholic Education in America,* 59; Nolan, *Pastoral Letters,* 90.

18. McCluskey, *Catholic Education in America,* 63; Nolan, *Pastoral Letters,* 109.

19. McCluskey, *Catholic Education in America,* 63.

20. McCluskey, *Catholic Education in America,* 61; Nolan, *Pastoral Letters,* 94.

21. McCluskey, *Catholic Education in America,* 78–94; Nolan, *Pastoral Letters,* 128–88.

22. For background on Kenrick, see Hugh J. Nolan, *The Most Reverend Francis Patrick Kenrick, Third Bishop of Philadelphia, 1830–1851* (Washington, D.C., 1948); on Hughes, see Richard V. Shaw, *Dagger John: The Unquiet Life and Times of Archbishop John Hughes* (New York, 1977).

23. Lannie and Diethorn, "For the Honor and Glory of God," 44–72; Nolan, *Francis Patrick Kenrick,* 288–342.

24. Nolan, *Francis Patrick Kenrick,* 117–25, 141–45.

25. Shaw, *Dagger John,* passim; Timothy Walch, *Catholicism in America: A Social History* (Melbourne, Fla., 1989), 148–49; Lannie, *Public Money and Parochial Education,* 51–74.

26. Richard J. Purcell, "Hughes, John J.," *Dictionary of American Biography* (New York, 1933), 5:352–55.

27. Lannie, *Public Money and Parochial Education,* 75–258.

28. John G. Hassard, *The Life of the Most Reverend John Hughes, D.D.* (New York, 1866), 389, reprinted in Walch, *Catholicism in America,* 149.

Chapter 3: A Range of Educational Experiences

1. Timothy Walch, *The Diverse Origins of American Catholic Education: Chicago, Milwaukee, and the Nation* (New York, 1988), 75–120; Jay P. Dolan, ed., *The American Catholic Parish,* 2 vols. (New York, 1987), 2:282–326.

2. Walch, *Diverse Origins of American Catholic Education,* 19–43; Dolan, *American Catholic Parish,* 2:282–36; Gerald R. Fogarty, ed., *Patterns of Episcopal Leadership* (New York, 1989), 85–89.

3. James W. Sanders, "Boston Catholic Schools and the Social Question, 1825–1870," in Brian Mitchell, ed., *Building the American Catholic City: Parishes and Institutions* (New York, 1988), 151–83; Thomas H. O'Connor, *Fitzpatrick's Boston, 1846–1866* (Boston, 1984).

4. Sanders, "Boston Catholic Schools," 156–57; Donna Merwick, *Boston Priests, 1848–1910* (Cambridge, 1973), 19.

5. Brian C. Mitchell, "Educating Irish Immigrants in Ante-bellum Lowell," *Historical Journal of Massachusetts* 11 (1983): 94–103; James Burns, *Growth and Development of the Catholic School System in the United States* (New York, 1912), 285–89.

6. Mitchell, "Educating Irish Immigrants," 100; Burns, *Growth and Development of Catholic Schools,* 288–89.

7. For information on the variations of the Lowell Plan in other communities see Jay P. Dolan, *The American Catholic Experience* (New York, 1985), 270–76; Norlene M. Kunkel, *Bishop Bernard McQuaid and Catholic Education* (New York, 1988), 200; Timothy H. Morrisey, "Archbishop John Ireland and the Faribault-Stillwater School Plan of the 1890s: A Reappraisal," Ph.D. dissertation, University of Notre Dame, 1975, 98–105.

8. Jay P. Dolan, *The Immigrant Church: New York's Irish and German Catholics, 1815–1865* (Baltimore, 1975), 99–120; Carl Kaestle, *Evolution of an Urban School System: New York City, 1750–1850* (Cambridge, 1973), 145–48.

9. Kaestle, *Evolution of an Urban School System,* 146.

10. Vincent P. Lannie, *Public Money and Parochial Education* (Cleveland, 1968), 75–144.

11. Ibid., 166–244.

12. Quoted in John R. G. Hassard, *The Life of the Most Reverend John Hughes, D.D.* (New York, 1866), 389; reprinted in Walch, *Catholicism in America,* 149.

13. See Lannie, *Public Money and Parochial Education,* 245–58; Dolan, *Immigrant Church,* 105–6; Howard Weisz, "Irish American Attitudes and the Americanization of the English Language Parochial School," *New York History* 53 (1972): 157–67.

14. Michael Feldberg, *The Philadelphia Bible Riots of 1844: A Study of Ethnic Conflict* (Westport, Conn., 1975), and Vincent P. Lannie and Bernard

Diethorn, "For the Honor and Glory of God: The Philadelphia Bible Riots of 1844," *History of Education Quarterly* 8 (1968): 44–106.

15. Feldberg, *The Philadelphia Bible Riots of 1844*, 99–119, 143–61.

16. Quoted in Lannie and Diethorn, "For the Honor and Glory of God," 49.

17. Ibid., 56.

18. Ibid., 59.

19. Michael Feldberg, *The Philadelphia Bible Riots of 1844*, 78–99; Ray Allen Billington, *The Protestant Crusade* (New York, 1938), 221–35.

20. Quoted in Billington, *Protestant Crusade*, 230.

21. Quoted in Lannie and Diethorn, "For the Honor and Glory of God," 92–93.

22. Glen Gabert, *In Hoc Signo? A Brief History of Catholic Parochial Education* (Port Washington, N.Y., 1973), 68.

23. Dolan, ed., *The American Catholic Parish*, 2:282–326; Walch, *Diverse Origins of American Catholic Education*, 19–43; Edward A. Connaughton, *A History of Educational Legislation and Administration in the Archdiocese of Cincinnati* (Washington, D.C., 1946).

24. *Chicago Tribune* (April 22, 1853).

25. Heiss to Killian Kleiner, July 6, 1853, published in *Salesianum* 10 (1914).

26. Timothy Walch, "Catholic Social Institutions and Urban Development: The View from Nineteenth-Century Chicago and Milwaukee," *Catholic Historical Review* 64 (1978): 16–32.

27. William Wells to I. Haines, December 2, 1858, William Wells Papers, Chicago Historical Society.

28. Emmet H. Rothan, *The German Catholic Immigrant in the United States, 1830–1860* (Washington, D.C., 1946), 123–38.

29. J. B. Purcell in *The Catholic Telegraph* (March 26, 1853), as quoted in Connaughton, *A History of Educational Legislation and Administration in the Archdiocese of Cincinnati*, 43.

30. Colman Barry, "German Catholics and the Nationalist Controversy," in Philip Gleason, ed., *Catholicism in America* (New York, 1970), 65–80; Barry, *The Catholic Church and German Americans* (Milwaukee, 1953).

Chapter 4: The Campaign for Control

1. Ray Allen Billington, *The Protestant Crusade, 1800–1860* (New York, 1938), 247.

2. Lawrence Kehoe, *The Complete Works of the Most Reverend John Hughes*, 2 vols. (New York, 1865), 2:714–15.

3. Hugh J. Nolan, ed., *Pastoral Letters of the American Hierarchy, 1792–1970* (Huntington, Ind., 1970), 137–39; Neil G. McCluskey, ed., *Catholic Education in America* (New York, 1964), 78–81.

4. Nolan, *Pastoral Letters*, 138; McCluskey, *Catholic Education in America*, 81.

5. William K. Dunn, *What Ever Happened to Religious Education? The Decline of Religious Teaching in the Public Elementary School, 1776–1861* (Baltimore, 1958), 273–75; Harold A. Buetow, *Of Singular Benefit: The Story of U.S. Catholic Education* (New York, 1970), 155–56.

6. On McMaster's life and career, see Mary A. Kwitchin, *James Alphonsus McMaster: A Study in American Thought* (Washington, D.C., 1949), and Thomas T. McAvoy, "Public Schools versus Catholic Schools and James McMaster," *Review of Politics* 28 (1966): 19–46.

7. Richard J. Purcell, "McMaster, James Alphonsus," *Dictionary of American Biography* (New York, 1933), 6:140; McAvoy, "Public Schools versus Catholic Schools."

8. There is no complete biography of Sadlier. For basic biographical information, see Charles Fanning, *The Irish Voice in America* (Lexington, Ky., 1990), 114–40; Thomas N. Brown, "Sadlier, Mary Anne M.," *Notable American Women* (Cambridge, 1971), and Richard J. Purcell, "Sadlier, Mary Anne M.," *Dictionary of American Biography* (New York, 1933), 8:284.

9. For a general study of Catholic fiction, see Paul Messbarger, *Fiction with a Parochial Purpose* (Boston, 1971). On Sadlier, see Fanning, *The Irish Voice in America*, 114–40.

10. Preface to Mary Anne Sadlier, *Aunt Honor's Keepsake* (New York, 1866).

11. Mary Anne Sadlier, *The Blakes and the Flanagans* (Boston, 1855), 390.

12. There are several biographies of this controversial Catholic leader. The best study is Thomas Ryan, *Orestes Brownson: A Definitive Biography* (Huntington, Ind., 1976). On education, see James M. McDonnell, *Orestes A. Brownson and Nineteenth-Century Catholic Education* (New York, 1988).

13. James A. McMaster and later Bernard McQuaid led the conservative campaign for a total church commitment to Catholic education. On McMaster, see McAvoy, "Public Schools versus Catholic Schools and James McMaster." On McQuaid, see Norlene M. Kunkel, *Bishop Bernard J. McQuaid and Catholic Education* (New York 1988).

14. Harold A. Buetow, *Of Singular Benefit*, 154–61; Timothy Walch, *The Diverse Origins of American Catholic Education* (New York, 1988), 45–74; Thomas T. McAvoy, *A History of the Catholic Church in the United States* (Notre Dame, Ind., 1969), 229–31.

15. McAvoy, "Public Schools versus Catholic Schools and James McMaster," 22–25; McAvoy, *A History of the Catholic Church*, 229–30; Neil G. McCluskey, *Catholic Education Faces Its Future* (Garden City, N.Y., 1970), 67–77.

16. McCluskey, *Catholic Education Faces Its Future*, 71–74; McAvoy, "Public Schools versus Catholic Schools and James McMaster," 30–31.

17. McAvoy, "Public Schools versus Catholic Schools and James McMaster," 33; McCluskey, *Catholic Education Faces Its Future*, 72–73.

18. McAvoy, "Public Schools versus Catholic Schools and James McMaster," 35.

19. Neil G. McCluskey, ed., *Catholic Education in America: A Documentary*

History (New York, 1964), 121–26; McAvoy, "Public Schools versus Catholic Schools and James McMaster," 36–43; McCluskey, *Catholic Education Faces Its Future*, 74–77.

20. McCluskey, *Catholic Education in America*, 121–26.

21. For a general history of education at the Third Plenary Council, see Philip Gleason, "Baltimore III and Education," *U.S. Catholic Historian* 4 (1985): 273–313; Francis P. Cassidy, "Catholic Education in the Third Plenary Council of Baltimore," *Catholic Historical Review* 34 (1948–49): 257–305, 414–36; and Bernard J. Meiring, *Educational Aspects of the Legislation of the Councils of Baltimore, 1829–1884* (New York, 1978).

22. McCluskey, *Catholic Education in America*, 93; Hugh J. Nolan, ed., *Pastoral Letters of the American Hierarchy, 1792–1970* (Huntington, Ind., 1971), 115.

23. McCluskey, *Catholic Education in America*, 94.

24. William Scanlon, "The Development of the American Catholic Diocesan Board of Education, 1884–1966," Ed.D. dissertation, New York University, 1967.

25. See M. C. Klinkhamer, "The Blaine Amendment of 1875: Private Motives for Political Action," *Catholic Historical Review* 52 (1956): 15–49; John Tracy Ellis, ed., *Documents of American Catholic History* (Milwaukee, 1956), 407–9; Harold A. Buetow, *Of Singular Benefit*, 154–61; Richard M. Jensen, *The Winning of the Midwest* (Chicago, 1972).

26. Ellis, *Documents of American Catholic History*, 408; Buetow, *Of Singular Benefit*, 154–61.

27. Klinkhamer, "The Blaine Amendment"; Buetow, *Of Singular Benefit*, 158.

28. Daniel W. Kucera, *Church-State Relationships in Education in Illinois* (Washington, D.C., 1955), 111–12; *Laws Passed by the General Assembly for the Year 1889* (Springfield, Ill., 1890), 237ff.

29. Kucera, *Church-State Relationships*, 111–12.

30. *Chicago Tribune* (November 10, 1892).

31. Jensen, *Winning of the Midwest*, 123–53; Paul Kleppner, *The Cross of Culture* (New York, 1971); M. Justile McDonald, *The Irish in Wisconsin during the Nineteenth Century* (Washington, D.C., 1954), 159–63; *Lutheran Witness* (July 21, 1889) as cited in Jensen, *Winning of the Midwest*, 124.

32. *Milwaukee Sentinel* (December 30, 1889, March 12, 1890); Jensen, *Winning of the Midwest*, 124, 133; *Chicago Tribune* (August 27, 28, 1890).

33. John Spooner to H. M. Kulitin, November 18, 1890, as cited in Jensen, *Winning of the Midwest*, 122.

34. Quoted in Harry Heming, ed., *The Catholic Church in Wisconsin*, 4 vols. (Milwaukee, 1895–99), 1:172.

Chapter 5: New Models for Parish Schools

1. Among the general overviews of the different models of American parochial education is Jay P. Dolan, *The American Catholic Experience* (Garden City, N.Y., 1985), 269–93. See also Robert D. Cross, "Origins of the

Catholic Parochial School in America," and Howard Weisz, "Irish American Attitudes and the Americanization of English Language Parochial Schools," both republished in F. Michael Perko, ed., *Enlightening the Next Generation* (New York, 1988).

2. On the Lowell experiment, see Brian Mitchell, *The Paddy Camps: The Irish of Lowell, 1821–1861* (Urbana, Ill., 1987); on the Savannah parochial schools, see Michael V. Gannon, *Rebel Bishop: The Life and Era of Augustin Verot* (Milwaukee, 1964). On Poughkeepsie, see Clyde and Sally Griffin, *Natives and Newcomers: The Ordering of Opportunity in Mid-Nineteenth-Century Poughkeepsie* (Cambridge, 1978).

3. Griffin, *Natives and Newcomers*, 28.

4. James A. Burns, *The Growth and Development of the Catholic School System in the United States*, 256–58; Harold A. Buetow, *Of Singular Benefit* (New York, 1970), 159–61.

5. Griffin, *Natives and Newcomers*, 29.

6. Ibid., 44.

7. Burns, *Growth and Development*, 265–69.

8. See Weisz, "Irish American Attitudes," and Cross, "Origins of Catholic Parochial Education," in Perko, ed., *Enlightening the Next Generation*.

9. *Western Catholic* (February 23, 1884).

10. Weisz, "Irish American Attitudes," in Perko, ed., *Enlightening the Next Generation*, 163.

11. Quoted in ibid., 168.

12. Ibid.

13. Ibid., 165.

14. See Timothy Walch, "Catholic Schoolbooks and American Values: The Nineteenth-Century Experience," *Religious Education* 73 (1978): 582–91.

15. See Ruth Miller Elson, *Guardians of Tradition* (Lincoln, Neb., 1964), and Richard D. Moser, *Making the American Mind: Social and Moral Ideas in McGuffey Readers* (New York, 1965).

16. Burns, *Growth and Development of Catholic Schools in the United States*, 143.

17. *Sadlier's Excelsior Third Reader* (New York, 1876–78). For a general overview of the themes developed in Catholic schoolbooks, see Timothy Walch, "Catholic Schoolbooks and American Social Values."

18. *Sadlier's Excelsior Fourth Reader* (New York, 1876–78), 100–101.

19. Richard Gilmour, "Catholic National Series of Readers" (New York, 1877).

20. *The Little Bee* (Chicago), no. 1 (December 1884); *Sadlier's Excelsior Studies in the History of the United States for Schools* (New York, 1879).

21. Weisz, "Irish American Attitudes," in Perko, ed., *Enlightening the Next Generation*, 175.

22. See Richard M. Linkh, *American Catholicism and European Immigrants, 1900–1924* (New York, 1975), 103–31; Charles Shanabruch, *Chicago's Catholics: The Evolution of an American Identity* (Notre Dame, Ind., 1981), 78–104; Ellen M. Kuznicki, "The Polish American Parochial Schools," in Frank

Mocha, ed., *Poles in America* (Stevens Point, Wis., 1978), 435–60; Josef Barton, *Peasants and Strangers* (Cambridge, 1975). 145–69.

23. Quoted in Emmet Rothan, *German Catholic Immigrants in the United States (1830–1860)* (Washington, D.C., 1946), 126.

24. Quoted in Shanabruch, *Chicago's Catholics*, 91.

25. Philip Gleason, "Immigration and the American Catholic Intellectual Life," *Review of Politics* 26 (April 1964): 147–73. See also A. H. Walburg, "The Question of Nationality in Its Relation to the Catholic Church in the United States" (1889), reprinted in part in Aaron I. Abell, ed., *American Catholic Thought on Social Questions* (Indianapolis, 1968), 37–51.

26. Rudolph J. Vecoli, "Prelates and Peasants: Italian Immigrants and the Catholic Church," *Journal of Social History* 2 (Spring 1969): 248.

27. Ibid., 249.

28. Ibid., 251.

29. John Bodnar, "Materialism and Morality: Slavic Immigrants and Education, 1890–1940," *Journal of Ethnic Studies* 3 (1976): 1–19.

30. Ibid., 6.

31. Joseph Cada, *Czech-American Catholics, 1850–1920* (Lisle, Ill., 1964), 54.

32. Quoted in M. Mark Stolarik, "Immigration, Education, and the Social Mobility of Slovaks, 1870–1930," in R. M. Miller and T. D. Marzik, eds., *Immigrants and Religion in Urban America* (Philadelphia, 1977), 106.

33. Ibid., 107.

34. Ibid., 108. See also Josef J. Barton, *Peasants and Strangers*, 147.

35. William J. Galush, "Faith and Fatherland: Dimensions of Polish-American Ethno Religion, 1875–1975," in Miller and Marzik, eds., *Immigrants and Religion in Urban America*, 93.

36. Ellen Marie Kuznicki, "The Polish American Parochial Schools," 435–60.

37. Quoted in Anthony J. Kuzniewski, "The Catholic Church in the Life of Polish Americans," in Mocha, ed., *Poles in America*, 410.

38. Ibid.

39. Quoted in Daniel S. Buczek, "The Polish American Parish as an Americanizing Factor," in C. A. Ward, P. Shashko, and D. E. Pienkos, eds., *Studies in Ethnicity: The East European Experience in America* (New York, 1980), 157.

40. Kuzniewski, "Catholic Church in the Life of Polish Americans," 415; Buczek, "Polish American Parish," 159–63; Kuznicki, "Polish American Parochial Schools," 454–55.

41. Kuznicki, "Polish American Parochial Schools," 454; Kantowicz, *Corporation Sole*, 77–82; Galush, "Faith and Fatherland," 95–97.

42. Jay P. Dolan, *The American Catholic Parish*, 2 vols. (Mahwah, N.J., 1987).

Chapter 6: The School Controversy

1. Among the best studies of these "energetic individuals" is Robert Cross's classic, *The Emergence of Liberal Catholicism in America* (Cambridge,

1958), 130–45 and 162–81. The term "energetic individuals" comes from Cross. Another useful work is Colman J. Barry, *The Catholic Church and the German Americans* (Milwaukee, 1953), 183–236. See also the biographies of individual prelates noted below as well as the essays in F. Michael Perko, ed., *Enlightening the Next Generation: Catholics and Their Schools, 1830–1980* (New York, 1988), and William L. Portier, ed., *The Inculturation of American Catholicism, 1820–1900* (New York, 1988).

2. On Ireland, see Marvin R. O'Connell, *Archbishop John Ireland and American Catholicism* (St. Paul, 1988), and James H. Moynihan, *The Life of Archbishop John Ireland* (New York, 1953).

3. Quoted in Timothy H. Morrisey, "A Controversial Reformer: Archbishop John Ireland and His Educational Beliefs," in F. Michael Perko, ed., *Enlightening the Next Generation* (New York, 1988), 57.

4. Ibid., 59.

5. Robert Emmett Curran, "Conservative Thought and Strategy in the School Controversy, 1891–93," in F. Michael Perko, ed., *Enlightening the Next Generation* (New York, 1988), 77–96.

6. The best biography of McQuaid is Norlene M. Kunkel, *Bishop Bernard J. McQuaid and Catholic Education* (New York, 1988). See also Frederick J. Zwierlein, *The Life and Letters of Bishop Bernard McQuaid*, 3 vols. (Rochester, 1925–27).

7. As printed in the *West End Journal* (May 1871) and cited in Norlene M. Kunkel, "Consolidating an American Catholic School System: Bishop Bernard McQuaid's Rationale," in David J. Alvarez, ed., *An American Church* (Moraga, Calif., 1979).

8. Archbishop Austin J. Dowling in a review of Zwierlein, *Life of McQuaid* in *American Historical Review* 33 (April 1928): 702.

9. Morrisey, "Controversial Reformer," 61–74.

10. John Ireland, "State Schools and Parish Schools" (1890), reprinted in Neil G. McCluskey, ed., *Catholic Education in America* (New York, 1964), 128.

11. The most complete study of the so-called school controversy is Timothy H. Morrisey, "Archbishop John Ireland and the Faribault-Stillwater School Plan of the 1890s: A Reappraisal," Ph.D. dissertation, University of Notre Dame, 1975; see also Daniel F. Reilly, *The School Controversy (1891–1893)* (Washington, D.C., 1943), and John Tracy Ellis, *The Life of James Cardinal Gibbons*, 2 vols. (Milwaukee, 1952), 1:653–707.

12. The liberal position on parochial schools is articulated in the two works cited in note 2; also of value is Robert D. Cross, *The Emergence of Liberal Catholicism in America* (Cambridge, 1958), 130–45; David J. O'Brien, *Public Catholicism* (New York, 1989), 103–12; and Marvin R. O'Connell, *Archbishop John Ireland and the American Catholic Church* (St. Paul, 1988).

13. The conservative position on parochial schools is articulated in Curran, "Conservative Thought and Strategy in the School Controversy, 1891–1893," in F. Michael Perko, ed., *Enlightening the Next Generation* (New York, 1988), 77–96; see also Curran, *Michael Augustine Corrigan and the Shap-*

ing of Conservative Catholicism in America, 1878–1902 (New York, 1978) and Kunkel, *Bishop Bernard J. McQuaid and Catholic Education* (New York, 1988).

14. On Ireland's intentions for his speech, see Ireland to Gibbons, December 1890, reprinted in John Tracy Ellis, ed., *Documents of American Catholic History* (Milwaukee, 1955), 490–95.

15. Ireland, "State Schools and Parish Schools," 140.

16. Ibid., 129.

17. Among the best accounts of the contempt of the conservative bishops for John Ireland and his views can be found in Kunkel, *Bishop Bernard McQuaid,* 177–221; Curran, *Michael Augustine Corrigan,* passim; and Curran, "Conservative Thought," 77–95.

18. Ireland to Gibbons, December 1890, as reprinted in John Tracy Ellis, ed., *Documents of American Catholic History,* 490–95. Also reprinted in McCluskey, ed., *Catholic Education in America,* 141–50.

19. McCluskey, *Catholic Education in America,* 148.

20. Ibid., 147.

21. Quoted in John Tracy Ellis, *Life of Gibbons,* 665.

22. Ibid., 667–72; Harold A. Buetow, *Of Singular Benefit* (New York, 1970), 170–75.

23. Curran, "Conservative Thought," 46.

24. Ibid., 51–52; Kunkel, *Bishop Bernard McQuaid,* 213–15.

25. Ellis, *Life of Gibbons,* 1:670–73; Curran, "Conservative Thought," 49.

26. Gibbons to Denis O'Connell, March 1, 1892, quoted in Ellis, *Life of Gibbons,* 1:676.

27. Ellis, *Life of Gibbons,* 1:681–87; Curran, "Conservative Thought," 83–86.

28. Ellis, *Life of Gibbons,* 1:688; Curran, "Conservative Thought," 51–52.

29. Gibbons to Camillus Maes, June 16, 1892, as quoted in Ellis, *Life of Gibbons,* 1:691.

30. Ellis, *Life of Gibbons,* 1:694–702; Curran, "Conservative Thought," 87–89; McAvoy, *History of the Catholic Church,* 301–2.

31. Corrigan to Cardinal Rampolla, December 16, 1892, as quoted in Curran, "Conservative Thought," 91.

32. Corrigan to Gibbons, June 20, 1893, as quoted in Ellis, *Life of Gibbons,* 1:702.

33. Quoted in F. J. Zwierlein, *The Life and Letters of Bishop Bernard McQuaid* 3 vols. (Rochester, 1927), 3:187.

34. Robert D. Cross, *The Emergence of Liberal Catholicism in America* (Cambridge, 1958), 145.

Chapter 7: The Search for Order

1. Morgan M. Sheedy, "The Catholic Parochial Schools of the United States," *Report of the U.S. Commissioner of Education for 1903* (Washington, D.C., 1903), 1079.

2. I am indebted to Robert H. Wiebe and his extraordinary book *The Search for Order, 1877–1920* (New York, 1967) for the title and the framework for this chapter. Wiebe's work is highly recommended for anyone interested in understanding the broad changes in American society during these decades.

3. Sheedy, *Report*, 1096.

4. E. F. Gibbons, "School Supervision: Its Necessity, Aims, and Methods," *CEA Bulletin* 2 (1905): 167.

5. James A. Burns, s.v. "Schools, In the United States," *Catholic Encyclopedia* (New York, 1907–12).

6. William Scanlon, "The Development of the American Catholic Diocesan Board of Education, 1884–1966," Ed.D. dissertation, New York University, 1967, Figure 10.

7. Michael J. Relihan, "The Parish School System as the Lay Educator Sees It," *NCEA Bulletin* 25 (1928): 480–92.

8. Scanlon, "Development of the American Catholic Diocesan Board of Education," Figures 1–10.

9. Ibid.

10. Ibid., figures 4 and 6.

11. Ibid., figures 3, 5, and 7.

12. Ibid., figures 7, 8, and 9.

13. Ibid., figure 10.

14. Elizabeth McKeown, "The National Bishops Conference: An Analysis of Its Origins," *Catholic Historical Review* 66 (1968): 565–83, and McKeown, *War and Welfare: American Catholics and World War I* (New York, 1988). See also Donald C. Horrigan, *The Shaping of the NCEA* (Washington, D.C., 1978), and Edgar McCarren, "The Origins and Early Years of the National Catholic Educational Association," Ph.D. dissertation, Catholic University of America, 1966.

15. Horrigan, *Shaping of the NCEA*, 3.

16. Ibid., 4.

17. Conaty as quoted in James H. Plough, "Catholic Colleges and the Catholic Educational Association: The Foundation and Early Years of the CEA, 1899–1919," Ph.D. dissertation, University of Notre Dame, 1967, 163.

18. *Report of the Proceedings of the First Annual Meeting of the CEA [CEA Bulletin]* 1 (1904): 9–10, and Buetow, *Of Singular Benefit*, 181.

19. Horrigan, *Shaping of the NCEA*, 4.

20. Ibid., 4–5.

21. Francis Howard, s.v. "Educational Association," *Catholic Encyclopedia*.

22. Horrigan, *Shaping of the NCEA*, 5, Burns, *Catholic Education*, 75–83.

23. Horrigan, *Shaping of the NCEA*, 5, and James A. Burns, *Catholic Education: A Study of Conditions* (New York, 1917), 75–83.

24. Paul J. Schuler, "The Reaction of American Catholics to the Foundations and Early Practices of Progressive Education in the United States, 1892–1917," Ph.D. dissertation, University of Notre Dame, 1970, 371–74.

25. William F. Lawlor, "Are Any Changes Needed in Our Elementary Schools to Meet Post-War Conditions?" *CEA Bulletin* 16 (1919): 331–35.

26. Ibid., 335.

27. Joseph M'Clancy in comment on ibid., 337.

28. Albert L. Hollinger, "Getting Full Value Out of Catholic Education," *CEA Bulletin* (1920): 264.

29. Francis I. Bredestege, "Present-Day Trends in Education," *CEA Bulletin* 22 (1925): 372.

30. Ibid., 383.

31. Daniel J. Feeney, "Safeguarding Religious Spirit in Catholic Education, *NCEA Bulletin* 26 (1929): 327.

32. Horrigan, *Shaping of the NCEA*, 5–6; Plough, "Catholic Colleges," 515.

33. McKeown, "National Bishops Conference," 565–83; and McKeown, *War and Welfare*, passim.

34. McKeown, "National Bishops Conference," 574.

35. Ibid., 577.

36. Ibid., 578–84.

37. James H. Ryan, *A Catechism of Catholic Education* (Washington, D.C., 1922), 17; Fayette Veverka, *For God and Country: Catholic Schooling in the 1920s* (New York, 1988), 96–99.

38. Ryan as cited in Veverka, *For God and Country*, 99.

39. NCWC statement as cited in Veverka, *For God and Country*, 100.

40. Veverka, *For God and Country*, 102–5.

41. Ibid., 104.

42. Ibid., 102.

43. Ibid., 111; David B. Tyack, "The Perils of Pluralism: The Background of the Pierce Case," *American Historical Review* 74 (1968): 74–98.

44. Veverka, *For God and Country*, 116–23; Timothy Walch, *Catholicism in America* (Melbourne, Fla., 1989), 68–69, 172–73.

45. NCWC statement as cited in Veverka, *For God and Country*, 123.

46. James H. Ryan, "What the Oregon Document Means for American Education," *NCWC Bulletin* 7 (1925): 10; Veverka, *For God and Country*, 123–25.

47. Michael Williams to John Burke (1922), cited in John B. Sheerin, *Never Look Back: The Career of John J. Burke* (New York, 1975), 85–86; Veverka, *For God and Country*, 107.

48. Veverka, *For God and Country*, 108; see also Patricia Byrne, "Saving Souls and Educating Americans, 1930–1945," in Jay P. Dolan et al., *Transforming Parish Ministry* (New York, 1989), 115–16.

Chapter 8: Catholic Education and Modern American Society

1. Lawrence A. Cremin, *The Transformation of the School* (New York, 1961), viii.

2. Paul J. Schuler, "Reaction of American Catholics to the Foundations and Early Practices of Progressive Education in the United States, 1892–1917," Ph.D. dissertation, University of Notre Dame, 1970, 378.

3. Ibid., 332.

4. Ibid.

5. The best biography of Shields is John F. Murphy, "Thomas E. Shields, Religious Educator," Ph.D. dissertation, Columbia University, 1971. See also Murphy, "Thomas Edward Shields, Progressive Educator," *Notre Dame Journal of Education* 5 (1974): 358–69.

6. Thomas E. Shields, *The Psychology of Education* (Washington, D.C., 1906), 2.

7. Murphy, "Thomas E. Shields" (dissertation), 95.

8. Shields, *Psychology of Education*, 89.

9. Shields, "Teaching the Children to Think," *Catholic Educational Review* 2 (1911): 949.

10. Schuler, "Reaction of American Catholics," 332.

11. Murphy, "Thomas Edward Shields," 364; Justine Ward, *Thomas Edward Shields* (New York, 1947), 138.

12. Bryce is quoted in Murphy, "Thomas E. Shields" (dissertation), 85–86.

13. Shields, "The Method of Teaching Religion," *CEA Bulletin* 5 (1908): 208.

14. Shields, *Psychology of Education*, 113–14; Murphy, "Thomas E. Shields" (dissertation), 107.

15. Murphy, "Thomas E. Shields" (dissertation), 108–9.

16. The best biography of Yorke is Joseph S. Brasher, S.J., *Consecrated Thunderbolt: Father Yorke of San Francisco* (New York, 1973). See also Mary Charles Bryce, "Four Decades of Roman Catholic Innovators," *Religious Education* 73 (1978): S37–S41.

17. Quoted in Murphy, "Thomas Edward Shields," 364.

18. Ibid.

19. Ibid.

20. Murphy, "Thomas E. Shields" (dissertation), 170.

21. Ibid., 84–91; Murphy, "Thomas Edward Shields," 366.

22. Shields, *Religion: First Book* (Washington, D.C., 1908), 92–96, quoted in Murphy, "Thomas Edward Shields," 362.

23. Shields to "Dr. O'Donnelly," October 14, 1913, as quoted in Murphy, "Thomas E. Shields" (dissertation), 172.

24. Shields to "Miss Clark," June 26, 1914, as quoted in Murphy, "Thomas E. Shields" (dissertation), 172–73.

25. Kane to Shields, November 21, 1914, quoted in Murphy, "Thomas E. Shields," 173, and Shields to Kane, February 25, 1918, as quoted in Murphy, "Thomas E. Shields" (dissertation), 179.

26. See Jeffrey M. Burns, "The Ideal Catholic Child: Images from Catholic Textbooks, 1875–1912," *Cushwa Center Working Papers Series* (Spring 1978).

27. There is no scholarly biography of Johnson; for basic details, see Neil G. McCluskey, "Johnson, George," *Dictionary of American Biography*, Supplement 3 (New York, 1973), 393. See also Sister Mary Giovanni Vidoni, S.N.D., "Monsignor George Johnson: His Principles and Their Application to the Curriculum of the Catholic Schools," M.A. thesis, Catholic University of America, 1952; Harold L. Buetow, *Of Singular Benefit: The Story of U.S. Catholic Education* (New York, 1970), 218–41.

28. McCluskey, "Johnson, George."

29. Donald C. Horrigan, *Shaping of the NCEA* (Washington, D.C., 1979), 8–9.

30. McCluskey, "Johnson, George."

31. George Johnson, "Principles of Standardization," *CEA Bulletin* 19 (November 1922): 82–83. See also Fayette Veverka, *For God and Country: Catholic Schooling in the 1920s* (New York, 1988), 126–50.

32. Johnson, "Principles of Standardization," 89.

33. Johnson, "The Need of a Constructive Policy for Catholic Education in the United States," *Catholic Educational Review* 23 (1925): 385–94.

34. Horrigan, *Shaping of the NCEA*, 9.

35. Johnson, "Address of the Reverend Doctor George Johnson," *NCEA Bulletin* 26 (1929): 43.

36. Horrigan, *Shaping of the NCEA*, 12.

37. Vidoni, "George Johnson," 82–91; Buetow, *Of Singular Benefit*, 231–46; Thomas Blantz, *A Priest in Public Service: Francis J. Haas and the New Deal* (Notre Dame, Ind., 1982), 176–77.

38. Quoted in John J. Bonner, "Tribute to the Memory of Monsignor Johnson," *NCEA Bulletin* 41 (1944): 40.

39. George Johnson, "Federal Aid to Education in the Emergency," *Catholic Educational Review* 32 (1934): 77.

40. Ibid., 78.

41. Ibid., 80.

42. George Johnson, "Report of the Secretary General," *NCEA Bulletin* 39 (1942): 75.

43. Vidoni, "Monsignor George Johnson," 84–91.

44. Ibid., 85.

45. Ibid., 91–93; Buetow, *Of Singular Benefit*, 239–40; Blantz, *Francis J. Haas*, 177.

46. Quoted in Blantz, *Francis J. Haas*, 177.

47. Vidoni, "Monsignor George Johnson," 83.

48. Edward B. Jordan, "Apostle of Catholic Education," *Catholic Educational Review* 42 (1944): 394–99; "Editorial," *Nation's Schools* (August 1944); John J. Bonner, "Tribute to the Memory of Monsignor Johnson," *NCEA Bulletin* 41 (1944): 40–41.

49. Jordan, "Apostle of Catholic Education," 399.

Chapter 9: The Making of Sister-Teachers

1. The historiography of Catholic sister-teachers is very limited. Two volumes that touch on the subject are Mary Ewens, *The Role of the Nun in Nineteenth-Century America* (New York, 1978), and Sister Bertrande Meyers, *The Education of Sisters* (New York, 1941). Histories of specific orders and congregations vary greatly in quality. In truth, the subject has yet to find its historian.

2. Jay P. Dolan, *The American Catholic Experience* (Garden City, N.Y., 1985), 277–79, 288–92; Dolan gathered these statistics from an unpublished paper by Mary Ewens entitled "The Impact of Sisters on the Nineteenth-Century Church," tables 1 and 2. See M. Jane Coogan, B.V.M., *The Price of Our Heritage*, 2 vols. (Dubuque, Iowa, 1975–78), on the Sisters of Charity of the Blessed Virgin Mary; Sister Maria Concepta, C.S.C., *The Making of a Sister Teacher* (Notre Dame, Ind., 1965), on the Sisters of the Holy Cross; and Sister JoAnn Euper, O.S.F., *First Century of Service: The School Sisters of St. Francis* (Milwaukee, 1976). These are three of the best studies of the contributions of specific orders of women religious to parochial education.

3. Meyers, *Education of Sisters*, 3–21.

4. Ibid., 7.

5. Ibid.

6. See Edward Kantowicz, *Corporation Sole: Cardinal Mundelein and Chicago Catholicism* (Notre Dame, Ind., 1982), 85. Although Kantowicz focuses on Chicago, his description of chaos is valid for many other dioceses.

7. Meyers, *Education of Sisters*, 3–49; John F. Murphy, "Professional Preparation of Catholic Teachers in the Nineteen Hundreds," in F. Michael Perko, ed., *Enlightening the Next Generation: Catholics and Their Schools, 1830–1980* (New York, 1988); Harold A. Buetow, *Of Singular Benefit: The Story of U.S. Catholic Education* (New York, 1970), 188–93, 246–51; Fayette Veverka, *For God and Country: Catholic Schooling in the 1920s* (New York, 1988), 151–86; and Mary J. Oates, "Learning to Teach: The Professional Preparation of Massachusetts Parochial School Faculty, 1870–1940," *Cushwa Center Working Paper Series* (Notre Dame, Ind., 1981). The most recent work on Catholic teacher training can be found in Patricia Byrne, "Saving Souls and Educating Americans," in Jay P. Dolan et al., *Transforming Parish Ministry* (New York, 1989), 118–23.

8. Henry J. Browne, "The American Parish School in the Last Half Century," *NCEA Bulletin* 50 (1953): 323–34; see also the annual volumes of the *Catholic Educational Review* from 1910 to 1920 and the *NCEA Bulletin* from 1904 to 1920 for the many articles and commentaries on teacher training; some of these essays are cited below.

9. Meyers, *Education of Sisters*, 9; Byrne, "Saving Souls and Educating Americans," 116–18.

10. Meyers, *Education of Sisters*, 3–48.

11. Ibid. See also Mary J. Oates, "Learning to Teach," passim.

12. Mary J. Oates, "Organized Volunteerism: The Catholic Sisters in Massachusetts, 1870–1940," *American Quarterly* 30 (1978): 654–57.

13. Ibid., 656.

14. Hugh J. Nolan, ed., *The Pastoral Letters of the American Hierarchy, 1792–1970* (Huntington, Ind., 1970), 178; Neil G. McCluskey, ed., *Catholic Education in America* (New York, 1964), 93–94; Buetow, *Of Singular Benefit* (New York, 1970), 152–53.

15. Harold A. Buetow, "The Teaching of Education at the Catholic University of America, 1889–1966," *Catholic Educational Review* 65 (1967): 3.

16. *Thirteenth Annual Report of the Rector of the Catholic University of America* (November 1902), quoted in ibid., 5.

17. Quoted in ibid., 6.

18. Thomas E. Shields, *The Education of Our Girls* (New York, 1907), 285–88, as quoted in Murphy, "Professional Preparation of Catholic Teachers," in Perko, ed., *Enlightening the Next Generation,* 247.

19. The story of the Sisters College can be found in Murphy, "Thomas E. Shields" (dissertation), 144–52; Murphy, "Professional Preparation of Catholic Teachers," 249–53; and Buetow, "The Teaching of Education at the Catholic University of America," 9–10.

20. Shields to Sister Josephine, June 12, 1915 as quoted in Murphy, "Thomas E. Shields" (dissertation), 144–45.

21. Ibid.

22. Murphy, "Professional Preparation of Catholic Teachers," 251.

23. Murphy, "Thomas E. Shields" (dissertation), 146–47; Murphy, "Professional Preparation of Catholic Teachers," 252.

24. Thomas E. Shields, "The Need of the Catholic Sisters College and the Scope of Its Work," *Catholic Educational Review* 17 (1919): 428–29.

25. See ibid.; see also Buetow, "The Teaching of Education at the Catholic University of America," 8–11.

26. Meyers, *Education of Sisters,* 14–15, 21–22; Oates, "Learning to Teach," 4.

27. Oates, "Learning to Teach," 4–5.

28. See James A. Burns, "The Training of Teachers," *Educational Brief* no. 5 (1904): 30–38; Thomas E. Shields, "The Sisters College," *Catholic Educational Review* 3 (1912): 1–12.

29. Burns, "The Training of Teachers," 38.

30. *Acts and Decrees of the Third Plenary Council of Baltimore* (Baltimore, 1886); the text is published in both English and Latin, 110.

31. Edwin V. O'Hara, "The Diocesan Teacher's Institute," *Catholic Educational Review* 2 (1911): 487.

32. See ibid.; see also Francis J. Macelwane, "A Diocesan Normal School," *CEA Bulletin* 21 (1924): 422–35; Leon A. McNeill, "The Diocesan Normal School," *NCEA Bulletin* 27 (1930): 382–89.

33. Oates, "Learning to Teach," 6–7.

34. Ibid., 15–16.

35. Meyers, *Education of Sisters,* 29–36; Veverka, *For God and Country,* 151–86; George Johnson, "A Plan for Teacher Certification," *Catholic Educational Review* 20 (1921): 446–52; P. J. McCormick, "Church Law and the Certifica-

tion of Teachers," *Catholic Educational Review* 20 (1922): 257–73; Ralph Hayes, "The Problem of Teacher Certification," *CEA Bulletin* 19 (1922): 364–69.

36. Meyers, *Education of Sisters*, 37–47; Veverka, *For God and Country*, 160–61, 166–73, 177–86; Byrne, "Saving Souls and Educating Americans," 118–23.

37. Meyers, *Education of Sisters*, 37–47.

38. "Superintendents Section," *CEA Bulletin* 16 (1919): 320.

39. Veverka, *For God and Country*, 155–56.

40. Paul L. Blakely, "The Certification of Teachers," *CEA Bulletin* 17 (1920): 450–53.

41. George Johnson, "A Plan of Teacher Certification," *CEA Bulletin* 18 (1921): 394.

42. Hayes, "Problem of Teacher Certification," 369.

43. Edward Jordan, "The Evaluation of Credits," *CEA Bulletin* 22 (1925): 493.

44. Veverka, *For God and Country*, 167.

45. Ibid., 168.

46. Meyers, *Education of Sisters*, 37–47.

47. Ibid., 101–2.

48. Veverka, *For God and Country*, 172.

49. Meyers, *Education of Sisters*, 70–73.

50. Veverka, *For God and Country*, 177.

51. Ibid., 177–79.

52. Mary Ewens, "The Leadership of Nuns in Immigrant Catholicism," in Rosemary R. Ruether and Rosemary S. Keller, eds., *Women and Religion in America*, 3 vols. (New York, 1981), 1:101.

53. Ibid., 1:101–2.

Chapter 10: The Church-State-School Question

1. One of the best summaries of the church-state-school question up to the date of its publication can be found in Richard E. Morgan, *The Supreme Court and Religion* (New York, 1972), 76–122. See also Sister Raymond McLaughlin, *A History of State Legislation Affecting Private Elementary and Secondary Schools in the United States, 1870–1945* (Washington, D.C., 1946), 82–175.

2. McLaughlin, *A History of State Legislation*, 60–83. See also Timothy Walch, *The Diverse Origin of American Catholic Education: Chicago, Milwaukee and the Nation* (New York, 1988), 45–74.

3. McLaughlin, *A History of State Legislation*, 91–116.

4. Ibid., 93.

5. Ibid., 95–96.

6. Ibid., 100–101.

7. Fayette Veverka, *For God and Country: Catholic Schooling in the 1920s* (New York, 1988), 60–67; McLaughlin, *A History of State Legislation*, 102–7.

8. *Nebraska District of Evangelical Lutheran Synods of Missouri, et al., v. McKelvie*, as quoted in McLaughlin, *A History of State Legislation*, 104–5; see also William G. Ross, *Forging New Freedoms: Nativism, Education, and the Constitution, 1917–1927* (Lincoln, Neb., 1994), 74–95.

9. *Meyer v. State of Nebraska* 262 U.S. 390 (1923). See McLaughlin, *A History of State Legislation*, 104–5; see also Ross, *Forging New Freedoms*, 115–33.

10. Thomas Elton Brown, "Patriotism or Religion? Compulsory Public Education and Michigan's Roman Catholic Church, 1920–1924," *Michigan History* (1980): 36–42; see also Ross, *Forging New Freedoms*, 134–47.

11. Brown, "Patriotism or Religion?" 40–42; Ross, *Forging New Freedoms*, 134–47.

12. There are three essays of note on the background of the Oregon case: David B. Tyack, "The Perils of Pluralism: The Background of the Pierce Case," *American Historical Review* 74 (1968): 74–98; Lloyd P. Jorgenson, "The Oregon School Law of 1922: Passage and Sequel," *Catholic Historical Review* 54 (1968): 455–66; and M. Paul Holsinger, "The Oregon School Bill Controversy, 1922–25," *Pacific Historical Review* 37 (1968): 327–42. The most recent account can be found in Ross, *Forging New Freedoms*, 148–73.

13. Holsinger, "Oregon School Bill," 332.

14. Ibid., 336.

15. Ibid., 337; Jorgenson, "Oregon School Law of 1922," 463.

16. Quoted in Holsinger, "Oregon School Bill," 338.

17. *Portland Catholic Sentinel* (April 3, 1923), as cited in Tyack, "Perils of Pluralism," 95.

18. Quoted in ibid., 96.

19. Quoted in ibid., 97.

20. *Pierce v. Society of Sisters* 268 U.S. 510 reprinted in John Tracy Ellis, ed., *Documents of American Catholic History* (Milwaukee, 1956), 635–38. See also Ross, *Forging New Freedoms*, 148–73, 185–200.

21. *New York Times* (June 2, 1925).

22. *Portland Oregonian* (June 2, 1925), as quoted in Lloyd P. Jorgenson, "Oregon School Law," 464.

23. Jorgenson, "Oregon School Law," 466.

24. Quoted in Edward G. Drouin, "The United States Supreme Court and Religious Freedom in American Education in Its Decisions Affecting Church-Related Elementary and Secondary Schools during the First Three Quarters of the Twentieth Century," Ph.D. dissertation, Catholic University of America, 1980, 184.

25. Ibid., 186–87.

26. Ibid.

27. *Cochran v. Louisiana State Board of Education* 281 U.S. 370 (1930). See also Drouin, "The United States Supreme Court," 189.

28. Cited in McLaughlin, *A History of State Legislation*, 154, 165.

29. Ibid., 166–68.

30. *Johnson v. Boyd*, as cited in ibid., 167.

31. Cited in Anson P. Stokes, *Church and State in the United States,* 3 vols. (New York, 1950), 3:693.

32. Ibid., 3:662–68.

33. Ibid., 3:664–66.

34. Ibid., 3:667.

35. *Everson v. Board of Education* 330 U.S. 1 (1947). See also Morgan, *Supreme Court and Religion,* 81–84, 90–95.

36. Morgan, *Supreme Court and Religion,* 80–81; Stokes, *Church and State,* 3:696–97.

37. The best background on the *Everson* case can be found in Daryl R. Fair, "Remote from the Schoolhouse: The Passage of the New Jersey Parochial School Bus Bill," *New Jersey History* (1981): 704–5.

38. *Everson v. Board of Education;* Morgan, *Supreme Court and Religion,* 90–92; Stokes, *Church and State,* 3:704–5.

39. *Everson v. Board of Education.*

40. Morgan, *Supreme Court and Religion,* 92.

41. *Washington Post* (February 13, 1947); Stokes, *Church and State,* 3:710–11.

42. Quoted in Robert I. Gannon, *The Cardinal Spellman Story* (New York, 1962), 310.

43. *New York Times* (June 14, 1947).

44. Quoted in Gannon, *The Cardinal Spellman Story,* 311. See also Joseph P. Lash, *Eleanor: The Years Alone* (New York, 1972), 155–68.

45. Gannon, *The Cardinal Spellman Story,* 312–13.

46. Ibid., 314–21. See also James Hennesey, *American Catholics* (New York, 1981), 298.

Chapter 11: A Generation of Crisis

1. There is no adequate history of Catholic education in the post–World War II era; worthy of review are Jay P. Dolan et al., *Transforming Parish Ministry: The Changing Role of Catholic Clergy, Laity, and Women Religious* (New York, 1989); James Hennesey, *American Catholics* (New York, 1981), 280–306; Jay P. Dolan, *The American Catholic Experience* (New York, 1985), 384–417; John Tracy Ellis, *American Catholicism,* rev. ed. (Chicago, 1969), 192–203; David J. O'Brien, *Public Catholicism* (New York, 1989), 212–15; Neil G. McCluskey, *Catholic Education Faces Its Future* (Garden City, N.Y., 1969), 107–37; and Harold Buetow, *Of Singular Benefit: The Story of U.S. Catholic Education* (New York, 1970).

2. See in particular, McCluskey, *Catholic Education Faces Its Future,* 185–214; Mary Perkins Ryan, *Are Catholic Schools the Answer?* (New York, 1964); Andrew M. Greeley and William C. Brown, *Will Catholic Schools Survive?* (New York, 1970).

3. Hennesey, *American Catholics,* 280.

4. Dolan et al., *Transforming Parish Ministry,* 134–35, 148–50; Hennesey, *American Catholics,* 296–300.

5. There are only a few studies of worth on these three dynamic figures. Of value are Steven Avella, *The Confident Church: Catholic Leadership and Life in Chicago, 1940–1965* (Notre Dame, Ind., 1992), Thomas J. McAvoy, *Father O'Hara of Notre Dame: The Cardinal Archbishop of Notre Dame* (Notre Dame, Ind., 1967), and Robert I. Gannon, *The Cardinal Spellman Story* (Garden City, N.Y., 1962). See also Thomas E. Blantz, "Stritch, Samuel A.," *Dictionary of American Biography, Supplement VI* (New York, 1980); Robert F. Trisco, "Meyer, Albert Gregory," *Dictionary of American Biography, Supplement VII* (New York, 1981), and Gerald P. Fogarty, "Spellman, Francis Joseph," *Dictionary of American Biography, Supplement VIII* (New York, 1988).

6. Florence D. Cohalan, *A Popular History of the Archdiocese of New York* (New York, 1983), 302.

7. "Current Comment," *America* (June 13, 1953): 289.

8. James W. Sanders, *Education of an Urban Minority: Catholics in Chicago, 1833–1965* (New York, 1977), 202–3; "Current Comment," *America* (September 8, 1956): 514.

9. James Connelly, ed., *History of the Archdiocese of Philadelphia* (Philadelphia, 1976), 457; Thomas Donaghy, *Philadelphia's Finest: A History of Education in the Catholic Archdiocese, 1692–1970* (Philadelphia, 1972), 235.

10. Quoted in Donaghy, *Philadelphia's Finest*, 251.

11. Joseph E. Cunneen, "Catholics and Education," *Commonweal* (August 7, 14, 1953); Urban Fleege, "Catholic Education Needs a 'New Look'" *America* (April 24, 1954): 96–101; Robert Hartnett, "On Asking the Right Question," *America* (April 24, 1954): 102–3.

12. Harold T. O'Donnell, "The Lay Teacher in Catholic Education," in F. Michael Perko, ed., *Enlightening the Next Generation: Catholics and Their Schools, 1830–1900* (New York, 1988); Annette Cronin, "Catholic Schools Need Lay Teachers," *America* (April 24, 1954); John J. Reilly, "Idea for More Teachers," *America* (April 24, 1954).

13. McAvoy, *O'Hara of Notre Dame*, 385.

14. Ibid., 391–93.

15. William E. McManus, "How Good Are Catholic Schools? *America* (September 8, 1956): 522.

16. Ibid., 523.

17. Quoted in McAvoy, *O'Hara of Notre Dame*, 429.

18. John P. Sullivan, "The Growth of Catholic Schools," *America* (November 16, 1957): 205; Dolan et al., *Transforming Parish Ministry*, 148–50.

19. Hennesey, *American Catholics*, 314; Dolan, *Transforming Parish Ministry*, 150–53.

20. "How Big Is the Crisis for Catholic Schools?" *U.S. News and World Report* (February 3, 1964): 60–61; see also "Schools under Strain," *Time* (March 20, 1964): 75.

21. Quoted in "No First Grade," *Newsweek* (March 16, 1964): 98.

22. Mary Perkins Ryan, *Are Catholic Schools the Answer?* (New York, 1964).

23. James A. O'Conner, "The Modest Proposal of Mary Perkins Ryan," *Catholic World* (July 1964): 220; John N. Kotre, *The Best of Times, The Worst*

of Times: Andrew M. Greeley and American Catholicism, 1950–1975 (Chicago, 1978).

24. "Schools under Strain," 75.

25. Lawrence J. Sheehan, "The Parochial School," *America* (April 4, 1964): 481–83.

26. Francis Canavan, "The School: Whose Is It?" *America* (August 15, 1964): 153–56; Olin J. Murdick, "Preparing for Change in Parochial Schools," *America* (February 27, 1965): 282–84; Joseph M. Cunneen, "Negroes in Catholic Schools," *Commonweal* (October 7, 1966): 13–16; Andrew M. Greeley, "Catholic Education," *America* (April 17, 1965): 522–28.

27. Glen Gabert, *In Hoc Signo? A Brief History of American Catholic Parochial Schools* (Port Washington, N.Y., 1973), 131–32; Patricia Byrne, "A Tumultuous Decade, 1960–1970," in Dolan et al., *Transforming Parish Ministry*, 170–75.

28. "Trouble in the Classroom," *Time* (June 2, 1967); "Catholic Education: Why Its Special Problems Are Increasing," *U.S. News and World Report* (September 11, 1967); "A Fiscal Crisis," *Time* (March 28, 1969); "Crisis Hits Catholic Schools," *U.S. News and World Report* (September 29, 1969).

29. Donald C. Horrigan, *The Shaping of the NCEA* (Washington, D.C., 1978), 20.

30. C. Albert Koob as quoted in ibid., 23.

31. Ibid., 24.

32. Ellis, *American Catholicism*, rev. ed., 197.

33. "Statement of the Washington Symposium," reprinted in C. Albert Koob and Russell Shaw, eds., *Trends and Issues in Catholic Education* (Washington, D.C., 1969), 310.

34. James C. Donohue, "New Frontiers in Catholic Education," *America* (April 13, 1968): 476–79. Russell Shaw, "Financing Catholic Education?" *America* (September 28, 1968): 240–43; Mary Kavanagh, "Who Killed Parochial Education," *America* (November 16, 1968): 472–73; Franklin E. Fitzpatrick, "The Missing Ingredient in Catholic Schools," *America* (April 5, 1969): 406–7.

35. "A Fiscal Crisis," *Time* (March 28, 1969): 42–43; Buetow, *Of Singular Benefit*, 286–87.

36. "A Fiscal Crisis"; "Crisis Hits Catholic Schools," *U.S. News and World Report* (September 29, 1969): 33–34; "Will Catholic Schools Survive?" *America* (April 19, 1969): 460.

37. Neil G. McCluskey, "Neil G. McCluskey on Catholic Schools," *America* (January 10, 1970): 22–23; Michael O'Neill, "Giving Americans a Choice — Alternatives to Public Education," *America* (January 24, 1970); C. Albert Koob, "Where Is the Catholic School Heading?" *America* (September 19, 1970).

38. C. Albert Koob and Russell Shaw, *S.O.S. for Catholic Schools* (New York, 1970), 132–50.

39. William C. Brown and Andrew M. Greeley, *Can Catholic Schools Survive?* (New York, 1970), 22, 24.

40. "School and Parish," *Commonweal* (January 29, 1971).

41. "The Catholic School Crisis," *Newsweek* (October 4, 1971): 83–84.

42. Ibid., 84; see also "Untangling Parochial Schools," *Time* (July 12, 1971), and "Can Catholic Schools Survive?" *U.S. News and World Report* (July 12, 1971).

43. Edward F. Spiers, "The Youngstown Plan," *America* (June 24, 1972): 650–51; Harold J. O'Donnell, "Catholic Schools — the Problem Is One of Values," *America* (September 15, 1973): 171; William E. McManus, " 'Project Choose' — The Chicago Plan," *America* (April 1, 1972): 347; George Elford, "The Chicago Report," *Commonweal* (January 28, 1972): 390–93; Ed Marciniak, "The Games They Play in Catholic Schools," *Commonweal* (October 6, 1972).

44. Andrew M. Greeley, "The Catholic Schools Are Committing Suicide," *New York Times Magazine* (October 21, 1973).

45. S. Francis Overlan, "Why Are Parochial Schools Closing?" *America* (September 14, 1974): 111–13.

46. "Catholic Schools in Black Areas," *America* (February 7, 1976): 86.

47. Quoted in Horrigan, *Shaping of the NCEA*, 28.

48. For statistics on declining enrollments, see Andrew D. Thompson and Eugene F. Hemrick, *The Last Fifteen Years: A Statistical Survey of Catholic Elementary and Secondary Formal Education, 1965–1980* (Washington, D.C., 1982).

49. *New York Times* (May 15, June 25, 1977).

50. Mary Sherry, "Is State Aid the Saving Grace of Catholic Education?" *America* (April 9, 1977).

51. "Comeback in Catholic Schools," *U.S. News and World Report* (March 20, 1978): 54; *New York Times* (June 4, 1978).

52. *New York Times* (March 25, June 6, September 30, 1978; May 13, 1979; April 21, October 9, October 12, October 21, November 16, December 27, 1980).

Chapter 12: Catholic Schools Observed

1. Myron Leiberman, "Parochial Schools and Public Leadership," *NCEA Bulletin* 57 (1960): 242; Harold Buetow, *Of Singular Benefit: The Story of U.S. Catholic Education* (New York, 1970), 295.

2. Leonard V. Koos, *Private and Public Secondary Education* (Chicago, 1931); Michael O'Neill, *How Good Are Catholic Schools?* (Washington, D.C., 1968), 9.

3. Paul Blanshard, *American Freedom and Catholic Power* (Boston, 1951).

4. Joseph H. Fichter, *Parochial School: A Sociological Study* (Notre Dame, Ind., 1958).

5. Gerhard Lenski, *The Religious Factor* (Garden City, N.Y., 1963), 267.

6. Ibid., 268–70.

7. Ibid., 270–71.

8. Ibid., 271.

9. Ibid., 272–73.

10. Ibid., 273–74.

11. Ibid., 274–76.

12. Ibid., 278–80.

13. Reginald A. Neuwien, ed., *Catholic Schools in Action* (Notre Dame, Ind., 1966); Peter H. Rossi and Andrew M. Greeley, *The Education of Catholic Americans* (Chicago, 1966).

14. Neuwien, ed., *Catholic Schools in Action;* O'Neill, *How Good Are Catholic Schools?* 15–17.

15. O'Neill, *How Good Are Catholic Schools?* 8–9.

16. Buetow, *Of Singular Benefit,* 295–96.

17. Rossi and Greeley, *The Education of Catholic Americans;* John N. Kotre, *Best of Times, Worst of Times: Andrew M. Greeley and American Catholicism, 1950–1975* (Chicago, 1978), 49–72.

18. Kotre, *Best of Times, Worst of Times,* 53–55.

19. Rossi and Greeley, *Education of Catholic Americans,* 229; Buetow, *Of Singular Benefit,* 298–99.

20. Rossi and Greeley, *Education of Catholic Americans,* 220; Buetow, *Of Singular Benefit,* 299.

21. Rossi and Greeley, *Education of Catholic Americans,* 231; Buetow, *Of Singular Benefit,* 300.

22. Rossi and Greeley, *Education of Catholic Americans,* 227–28; Buetow, *Of Singular Benefit,* 300.

23. Edward B. Fiske, "Study Evaluates Catholic Schools," *New York Times* (July 25, 1966); Daniel Callahan, "Review of *The Education of Catholic Americans*," *Commentary* (January 1967): 83; "Review of *The Education of Catholic Americans*," *Harvard Educational Review* (Summer 1967); C. Albert Koob and Russell Shaw, *Trends and Issues in Catholic Education* (Washington, D.C., 1969), 61.

24. *NCEA News* (February 13, 1969), as cited in Buetow, *Of Singular Benefit,* 300.

25. Buetow, *Of Singular Benefit,* 301–2.

26. Louis Mayock and Allan Glatthorn, "NCEA and the Development of the Post-Conciliar Catholic School," *Momentum* (December 1980): 10.

27. Andrew M. Greeley, Kathleen McCourt, and William McCready, *Catholic Schools in a Declining Church* (Kansas City, Mo., 1976), 10.

28. Ibid., 221.

29. Ibid., 233–34.

30. Ibid., 235.

31. Ibid., 243.

32. Ibid., 325.

33. Ibid., 236.

34. James R. Kelly, " 'Catholic Schools in a Declining Church': A Review Article," *America* (May 15, 1976): 424–26; Andrew M. Greeley, *American Catholics: A Sociological Portrait* (New York, 1977), 164–86.

35. Philip E. Lampe, "Parochial Schools: How Un-American Are They?" *America* (September 13, 1975): 116–17.

36. James G. Cibulka, Timothy O'Brien, and Donald Zewe, *Inner City Private Elementary Schools: A Study* (Milwaukee, 1982). See also a summary of the findings published in pamphlet form by the Catholic League for Religious and Civil Rights. All citations below are to the Catholic League publication.

37. Ibid., 4.

38. Ibid., 9.

39. Ibid., 16.

40. Ibid., 31–32.

41. Ibid., 43.

42. Ibid., 55–58.

43. Andrew D. Thompson and Eugene F. Hemrick, *The Last Fifteen Years: A Statistical Summary of Catholic Elementary and Secondary Formal Religious Education, 1965–1980* (Washington, D.C., 1982), 6–7.

Chapter 13: The Church-State-School Question Revisited

1. *Everson v. Board of Education* 330 U.S. 1 (1947); Richard E. Morgan, *The Supreme Court and Religion* (New York, 1972), 81–84, 90–95; Anson P. Stokes, *Church and State in the United States*, 3 vols. (New York, 1950), 3:704.

2. The best discussion of the church-state-school issue from 1950 through 1971 is Morgan, *The Supreme Court and Religion*, 76–144. See also Morgan, "The Establishment Clause and Sectarian Schools: A Final Installment?" in Philip B. Kurland, ed., *Church and State: The Supreme Court and the First Amendment* (Chicago, 1975), 232–75.

3. Neil G. McCluskey, *The Catholic Viewpoint on Education* (Garden City, N.Y., 1959), 153.

4. Ibid., 153–54.

5. Lerond Curry, *Protestant-Catholic Relations in America: World War I through Vatican II* (Lexington, Ky., 1972), 63–67.

6. Ibid., 70–79; Paul Blanshard, *God and Man in Washington* (Boston, 1960); Theodore H. White, *The Making of a President, 1960* (New York, 1961); John Cogley, *A Canterbury Tale* (New York, 1976), 83–87.

7. *Look Magazine* (March 3, 1959); Blanshard, *God and Man in Washington*, 200–205.

8. *Look Magazine* (March 3, 1959).

9. Quoted in Blanshard, *God and Man in Washington*, 200–205.

10. Ibid.

11. Robert I. Gannon, *The Cardinal Spellman Story* (Garden City, N.Y., 1962), 323–25.

12. Ibid., 323; "Under Catholic Church Fire: Kennedy's School Plan," *U.S. News and World Report* (January 30, 1961): 54–55; "The Cardinal's Claim," *Time* (January 27, 1961).

13. John F. Kennedy, "Special Message to the U.S. Congress on Education, February 20, 1961," *Public Papers of the Presidents: John F. Kennedy, 1961* (Washington, D.C., 1962), 109; Hugh Douglas Price, "Race, Religion, and the

Rules Committee: The Kennedy Aid-to-Education Bills," in Alan F. Weston, ed., *The Uses of Power* (New York, 1962), 24.

14. Price, "Race, Religion, and the Rules Committee," 25. See also Eugene Eidenberg and Ray D. Morey, *An Act of Congress* (New York, 1969), 22–23.

15. Price, "Race, Religion, and the Rules Committee," 28.

16. John F. Kennedy, "Press Conference, March 8, 1961," *Public Papers of the President: John F. Kennedy, 1961* (Washington, D.C., 1962), 154–56.

17. Hugh Price, "Race, Religion, and the Rules Committee," 30.

18. Ibid., 39.

19. Ibid., 47.

20. Ibid., 62.

21. Ibid., 68. See also Gannon, *The Cardinal Spellman Story*, 327–29.

22. For the history of Johnson's aid to education legislation, see Eidenberg and Morey, *An Act of Congress*, 58–70, 81–89, and 182–83.

23. Quoted in ibid., 64.

24. Diane Ravitch, *The Troubled Crusade: American Education, 1945–1980* (New York, 1983), 148–49; Harold A. Buetow, *Of Singular Benefit: The Story of U.S. Catholic Education* (New York, 1970), 330–33; and Neil G. McCluskey, *The Catholic Viewpoint on Education* (New York, 1959), 163–70.

25. See Eidenberg and Morey, *An Act of Congress*, 182–83, and Michael O'Neill, "Catholic Schools, Innovation and Title III," *America* (January 25, 1975): 49–50.

26. Neil G. McCluskey, *Catholic Education Faces Its Future* (Garden City, N.Y., 1969), 142–44; Buetow, *Of Singular Benefit*, 334–35.

27. *Flast v. Cohen* 392 U.S. 83 (1968); Morgan, *The Supreme Court and Religion*, 96–100; Peter M. J. Stravinskas, *Constitutional Rights and Religious Prejudice: Catholic Education as the Battleground* (Milwaukee, 1982), 82.

28. *Board of Education v. Allen* 392 U.S. 236 (1968); Morgan, *Supreme Court and Religion*, 100–103; Buetow, *Of Singular Benefit*, 336–37; Stravinskas, *Constitutional Rights and Religious Prejudice*, 99–101.

29. *Lemon v. Kurtzman, Earley v. DiCenso* 403 U.S. 602 (1971); "New Trend: State Money for Private Schools," *U.S. News and World Report* (May 4, 1970): 34–36; Morgan, *Supreme Court and Religion*, 100–112; Stravinskas, *Constitutional Rights and Religious Prejudice*, 99–101.

30. Morgan, *Supreme Court and Religion*, 110–11, 242–43; "Untangling Parochial Schools," *Time* (July 12, 1971): 55; "The Parochial School Tangle," *Saturday Review* (August 21, 1971); Charles M. Whelan, "Lessons from the School Aid Decisions," *America* (July 24, 1971): 32–33.

31. *Lemon v. Kurtzman* 411 U.S. 192 (1973); Morgan, "The Establishment Clause and Sectarian Schools," 245–46; Stravinskas, *Constitutional Rights and Religious Prejudice*, 101.

32. *Levitt v. Committee for Public Education and Religious Liberty*, 413 U.S. 472 (1973); Morgan, "The Establishment Clause and Sectarian Schools," 245–48; "Church, State, and School," *Newsweek* (July 9, 1973); Charles M. Whelan, "The School Aid Decisions: 'Not Dead but Sleeping,'" *America* (July 7, 1973): 6–8.

33. *Levitt v. Committee;* Morgan, "The Establishment Clause v. Sectarian Schools," 247.

34. *Committee for Public Education and Religious Liberty v. Nyquist* 413 U.S. 756 (1973); Morgan, "The Establishment Clause and Sectarian Schools," 249–50.

35. *Sloan v. Lemon* 413 U.S. 825 (1973); Morgan, "The Establishment Clause and Sectarian Schools," 250–51.

36. "Church, State, and School," 64.

37. Whelan, "School Aid Decisions," 8.

38. "Church, State, and School," 64.

39. Ibid.

40. Whelan, "School Aid Decisions," 8.

41. *Committee for Public Education and Religious Liberty v. Regan,* 444 U.S. 646 (1980); Stravinskas, *Constitutional Rights and Religious Prejudice,* 106.

42. *America* (July 9, 1977): 3.

43. Fred Barbash, "Court Relaxes Restrictions on Aid to Religious Schools," *Washington Post* (June 30, 1983).

44. *Mueller v. Allen,* as cited in Linda Greenhouse, "High Court Backs State Benefit for School Costs," *New York Times* (June 30, 1983); "The Court, Education, and Religion," *Washington Post* (June 30, 1983).

45. Jim Castelli, "Impact of Supreme Court Ruling Will Be Felt for Years, *Our Sunday Visitor* (July 31, 1983); "The Court, Education, and Religion," *Washington Post* (June 30, 1983); "The Minnesota School Aid Case," *America* (July 16, 1983).

46. Robert Pear, "Ruling Touches Off New Debate on the Prospects of Tuition Credits," *New York Times* (June 30, 1983); Felicity Barringer, "Tuition Tax Credit Advocates Sing Muted Hosannas," *Washington Post* (June 30, 1983).

47. Al Kamen, "Supreme Court to Hear Arguments in 'Parochiaid' Case of Wednesday," *Washington Post* (December 4, 1984); Kamen, "Court Urged to Sanction Parochial School Aid," *Washington Post* (December 6, 1984); Tom Diaz, "High Court Hears Two Cases on State Aid to Private Schools," *Washington Times* (December 6, 1984).

48. Al Kamen, "High Court Rejects Public Aid for Paying Parochial Teachers," *Washington Post* (July 2, 1985); Linda Greenhouse, "Public Teachers Can't Hold Class in Church Schools," *New York Times* (July 2, 1985).

49. William E. McManus, "Court Closed Its Eyes to Facts in Education Ruling," *Our Sunday Visitor* (August 4, 1985); Joseph Duer, "Church-State: Court's 'Old Majority' Intact," *Our Sunday Visitor* (August 4, 1985).

50. John Manuel Andriote, "Court Stops Catholic Schools," *National Catholic Register* (August 11, 1985); Harry J. Byrne, "Tragic Paranoia: The Supreme Court and Parochial Schools," *America* (October 5, 1985).

51. Dick Goldencamp, "Parochial School Program Sent Back to Square One," *Our Sunday Visitor* (September 15, 1985).

52. Keith Richberg, "Bennett Backs Suits over Title One Rule," *Washing-

ton Post (August 16, 1985); Ivan Kauffman, "Voucher System Brought into Political Limelight," *Our Sunday Visitor* (March 30, 1986).

Chapter 14: A Decade of Doubt and Resolve

1. Gene I. Maeroff, "Catholic Schools Expecting a Turnaround in Fortunes," *New York Times* (April 26, 1981).
2. William C. McCready, "Let's Support Catholic Schools at Any Price," *U.S. Catholic* 46 (November 1981): 12–17; Sister Mary Ann Walsh, "Can Catholic Schools Survive the Economic Crunch of the 1980s?" *Our Sunday Visitor* (December 13, 1981): 4, 16–17; Kris Tuberty, "Catholic Grade Schools: An Idea Whose Time Has Passed?" *U.S. Catholic* 47 (November 1982): 18–23; Dan Herr, "Stop Killing Catholic Schools," *U.S. Catholic* 49 (October 1984): 13–18; Julie Sly, "Keeping Catholic Schools Open Is a Family Affair," *Our Sunday Visitor* (April 21, 1985): 3.
3. McCready, "Let's Support Catholic Schools at Any Price," 12.
4. Ibid., 15.
5. Quoted in Sister Mary Ann Walsh, "Planning for the Future," *Our Sunday Visitor* (December 13, 1981): 5.
6. William McGurn, "Our Catholic Schools"; Barry B. Bun, "Chicago: The Church Makes You Human"; Jane Frawley, "New York: Stressing Basics"; and Jim Orso, "St. Louis: Renewed Spirit"; all in the *National Catholic Register* (September 12, 1982). See also Vivian Dudro, "Hitting the Books," *National Catholic Register* (September 9, 1984), and Theodore M. Hesburgh, "Catholic Education in America," *America* (October 4, 1986): 160–64.
7. Ronald Reagan, "Remarks to the National Catholic Educational Association, April 15, 1982," *Public Papers of the Presidents: Ronald W. Reagan, 1982*, 2 vols. (Washington, D.C., 1983), 1:465–69.
8. Quoted in "Tuition Tax Credits for Tuition?" *Newsweek* (April 26, 1982).
9. "Mr. Reagan and Tuition Tax Credits," *America* (May 1, 1982); "Educational Voucher Raises Questions," *Our Sunday Visitor* (May 8, 1982); Charles R. Babcock, "Reagan Sends Tuition Tax Credit Bill to Hill," *Washington Post* (June 23, 1982); "Tuition Tax Credits Are Formally Asked by Reagan," *Wall Street Journal* (June 23, 1982); Robert Pear, "Debate Begins on Tuition Tax Credits," *New York Times* (July 17, 1982); Charles R. Babcock, "Changes Sought in Tuition Credit Plan," *Washington Post* (August 10, 1982); Babcock, "Tuition Tax Credit Actions Blocked by Democrats," *Washington Post* (August 12, 1982); Lou Cannon, "Senate Group Seeks to Save President's Tuition Tax Credits," *Washington Post* (September 14, 1982).
10. Marjorie Hyer, "Catholic Schools' Rate of Decline Has Slowed," *Washington Post* (April 28, 1984), and Ann Mariano, "Transformation of Catholic Schools," *Washington Post Education Review* (April 21, 1985).
11. Virgil C. Blum, "Catholic Parents Are Political Pygmies," *Newsletter of the Catholic League for Religious and Civil Rights* 10 (January 1983).

12. "Reagan Again Asks Congress for Tax Credits for Tuition," *Washington Post* (February 17, 1983); Juan Williams, "White House Pushes for Tuition Tax Credit," *Washington Post* (March 5, 1983); Williams, "Reagan Vows to Fight for Tuition Tax Credit," *Washington Post* (April 8, 1983).

13. Juan Williams, "Reagan Pushes Tuition Tax Credits," *Washington Post* (November 16, 1983); Helen Dewar, "Senate Approves Debt Ceiling, Rejects Tuition Tax Credits," *Washington Post* (November 17, 1983); "Senate Tables Tuition Tax Credit Amendment," *Our Sunday Visitor* (November 27, 1983).

14. " '84 Tuition Tax Credit Campaign to Begin," *National Catholic Register* (February 5, 1984); Michael Schwartz, "For Tuition Tax Credits, a Crossroads," *National Catholic Register* (February 19, 1984); Pete Sheehan, "Tuition Tax Credits: Who Would Benefit the Most?" *Our Sunday Visitor* (August 9, 1984); Stephen O'Brien, "Let's Back Tuition Tax Credits," *U.S. Catholic* 50 (January 1985): 12–17.

15. McGurn, "Our Catholic Schools," 8.

16. Sister Mary Ann Walsh, "Most Parents Can Afford Catholic Education," *Our Sunday Visitor* (January 30, 1983). See also Walsh, "Can Catholic Schools Survive?"; Tuberty, "Catholic Grade Schools?" 20–23; Sly, "Keeping Catholic Schools Open"; Peter J. Feuerherd, "Catholic Elementary Schools: Are They in Trouble?" *Our Sunday Visitor* (October 13, 1985); Julie Sly, "Catholic Schools: The Best and Worst of Times," *Our Sunday Visitor* (June 21, 1987).

17. Nick Thimmish, "Learning: The Catholics," *Washington Post* (April 18, 1983).

18. David K. O'Rourke, "Resolution and Alienation in the American Church," *Commonweal* (February 11, 1983): 76–79; Ann Mariano, "Social Shifts Lead Catholics to Sell Schools," *Washington Post* (November 10, 1984).

19. O'Rourke, "Revolution and Alienation in the American Church," 76.

20. Ibid., 78; see also Dan Herr, "Stop Killing Catholic Schools," 14.

21. Andrew M. Greeley, "Catholic Schools: A Golden Twilight?" *America* (February 11, 1989): 106–8, 116–18.

22. Ibid., 118.

23. Quoted in Gene I. Maeroff, "Private Schools Look to Bright Future," *New York Times* (January 4, 1981).

24. Quoted in Sister Mary Ann Walsh, "Are They Learning Catholic Values," *Our Sunday Visitor* (November 29, 1981).

25. James J. Digiacomo, "Teaching the New Breed," *America* (June 27, 1981): 518–20; Sister Mary Anne Walsh, "The Fight to Keep a Catholic Image," *Our Sunday Visitor* (December 20, 1981).

26. James P. Emswiler, "What Are Catholic Schools Teaching Kids about Religion?" *U.S. Catholic* (January 1983): 37.

27. Quoted in Paula Herbert, "Using Bishop's Letter in Daily Life," *Washington Post* (April 9, 1983).

28. "Catholic Schools to Teach Pastoral," *National Catholic Register* (July 17, 1983); "Catholic Educators Work to Implement Peace Pastoral,"

Our Sunday Visitor (July 17, 1983); and Chester E. Finn, Jr., "Catholic Schools Veer toward Pacifism," *Wall Street Journal* (December 27, 1983).

29. Jerry Becan, "What Was Wrong with the Catechism Anyway?" *America* (July 2, 1983): 12.

30. Ibid.

31. Ibid., 13.

32. William Odell, "Do We Need a Return to the Baltimore Catechism?" *Our Sunday Visitor* (September 11, 1983); Sister Mary Ann Walsh, "Religious Illiteracy: Are There Any Answers?" *Our Sunday Visitor* (July 31, 1983).

33. Odell, "Do We Need a Return to the Baltimore Catechism?"

34. Francis D. Kelly, "A Church at Risk: Toward Balance in Catechetics," *America* (October 8, 1983); Walsh, "Religious Illiteracy."

35. Emswiler, "What Are Catholic Schools Teaching Kids about Religion?"; Julie Sly, " 'Community of Faith' Attracts Parents to Schools," *Our Sunday Visitor* (July 5, 1987); Mitch Finley, "Into the Quiet Mystery: Why We Send Our Children to a Catholic School," *America* (March 26, 1988).

36. A Vatican Salute to Catholic Lay Teachers," *America* (October 30, 1982).

37. William Ryan, "Portrait: The Catholic Lay Teacher," *Our Sunday Visitor* (February 27, 1983): 6–7.

38. "The Nosiest Catholic in America: The Editors Interview William C. McCready," *U.S. Catholic* (June 1983): 19–25; "Catholic Lay Teachers: A 'New Religious Order,' " *Our Sunday Visitor* (June 5, 1983).

39. Barbara Mahany, "The Rugged Devotion of Teachers in Catholic Schools," *U.S. Catholic* (September 1984): 30.

40. Madeline McGuire quoted in ibid.

41. Ibid.

42. Jim Castelli, "Study: 'Schools Run Great Risk of Losing Their Sense of Mission,' " *Our Sunday Visitor* (May 6, 1984); Bruno V. Manno, "Lay Involvement in Catholic Schools," *America* (October 27, 1984): 246.

43. Cited in Mary Ann Walsh, "Minorities in Catholic Schools: Tokenism or Commitment?" *Our Sunday Visitor* (December 6, 1981).

44. Coleman as quoted in ibid.; Greeley as quoted in "The Bright Flight," *Newsweek* (April 20, 1981).

45. Lorraine Ferris as quoted in Fred Reed, "The Color of Education," *Harper's Magazine* 262 (February, 1981): 28.

46. Jerome Porath of Albany as quoted in Mary Ann Walsh, "Minorities in Catholic Schools." See also Jim Orso, "Black Leaders Urge Strong Catholic Identity," *National Catholic Register* (August 7, 1983).

47. Louis H. Pumphrey, "Portrait of an Inner City Catholic School," *Our Sunday Visitor* (February 1, 1981); Alfredo S. Lanier, "Let Us Now Praise Catholic Schools," *Chicago* (October 1982): 147–53; Barry Bun, "Ghetto School: Strong and Growing," *National Catholic Register* (September 5, 1982); John W. Donohue, "One School's Secret," *America* (April 2, 1983); Carol Krucoff, "A World of New Freedoms, Old Problems," *Washington Post*

(December 20, 1983); Danielle Schultz, "What Makes Schools Good?" *Washington Monthly* (November 1983).

48. Bruno V. Manno, "Catholic Schools: Common, Public, Serving Minority Interests," *America* (October 25, 1986): 230–31.

49. Ibid.

50. Ibid.

Conclusion

1. David Le Duc, "The Four Rs," *Notre Dame Magazine* (Spring 1990): 27.

2. "Catholic Schools: New Testing Adds More Evidence of Good Results" (Catholic News Service story), *Davenport Catholic Messenger* (July 4, 1991); Ari Goldman, "Money Problems Put Some Catholic Schools in Danger of Closing," *New York Times* (February 16, 1992).

3. Peter J. Daly, "Who Needs Catholic Schools?" *Washington Post* (September 1, 1991).

4. William J. Byron, "Catholic Education in America," *Vital Speeches of the Day* 61 (June 1, 1990): 489.

5. Ibid.

6. David J. O'Brien, "American Catholicism and Diaspora," *Cross Currents* 16 (Summer 1966): 308–9. See also Marvin Lazerson, "Understanding American Catholic Educational History," *History of Education Quarterly* (Fall 1977): 298–99.

7. Meg Sommerfeld, "Study Compares Religious Education of Parish Programs, Catholic Schools," *Education Week* (August 3, 1994); "Educators Are Doing a Good Job," Catholic News Service story as published in *Davenport Catholic Messenger* (July 28, 1994) and other Catholic newspapers.

8. Anthony S. Bryk, Valerie E. Lee, and Peter B. Holland, *Catholic Schools and the Common Good* (Cambridge, Mass., 1993).

9. Peter Steinfels, "Why Catholic Schools Succeed: A Community of Shared Values," *New York Times* (April 17, 1994).

10. Quoted in Joseph P. McDonald, "The Greening of St. Madeline's," *New York Times Book Review* (September 5, 1993).

11. David Gonzalez, "Poverty Raises Stakes for Catholic School," *New York Times* (April 17, 1994); Marla K. Kale, "Inner-city Schools: What's in It for Catholics?" *U.S. Catholic* (April 1992): 21–28; Peter J. Daly, "Who Needs Catholic Schools?" *Washington Post* (September 1, 1991).

12. Daly, "Who Needs Catholic Schools?"

Index